NEVER FORGET

ReganBooks
An Imprint of HarperCollins*Publishers*

NEVER FORGET

AN ORAL HISTORY OF SEPTEMBER 11, 2001

Mitchell Fink and Lois Mathias

HarperCollins books may be purchased for educational, business, or sales promotional use. For information please write: Special Markets Department, HarperCollins Publishers Inc., 10 East 53rd Street, New York, NY 10022.

FIRST EDITION

Printed on acid-free paper

Library of Congress Cataloging-in-Publication Data has been applied for.

ISBN 0-06-051433-7

02 03 04 05 06 RRD 10 9 8 7 6 5 4 3 2 1

—

To those who lost their lives on
September 11, 2001, and to those who are now charged
with the responsibility of keeping their memories alive

—

CONTENTS

INTRODUCTION

On September 11, 2001, I watched the Twin Towers fall on an overhead TV monitor above my desk at the New York *Daily News*. For a long time I sat there stunned, unable to speak. I didn't want to run those few miles south to the attack site, and I couldn't run away. As a gossip columnist for the past fifteen years, I occupied a unique vantage point from which to view America's ongoing fascination with celebrities. We were a celebrity-driven culture and our chief export was fame. And I was lucky enough to be in the middle of it all, telling stories, breaking stories, and carrying goody bags home at the end of the night.

But this endless parade of famous people, which seemed to first mobilize in the mid-1970s with the dual births of *People* magazine and *Saturday Night Live,* was now screeching to a halt in front of my eyes. And the sudden realization that readers of the next day's papers would not want to hear any more nonsense about Whitney Houston's sunken eyes or Pamela Anderson's romance with Kid Rock did little to calm the conflict within me. I felt a little like Frankie Valli and the Four Seasons in a world about to explode with the Beatles.

The world indeed changed on the morning of September 11, and I would somehow have to find the strength and means to change with it. On that day and for days afterward I suspected that those changes would occur mostly in the tone of what I wrote. Little did I know that the real change required of me would manifest into something I never could have predicted.

When I left the *Daily News* in early January of 2002, one of the first calls I received was from Judith Regan. I had known Judith during all those years of writing my columns. You couldn't possibly be in my line of work and not have come across Judith. The stunning success she has achieved as an editor and a publisher, and her instincts about our culture, commercial and otherwise, have made her a far more interesting public figure than her literary peers.

And so, when she said simply, "I have an idea. We should talk," you can bet I took her seriously.

Her idea was this book, an oral history about a day in history no one living would ever forget.

I agreed to do it, having no real idea how I might actually complete the task. After all, I heard Judith's idea for the first time in January, and she wanted the book out by September.

On my way home that night, I began formulating a plan: I would scour the important magazines and newspapers in an effort to find the most relevant first-person accounts of the tragedy. I would then call these publications and beg for the rights to reprint those stories in our book. Surely I would have little time to do much more than that.

And then a remarkable thing happened when I got home: I told my wife, Lois, about Judith's offer, and her response was like nothing I'd ever heard from her. She said, "I want to help you do it."

Lois and I had never worked together professionally. We'd raised two incredible sons and carved out a life together that I'm sure neither of us would ever want to change. But work together? That never seemed possible. Lois had always resisted the celebrity lifestyle, with its many opening nights, endless cocktail parties, and the idle banter that accompanies most high-profile events. Whether it was the Academy Awards, a party with the Clintons, or a junket to the Bahamas, her answer was almost always the same: "Not interested."

But this, she said, was different. You don't find stories like these on the red carpet. A much deeper emotional connection, something Lois has always demanded of herself and of those around her, was needed here. And her ability to connect with people made her a perfect partner for this project.

And so it began. On January 31, Lois conducted the first interview for this book with Sean Crowley, an NYPD captain who remains haunted by the image of five people holding hands and jumping together as a group from high up in the North Tower.

The following day I spoke with Michelle Wiley, a downtown musician who called 911 with news of a plane "flying very low, but very steady," toward the World Trade Center. With seconds still to go before impact, the 911 operator had no idea what she was talking about.

The next day Lois and I went to Ground Zero, where we interviewed three amazingly dedicated construction workers—Gregg Nolan, Tim Cahill, and Joseph Bradley. Each of their stories was different from the next except for the one common thread that now ties these men together for life: all three talked separately about finding a spiritual life down at Ground Zero. Their stories were like nothing we could have imagined.

Before going home that day, we stopped in the back of a seedy bar in Little Italy to meet with retired police lieutenant Tim McGinn. All he did on September 11 was save the lives of at least thirty people who were all suffocating in front of 1 World Financial Center when the South Tower collapsed.

In a span of less than forty-eight hours, we had interviewed six people with six extraordinary stories. Our time with these people gave us the inspiration to go after every interview ourselves. And that's precisely what happened. The cutting and pasting was no longer necessary. Every person in this book was either interviewed by me, or by Lois, or by the two of us together. And for that I am indeed grateful to my wife. I simply could not have done this without her.

In the months we spent interviewing and editing, I learned a great deal about myself. I already knew that Lois's personality would make it hard for her to detach from the people with whom she came in contact. But that was not supposed to happen to me. I was the big-shot journalist who did what he did and moved on. Only I'm not moving on so easily. Before I became a gossip columnist I was a hard-news reporter who regularly struggled with the emotions of having to watch people suffer and then report on it. Turning to gossip in those days was like being handed a "get out of jail free" card.

But here I am fifteen years later working on hard-news accounts that have rarely in history been this hard. And I'm not ashamed to say that I still can't handle it. The people in this book have gotten into my head and my heart and I feel they are here to stay.

When writer Spencer Kobren speaks of the humiliation of being hosed down after having to strip naked outside Staten Island Hospital, I can't help but think of what was done to people in Nazi Germany, and then in the American South.

When NYPD Chief of Detectives William Allee describes himself in the dust cloud as "an hourglass filling up," I can't help but wonder how the health-care industry will deal with these survivors years from now should they become sick.

And when Deena Burnett's husband, United Flight 93 passenger Tom, scolds her for needlessly worrying his parents by telling them about the hijacking of his plane, I can't help but imagine what I might have said to my wife under similar circumstances.

It is often said that the best accolade a book can receive is when someone says, "I couldn't put it down." Trust me, this is not one of those books. This is one you may need to put down, or risk being overwhelmed by the voices within it. The subject matter, after all, is without precedent. No one alive that day had any prior experience in dealing with events like these, and as a result many of the images described herein had never been imagined—not by the government, not by the local emergency services, and not even by Stephen King.

—Mitchell Fink

On December 15, 2000, I suffered an early heart attack and survived what I thought was one of the most difficult days of my life. I spent most of the year 2001 in recovery and getting used to my own vulnerability and the randomness of life and death. I knew I had been given another chance at life. Each day I woke up I was thankful to be alive.

On September 11, I was on the treadmill at the cardiac rehabilitation center in a Connecticut hospital watching the news when there was a breaking story. Incredibly, a plane had crashed into the North Tower of the World Trade Center. I immediately thought of terrorism and watched in horror as a second plane hit the South Tower.

I stopped the treadmill and stared at the television until I could no longer stand it. I felt an enormous need to contact my family and make sure they were all okay.

I have never watched scary movies, and I no longer read scary books. I don't watch the news late at night because it is too upsetting. I have always purposely stayed away from graphic accounts of the Holocaust, and the one time I went to the Vietnam Memorial in Washington I couldn't stop crying.

September 11 changed my life and was yet another turning point for me. Any and all illusions of control were shattered. I was truly rocked to my core. Life as I knew it had changed.

After September 11, many people I know said they felt compelled to go down to Ground Zero. I felt no such pull.

When my husband told me he had an opportunity to do a book about September 11, I heard this voice come out of my mouth saying, "I want to help you do it." I turned around to see who had said that, and it was indeed me. I had no idea of the impact this project would have on me, or that I would have to challenge myself on so many levels. I surely didn't expect my life to intersect with some of the most amazingly brave, selfless, and determined people I have ever encountered.

It continues to be an honor for me to be involved in something so profound. I understand that I am simply a conduit for the people who have been willing to speak to me and I feel privileged by the opportunity they have given us. I have talked to people at the most traumatic and horrific time in their lives, listening to stories that I could barely wrap my mind around. And in each case there was nothing to do but listen, and bear witness to their experiences. There was simply no way to make it better.

Often at the end of an interview I would just walk around or sit quietly. I would sometimes cry at the devastation, the descriptions of damaged psyches and souls. There was always a moment during each interview when I saw or heard the person going back to where they were on that day, and I couldn't help but see through their eyes the hellish nightmare they endured.

I can never properly thank these people for their trust in allowing us to present their voices in the most authentic way possible. This project was a true gift for me, and I will always be grateful to the people I've spoken with and met during this process, people who were willing to share the unthinkable with us. I have renewed faith in what people can endure, and that we truly are all in this life together.

I would also like to thank my children for being so supportive, and lastly, my husband, Mitchell, who has been a true partner every step of the way. I want to thank him for hearing me that day, and allowing me to participate in this life-changing project.

—Lois Mathias

For millions of Americans, September 10, 2001, was like so many other days before it: The nation was at peace. There was relative prosperity throughout the land. Children were beginning a new school year.

In New York, Michael Jackson was performing the second of two sold-out shows at Madison Square Garden. A few miles north in the South Bronx, umpires called the Yankees game on account of rain.

In Washington, Secretary of Defense Donald Rumsfeld was railing against the bureaucracy at the Pentagon and promising to streamline management and make the military more efficient.

And in Somerset County, Pennsylvania, local pride swelled when the Shanksville–Stony Creek school district was awarded a $54,033 grant as part of a statewide "safe school" program.

Certainly nobody in these regions, or practically anywhere, had any reason to believe that on the following morning nineteen Middle Eastern terrorists would hijack four commercial jetliners and change the course of world events.

MICHELLE WILEY
52, Musician

~

"I THOUGHT I WAS DEAD BECAUSE EVERYTHING WENT BLACK."

The day was very bright and very clear. Paul left early that morning, probably on the last train out. We live in an apartment in Gateway Plaza, a block over from the World Trade Center. Normally I'm up with him and dressed. But I sort of stayed in my nightgown and shower shoes and decided I would practice on the piano. I often play "Autumn Leaves" in all twelve keys, just to get my head going.

The piano (actually a Kurzweil synthesizer/sequencer in the body of a small baby grand) is in a studio which looks out at the World Trade Center. My dad was an old air force lifer, so I know planes. I've been around them since I was little. I think I was in the second chorus of "Autumn Leaves" when I paused, just to stretch. I stood up by the window looking out at the Center when I see this plane flying very low, but very steady, toward the World Trade. I immediately said to myself, "This plane is going to hit it. It's not spiraling, it's not smoking, it doesn't look out of control."

I picked up the phone and dialed 911. I don't know why. I said, "There's a plane flying into the World Trade Center." And the operator said, "My God, I didn't know that." By the time I finished the sentence, the plane was through the building. And she just sort of yelled at me, because I guess maybe someone else had gotten a call next to her, and she said, "Please stay on the phone." Then she said, "No, don't stay on the phone," and suddenly the phone went dead.

I got a couple of phone calls from friends, you know, "Are you all right?" "We heard that the plane hit the Trade Center." And I said, "Yeah, I'm fine. People are panicked and running around. I'm not going to go outside."

So I'm watching and I can't believe it. It reminded me of the movie *The Towering Inferno*. There's a building and the top of it is burning, like a huge candle. I turned on the television, and then I got another call from a DJ in Detroit. I coach professional singers and one of my students in the Detroit area had been trying to reach me and couldn't. So she called a DJ friend, Johnny Burke, and he got through. He asked me to describe the scene, and I described what I saw. I could see people jumping from the building. I don't know how many, but it was more than two, I know that. Some things I don't remember. Some things I just block out. But I knew things were escalating. I saw people leaning out of the tower. They were waving towels, trying to get the smoke out or trying to signal people.

I thought about trying to run to the place where our car was parked, and just get in and drive out, but thank God I didn't because that's when the second plane hit. Now I was conflicted about what to do.

Then the South Tower collapsed.

I remember standing in front of the window and feeling the ground start to vibrate. It was as though someone had just put a huge sock over our entire building. I mean, it went from that bright crisp morning to just total blackness, and then it felt like an earthquake. I thought I was dead because everything went black inside my apartment. My phone went out, the TV went out, and I was just sort of floating in the room, suspended there. I didn't feel my body or anything. I think I was in shock.

I started to shake, and I just fell to the floor and began crawling to my front door in my nightgown. Paul's leather jacket was hanging on the hook by the door. I knew I had to get out of the building at that point. I pulled the jacket on me. I felt along a corner of the floor for a pair of sneakers by the front door. And I put them on because I thought, Well, there is going to be glass and stuff down there. But in my haste and being so nervous, I guess, I still had the pair of shower shoes in my hand. I held onto them and I opened the door. I found my purse, but I couldn't find my cell phone. This is all happening in a matter of seconds.

When I got outside the door, my next-door neighbor was standing pinned against the wall. She just was frozen there, a young lady. We didn't really know each other that well, but I walked over to her and I took her arm and I said, "I want you to come with me." And we went down the stairwell. We could hear people from above and below, you know, falling down the steps because it was totally black. I didn't know if the building had been hit, or if it was on fire. The door to the lobby was jammed, but a man kicked it open. There were maybe fifty to one hundred people in the lobby and everyone started running outside. The air was cool and debris was everywhere. It looked like the surface of Mars, all this white sediment and piles of computer paper and pieces of desks and more paper just falling through the air.

I kept walking toward the front gate, and there was a very badly wounded policewoman standing there trying to get people to go back. But people panicked and kept running. I guess they thought they were going to try to get to the subway. But if you looked down that way, there were cars that were already all crunched up. I don't know why, but something told me to run back through the crowd. The door to an adjacent building was open and another door inside led out to the gate that leads to the promenade toward the river. I guess I thought I was going to swim.

There was a stench outside. I could feel something very itchy all over me. I pulled my coat over my nose. The air wasn't black anymore, but it was like a very heavy white fog. I turned right on the esplanade and starting running toward the right. I saw a group of men maybe one hundred yards down. They were loading injured firemen onto a tugboat that had pulled up next to the wall. There was one very badly wounded fireman that they couldn't move. I still see his face. I still have nightmares. His face still visits me. He was in so much pain. Every time they tried to pick him up, he just collapsed back down.

I made it onto the boat. There were other civilians on it. There was a hysterical woman next to me, I think she was Spanish. They gave us life vests and told us to stand toward the center of the boat or the boat would tip over. I tried to calm her down. I said, "Look, we're going to New Jersey. It's okay. We're lucky. We got out."

Then I looked to my right. There was another woman crying. Her legs were all cut up. She had run out of her shoes. So I handed her the shower shoes, the ones I had been carrying all this time, and I said, "You know something, I've been carrying these around. I guess they were for you."

SPENCER KOBREN
36, Writer

—

"ON TELEVISION IT LOOKED LIKE JUST A CLOUD OF
SMOKE. BUT IT WAS MONITORS AND DESKS AND CHAIRS,
FLYING THROUGH THE AIR, PIECES OF METAL."

I live on Greenwich Street, about two blocks south of the World Trade Center, and at first, I didn't even consider getting out of the building. After the first plane hit, I went on my terrace and I saw all these people on their rooftops and they were just looking. People were actually taking pictures. My girlfriend wasn't home at the time. She was uptown doing some shopping.

Then, I'm watching television and I see a plane coming on the screen about to hit tower 2. I could also see the shadow of the plane, and that wasn't on TV. The explosion threw me about four feet. I was in my living room. I live in a loft and I was thrown to the kitchen area, right on my back. I tried to be as calm as possible, but my back had gone out.

My girlfriend somehow made it back to the apartment, and she said, "Look, we gotta get out of here." We have a porno store on our block. It's open on New Year's Eve, Christmas. The place is never closed. She said, "That store is closed. We gotta get out of here." We tried to get out of the building, but there was just too much debris. We were told to wait in the building because too much stuff was falling.

All of a sudden I hear this sound, a noise like I've never heard in my life, the most frightening sound I've ever heard, like a thousand helicopters on top of us. And a rumbling like the earth was about to split apart. That was the first tower falling. We live on the eleventh floor, in a loft. Our windows shattered. Smoke started to come in, debris started to come in, and we were completely in darkness. I have two cats, so I had to get on my stomach and try to find them. I got them and put them in a bag. We made it out of the apartment on our stomachs and people were screaming. People had glass in their hair, completely gray, full of soot and bleeding. People were disoriented. I remember one girl who was talking on a cell phone, or she thought she was talking on her cell phone. I wanted to make a call and I asked her for her phone, and it was just a piece of her phone. The girl was in shock.

We couldn't get out of the building because once you got outside the door, you couldn't see a foot in front of you. So I ran back upstairs to get some towels and some water. I got on my stomach again, got the towels, found a bottle of water, I don't know how. I went back outside and wrapped my girlfriend's head and face with this towel. I wrapped one over my face and we left.

The debris was like snow. We saw twisted metal, blood, clothing. I saw a baby carriage. It was like a war and we were refugees. My back is out, we have the cats, and we're walking as fast as we can. You couldn't run in this debris. It was like trying to run in the sand. The only place we were able to go was south. I knew the Staten Island Ferry was at the end of the island, about eight or nine blocks away. People were running all over the place. There was no one to guide us. My girlfriend had gotten debris in her eyes and in her throat, so she couldn't really see for a while because the flakes were so big.

We never thought the other building was going to fall. And then all of a sudden we heard this rumbling and then some guy screams, "Run!" We turn around and it was like being in monster movie. We're just shooting through this alley of buildings, and it was right on our tail. We ran as fast as we could. Fortunately, we were younger than a lot of people out there, and I guess in better shape. Some of the people we were walking with were just left there. We saw them being knocked over by debris. On television it looked like just a cloud of smoke. But it was monitors and desks and chairs, flying through the air, pieces of metal.

It was like a mass pilgrimage down to the ferry area. We saw a few children, but mostly it was businesspeople. We get to the ferry, people are crowding, trying to jump on. There's not enough life vests for everybody. People are grabbing life vests from each other. It's like all hell is breaking loose. Finally, they close the door on people and people are trying to jump onto the ferry. People were hanging on the door. I remember this one kid just hanging on the door until he fell into the water. This is the kind of stuff they didn't show on the news.

Looking back at Manhattan from the ferry, about a half-mile out, it looked like the entire island had been taken out. You couldn't see any buildings. It was like they had just wiped out Manhattan and we were the last people to make it off. Everyone was just standing on the deck in silence. People were crying.

Once we got to Staten Island, we hobbled off the ferry trying to find a hospital. Couldn't find one, so we went to a hotel and it was just packed with people. We couldn't get a room, but this woman was nice enough to take us to her home. She and her husband gave us something to eat. Then we were taken to Staten Island Hospital, my girlfriend and myself. These guys in white shoes and bioterrorism suits came out to meet us. They waved and said, "Where are you guys coming from?"

We said, "Manhattan. We were in the Trade Center incident."

They waved us to another area and made us take off all our clothing. They showered us down in public, no clothes. They didn't want our clothes in the hospital. We were naked, both of us. There were a couple of other naked people. They tried to cordon us off. They were so terrified that it was chemical warfare.

They burnt our clothes. Our clothes were gone. Our shoes, her boots, whatever we were wearing. Our ID and credit cards were decontaminated for us. I never saw anybody talk about this on the news.

Then they brought us in as though we were lepers. They're treating us, they're holding us, and I'm naked. They don't even give me anything to wear. So we're wet and we're naked and it's cold, and I felt worse for my girlfriend than I did for me. She was embarrassed. Finally, they gave us some robes, some gowns. They checked us from head to toe. My girlfriend was so shocked, they gave her some Xanax. Then they let us go. But we had no clothes, they didn't give us any clothes to wear. So they found a pair of scrubs for us. They let me take a gown and no shoes.

We lost everything. I had a manuscript on my computer for a book that was due in October, and I lost the computer and the book. I had a backup, but who thought I'd have to keep it someplace else. You never think your home is going to be destroyed. When the second building fell, stuff just flew out of our apartment. But we were lucky enough to survive it.

When we tried to get back into the building, our building was a crime scene. They found body parts on terraces. They found a torso in a plane seat on our roof. Our building was one of the last buildings to be opened up. They had to reface it, decontaminate it, and of course put in all new windows. There was a luncheonette that we'd eat at in the morning, a block north from my apartment. It was completely destroyed, completely blown out, and I'm sure the place was full of people. They didn't talk a lot about those stories on the news either, all the ancillary places and the shop owners who may have lost their lives. I feel like I was in a war, for one day of my life. We were fighting for our lives to get out of there because we didn't know if we'd be alive one minute or dead the next.

STEVEN BIENKOWSKI
37, Harbor Unit Scuba Team, New York City Police Department

"PEOPLE WERE HANGING OUT OF THE BUILDING, GASPING FOR AIR. SOME WERE JUMPING AND OTHERS WERE ACCIDENTALLY BEING PUSHED BY PEOPLE BEHIND THEM WHO WERE JUST TRYING TO GET OUT OF THE SMOKE AND GET TO THE AIR."

I'm a police officer on the scuba team. We have divers in helicopters twenty-four hours a day, seven days a week, 365 days a year. We are the first responders for anything involving the water. We can pretty much get there faster than anybody else.

We got a call that a plane had hit the tower. Probably like so many other people, we were thinking it was a small private aircraft. But as we lifted up and came across Brooklyn, we saw that it was no small aircraft. There was a gaping hole in the North Tower and black smoke was pouring out.

It was pretty clear that people were trapped. There was nobody on the roof. About 80 percent of the roof was engulfed in black smoke. People were hanging out of the building, gasping for air. Some were jumping and others were accidentally being pushed by people behind them who were just trying to get out of the smoke and get to the air. Everything I've seen in my seventeen years as a police officer became minuscule. The past became insignificant. It was just so much more horrible than anything your mind could have ever conjured up.

People saw the helicopter and I'm sure many of them were thinking that we were going to be able to save them. In fact, we weren't able to do anything. We were as close as you could possibly be, and still we were helpless, totally helpless. There was no way of getting near anybody in a window. And then you're watching these people plunge to their death. We were so close.

Then we came around to the South Tower. We were still at the point of impact on the first building, seeing these poor people taking their plunge to certain death. I happened to be sitting in the back left side of the ship. There were two pilots, two crew chiefs, my partner, and I. We were on the southwest side of the South Tower, and I glanced over my shoulder and there came a United Airlines aircraft right at us, a little bit underneath where we were. And I do mean a little underneath us. It probably missed us by about three hundred feet, and it proceeded to fly right through the building, right in front of us. I must have gone numb. I don't remember hearing an explosion, although it must have been extremely loud. I don't remember the helicopter moving. I think it was all I could handle just to watch that happen.

When that second plane went into the building, it just looked like an evil magician's trick. It looked nothing like what I would have imagined a plane crashing into a building would look like. The plane just completely disappeared and turned into a giant fireball. Being there was surreal. I guess the brain tries to protect you in times like that. You have some kind of defense mechanism in there that shuts down some of your senses. It just doesn't allow you to believe.

And for me, the realization still hadn't set in that this was a terrorist attack. But the reality was becoming all too apparent. There was really no place to put the ship down in Manhattan because people were running like roaches. So we went and landed over on Governor's Island, just to regroup and refuel.

Coming back across Brooklyn again you could see that the South Tower was already down. The entire lower Manhattan was covered in a giant white dust cloud. And as you came around to the North Tower again, you could still see the people falling and jumping, except it didn't look so violent anymore because you weren't watching them hit the ground. It was almost peaceful because they were falling into a white cloud.

As we're coming around to the North Tower, I said, "Oh, my God, it looks like it's tilting." It came down a couple of minutes afterward, completely straight down, like a deck of cards.

The entire thickness of the cloud of dust was like nothing you've ever seen, and we watched the boats come in from everywhere. Our guys were down there, the scuba launch, the harbor launches, tugboats, and fishing boats were coming in. Boats from everywhere evacuated people over the sea wall. And after that we just went back to Floyd Bennett Field in total disbelief, trying to absorb the reality of it all.

Even though it's unreasonable and I know, rationally, that there was nothing we could do, it doesn't matter. The fact is, I was right there and I watched all those people die, and there wasn't a damn thing I could do about it. You sit there and you're powerless. It's like being forced to watch something with your hands tied. It was torture, total torture.

Joseph Pfeifer, right, with his late brother, Kevin.

JOSEPH PFEIFER
46, Chief, Battalion 1, New York City Fire Department

"IT WAS ALMOST LIKE THE CLOSER YOU WERE, THE LESS YOU KNEW."

I worked the night before in the firehouse, which is at 100 Duane Street, in lower Manhattan. Then that morning, somewhere around eight-thirty, we had a call to a possible gas leak in the street. So we went to the gas leak and there was a slight odor of gas in the street. No big deal. I had Engine 7 and Ladder 1 check some of the exposures. There was nothing inside the buildings. So we called Con Ed, and we were wrapping up with the operation there and standing around in the street. And then we hear this very loud plane coming overhead.

In Manhattan, you rarely hear planes because of the high buildings. So we all looked up. In almost disbelief, we see the plane pass, and it's flying so low. Our eyes followed it as it passed behind the buildings, and then it reappeared, and it appeared to me that it aimed right into the building. It smashed into the building. There was a large fireball. And then a couple of seconds later you heard the sound of the explosion. I told everybody to get in the rigs because we're going down there, to the Trade Center.

I got into a battalion car with Jules Naudet, the French film guy who made the *9/11* documentary tape. If you saw the tape, you saw our faces blank with disbelief that a plane was heading toward the Trade Center, followed by the actual impact. I picked up the department radio and I told them that a plane just hit the World Trade Center, and to transmit a second alarm. That was done immediately. That was the first official report of this happening.

We're heading down West Broadway, and I'm thinking to myself, What's the next step? What's the next thing I need to do? I picked up the radio again, and I told the dispatcher that this was a direct attack. I said I want a third alarm transmitted. "Have the second-alarm units report to the Trade Center, and the third-alarm units stage at Vesey and West Street."

We proceeded to the Trade Center. We pull up to the front, underneath the canopy. I get out of the car. The firefighters get their gear. I throw my gear on, and we proceed into the building. As we go in, we see a couple of people badly burned right in the lobby. I proceeded to the fire command center of the Trade Center. I was met by a deputy fire safety director. I asked him if he knew what floor the plane hit because it's very hard to tell from the outside exactly what floor. And he wasn't able to give me an exact floor. He said between 78 and 80, but he wasn't sure.

My first thought was to organize, to find out information and then try to organize the firefighters that I had asked for. I needed to find out if we had any elevators. In the Trade Center, each of the towers had ninety-nine elevators. So it wasn't a simple job. It was not just walking over and checking one elevator bank. I had to send a number of people, from a number of companies, to see if any of the elevators were available to us. And what we found out, after a couple of minutes, was that we had no elevators. So we had to send people upstairs to find out what was going on and to attempt a rescue. I knew that we had somewhere around twenty floors of people above the fire, and I knew they were trapped. I knew the fire itself was too big to put out.

Deputy Chief Peter Hayden came in and he took charge of the operation. My role was to support him, supply him with information, and continue communicating with the guys going up. Groups of firefighters were coming in. And we would brief them and then tell them the plan, and send them up. One of the engine companies that came in was Engine 33, which was my brother Kevin's. He was a lieutenant in 33, which is out of Great Jones Street, off the Bowery.

I was standing behind the fire command station, which is a high desk-type thing. And I remember seeing him walking over to me. And I said to myself, "What's he doing here?" He told me he was going to go on a special vacation and he was taking a number of mutuals off so he could study for the captain's test. So

I thought his last tour had been the day before. I was very surprised to see him. But he came over to me, and I told him where we thought the lowest level of the fire possibly was, at 78. And I told him we didn't have any elevators available. And then we just spent a couple of seconds just looking at each other, with a real feeling of concern for each other. It was just a couple of seconds of staring at each other. And then he knew what he had to do and he slowly walked away to his men, who were standing maybe twenty feet away. I watched him walk away, and that was the last time I saw him.

This was maybe five minutes before the second plane hit. A lot of the high-ranking citywide tour commanders of the fire department started coming in. We're trying to evaluate what's going on, what we have and who's coming in. We're trying to explain our rescue plan to people when the second plane hits the South Tower. We heard that. We saw debris coming down. A number of the chiefs got together: Deputy Chief Peter Hayden and myself, citywide tour commander Donald Burns and Battalion Chief Orio Palmer. It was decided that we'd just split the group in half. One group would go into the South Tower. The other would stay in the North Tower.

Pete Hayden said, "I need Joe Pfeifer to stay with me. We'll take North Tower." And Donald Burns said, "I'll take Orio, and we'll set up a command in tower 2."

What we tried to do at that point was to check out the repeater, the building repeater, because we were going to command channels. Orio and I tested it out together, and it failed. It did not work at all. So we had a communication difficulty right from the beginning.

So they went into the South Tower and we stayed with the North, knowing there was no communication between the two towers.

We tried a number of other communications solutions. We tried the repeater in the car. We also went to a different command channel. But our best system was knocked out with the first plane. Everything else from there would not be as good. High-rise communications are difficult at best because of the technology problems with radios.

I knew that the B stairs had a special standpipe phone, which meant they had a jack where you could plug in a phone and talk down to the fire command board. So I physically gave people red phones. I said, "Hey, listen, right next to the standpipe you'll see a box. Plug this in and we'll have direct hard-wire communication."

We tried every possible means of communication that day. But even cell phones weren't working. But what goes through my head is that with each of the systems we tried, the redundancy of the systems still failed. I felt very frustrated. You can almost see it in the *9/11* film, the frustration on my face. I'm trying to call different chiefs, trying to access what's going on upstairs, and not being able to get through. Some of the messages did get through. We found we were able to talk at different levels at different times and at different spots in the building. We had a lot of people trapped in elevators, and we had a number of firefighters having chest pains. And we got those messages down, and we started to get people up to assist. But it was spotty at best.

It was almost like the closer you were, the less you knew. That's what happened. We weren't getting full intelligence reports of what was going on. If you watched the *9/11* tape, I don't think you saw any ranking law enforcement in the lobby. The helicopters were up, but we had no means to communicate with them. We tried a number of times to do that, but it wasn't happening and no one was coming in to volunteer any of that information to us. As we look back, we were the least informed. Resources were up there. Helicopters were able to assess the damage. My question is "Who did they tell?" They didn't tell us. Or if they told anybody, whoever they told had a responsibility to tell us. But I think instead of blaming people, as we move forward I think we should just acknowledge that this is one of the areas that both departments need to work on, police and fire.

We heard this loud rumbling sound, which was the South Tower collapsing, but we didn't know that at the time. I thought that the elevators were coming down, or part of the building or the plane or something was crashing through the lobby, because it started to fill quickly with debris.

We ran around a little corner toward 6 World Trade. We pushed everybody around the corner. We actually huddled down at the base of the escalator, the escalator that leads up to 6 World Trade and then to the North Bridge over West Street. But now this whole area, which was brightly lit, became totally black. We stayed there until the rumbling stopped, and we knew we were alive.

But I thought it was a localized collapse. I never even suspected that the second tower collapsed. I figured whatever happened we're in the middle of it and we're okay.

I said, "Tower 1 command to all units. Evacuate the building. Evacuate the building." And that was heard. I got acknowledgment. Then I heard it go up farther, meaning that somebody, one of the chiefs, picked up the transmission. Then I heard it repeated again on the handy talkies, so I knew my call to get everybody out of the building was heard. And later on talking to firefighters, they said they heard me.

But I never knew the second tower collapsed. Nor did I hear any message of that. But I had to get the other guys out of the building because something was wrong and we were no longer able to assess what was going on. Now we're in a mode where we have to figure out how to escape. We didn't know what occurred, so the concern was to get everybody out and regroup.

We went across the West Bridge with Jules and an EMS lieutenant. I went back and forth a few times and still didn't know that the South Tower had collapsed. You couldn't see it. What you saw was smoke. Many times when you get a big fire, smoke covers the building and you don't see the building. But you know the building is still there. So when we looked, we were at a bad angle. It was just dust that covered where the building would be. A minute later Chief

Hayden came and was standing in the street, and still I did not know that the South Tower collapsed.

We were only out there a few minutes when we heard a loud rumbling sound, almost like a train if you're standing underneath an overpass. And somebody yelled, "The building's coming down. Run." I ran toward the river, and I guess Jules was with me. I had all my gear, the bunker gear, but I didn't have a mask. And I guess Jules ran faster than I, and as we get about twenty yards up the block, I see him huddled between a couple of cars in just a T-shirt. I figured, I have the helmet and the gear. I'll be able to protect him. So I actually jumped on top of him. He didn't know it was me at that time. And then I heard all the crashing and the steel and now the street goes totally black. As a firefighter you kind of expect blackness inside of a burning building. But outside in broad daylight, you don't.

At that point, I thought we were going to die. I could only think of my wife and my kids and how much I would like to see them again. I thought of Kevin right after. I thought, He's going to be okay. We told him to get out, he'll be okay. There are a lot of firemen around. It's hard for me to find him. He'll come and find me. You know, I'm there with a white helmet. I'm a lot more visible than all the other guys. All the other guys look the same. So I thought, He'll see the white helmet and he'll find me.

I tried to call him on the radio. It didn't work. And I said, "Okay, the radio's not doing well today anyway." And then a number of hours passed by and still no Kevin. So I decided to take a walk around the site. Let me see if there's anybody from 33. And I saw 33's rig, and for some reason I checked the riding list, even though I knew he was in the building.

I remember walking north on West Street, walking through the blackness of downtown because there were no lights. It was at that point I realized my brother was gone, and hundreds of firefighters were gone, and all I could think of was how much we really used to love working downtown, and all the times we used to talk on the phone, or at the house, or at parties about the job, and I realized that all that was gone.

We had the memorial for my brother. And then in February, I got a phone call to come to the Trade Center right away. And I knew they had found him. I went down to the Trade Center and they were in the process of digging him out. For me, that was the toughest part. I was pretty cool and calm in that command mode, but I think at that point I left it all behind and I just knelt there next to his body in the midst of all the steel and the rubble. And then we carried him through the field of twisted steel and it was almost overwhelming because everything became a reality of what took place there and how horrible it was.

We actually brought him up a dirt hill and we had about a hundred firefighters salute as we passed by with a flag over his body. We put him in the ambulance, and I jumped in. They closed the doors and I sat there. And there were a lot of tears. But after sitting there alone with him for a while, I started to remember all the good times we had. He only lived six blocks away from me in Middle

Village, so I always saw him. So in the middle of the tears, there was some sort of peace or tranquillity. I remember sitting in the ambulance saying how horrible this was. This was the worst I could imagine. And then after a few minutes I felt a calmness. It's very strange, but it was my time with him, which I'm really glad I had. Not only did I see him going into the towers, but I also brought him out.

A couple of days after September 11, I met Dennis Tardio, who was the captain of Engine 7. He stopped me on the stairs in the firehouse, and he said to me, "I owe my life to your brother."

I asked him what he meant. He said when he was coming down the stairs, he was coming down the C stairs, and for some strange reason he made eye contact with my brother. And my brother called him over and said, "Dennis, you can't get down these stairs. It leads you out into all the debris." He said, "You need to switch to the B stairs."

Dennis got out of the building and within thirty seconds the building came down. He said if it weren't for Kevin, he wouldn't be here. And I know for a fact, if they had gone down the other stairs, it would have led out onto the mezzanine level and there would never have been enough time to get out of the building.

ANTHONY R. WHITAKER
57, Captain, Port Authority Police Department

"I SAW A GIGANTIC FIREBALL COMING RIGHT TOWARD ME, AND IT
APPEARED AS IF IT WAS PUSHING PEOPLE IN FRONT OF IT, AND ALL
AROUND IT, AND INSIDE OF IT, JUST FREE-FLOATING."

On 9/11, I was—and I still am—the commanding officer of the World Trade Center police command. I was on duty on the morning of September 11, in my usual spot. I had a patrol philosophy of community policing, and so four days a week I routinely stood on the mall floor. We had seventy-five stores in the mall at the World Trade Center, and it was my habit to stand in front of one of the stores, Banana Republic, which is situated approximately fifty feet from the entrance doors to the lobby of building 1, which is the North Tower. So on that morning, between the hours of eight-thirty and the time of the impact of the first aircraft, that's where I was, standing in front of Banana Republic in the shopping mall of the World Trade Center.

I checked my timepiece at approximately 8:42 hours, and because it occurred to me at that moment that the traffic was fairly light for a Tuesday morning. It didn't dawn on me why. After the fact I realized it was because it was Election Day.

I normally stand in front of Banana Republic until about nine. Then I usually call my patrol sergeant, and the two of us do a perimeter walk around the entire complex, checking on illegal parkers and any other violations that may be visible on the street. Then we go back into the complex and make a tour of it before I go back to my office and start my paperwork.

So I was standing in front of Banana Republic when I heard what sounded to me like a roar, just a roar, and it just continued to get louder and louder and louder until it got so loud that it sounded like it was right next to me, right next to the left side of my face. So I looked to my left, and at that instant I saw a gigantic fireball coming out of the lobby of building 1 on the south side, which is the Marriott side. It was coming right toward me, and it appeared as if it was pushing people in front of it, and all around it, and inside of it, just free-floating. It was the eeriest thing I've ever seen. Instinctively, something told me to get out of the way of this thing. I didn't hesitate. I turned left and ran down the main corridor toward the lobby of building 2. There's a small hallway in between building 1 and building 2. When I got to that hallway, I dove in.

I don't know how long I was on the floor, but when I finally woke up or came out of whatever I was in, I dragged myself up to my knees and I just started feeling my body parts, just to make sure everything was there. I stumbled back out to the main hallway, and I stopped because it was quiet, just deadly quiet, no sounds at all. The lights were all off. And as I started to stumble back toward building 1, I became conscious. I became aware of the fact that I was stepping on things, and a voice inside of my head just said, "Don't look down." So I didn't, but it instinctively occurred to me what I was stepping on. I was walking on people, body parts. It just felt like I was walking on cushiony things.

At the same time, I saw two people out of the corner of my left eye, running toward me from the general direction of the lobby of building 1. And they were on fire. They ran toward me and then they ran right past me. They issued no sound. All their clothes were burnt off, and they were just smoldering.

About the same time as the two people ran past me, a transmission came over my radio and I think it snapped me out of whatever I was in. And it called for a Port Authority supervisor to respond to the north side of the lobby of building 1, to the fire command desk.

I acknowledged the radio transmission, and I contacted our police desk, which is located in building 5 on the mezzanine level. I ordered the cop at the desk to begin a full-scale evacuation of the entire complex. After 9/11, I was repeatedly asked, "Why did you give that order to evacuate at that particular time?" Now this is after the first aircraft came in and before the second aircraft came in. The only thing I can say is what I've been saying all along: It just occurred to me that whatever was going on—and I still didn't know what that was—was beyond my ability as a commanding officer of that facility to do anything about it. So, it seemed to me that the only prudent thing to do was start a full-scale evacuation and get everybody out of there. I then responded to the lobby of building 1, on the north side.

As I approached the fire command desk, I saw three friendly faces, three police officers from the Holland Tunnel that I've known practically my entire career: Donald Foreman, Walter McNeil, and Nathaniel Webb. I thought, How did they get here so fast? After 9/11, I've gone back over the sequence of events, and what has occurred to me is that I must have blacked out somewhere, and lost some time, which is why I couldn't account for how my three colleagues had gotten to the World Trade Center from the Holland Tunnel so quickly. I thought it was a matter of seconds, but it must have been five, ten, fifteen, twenty minutes that had passed since the time that I saw the fireball coming out of lobby 1.

Anyway, I responded to the fire control desk in lobby 1, and I rendezvoused with a representative from New York City's Office of Emergency Management and Fire Chief Joe Pfeifer. After I conferred with them, I took the three officers from the Holland Tunnel—Foreman, McNeil, and Webb—and I went over to the lobby of building 2 to establish a command presence there. I instructed Foreman and McNeil to establish land lines to our command police desk in Jersey City, a land line to the communications desk at the Holland Tunnel, and a land line to our communications desk at the World Trade Center. After I finished instructing those two, a New York City fire chief came in with about thirty to thirty-five firemen behind him. He approached me and he requested that I give him one of my uniformed police officers with a radio. So I turned to Nat Webb and I told him to go with the fire chief.

And Nat just gave me a funny look, which basically asked, "Why me?" After that, what happened between Nat and I was very strange, because we started a running conversation, but no words were spoken. It was a mental thing between us. And he just continuously kept asking me, "Why me?"

And I was busy telling him, "Look, there's nobody else. Foreman and McNeil had their job to do, and you have your job to do. Your job is to go with the fire chief." And all of this is transpiring between the two of us with no words, no spoken words. So Nat went walking off with the fire chief and thirty-some-odd firemen. And that's the last time I saw Nat Webb alive.

After Nat disappeared around the corner, I received another radio transmission from one of the Port Authority chiefs, and he asked me to rendezvous with him at the footbridge. I thought he meant the footbridge that leads over to Deutsche Bank on Liberty and Greenwich, so I got ready to respond to that location to rendezvous with him. I was looking at the exit doors onto Liberty Street from building 2, and I heard a voice in the back of my head, which said, "Don't walk out on Liberty Street." So I didn't. I reversed myself, and I walked through the lobby and into the mall area, made a right-hand turn, and walked down toward building 4. I walked through what we call the Sam Goody corridor, and I gained access to Liberty and Greenwich through that door. And when I got there, to the footbridge between building 2 and building 4, the chief wasn't there. No one was there.

After a few seconds, I turned around, I went back to the door, and I walked down toward the main corridor at the top of the PATH escalators, where J. Crew and Coach and other stores are located. I rendezvoused there with one of my sergeants from PATH, Sergeant Marty Duane. And again, here's where my memory lapses come in. I found out about some of what I did that day after 9/11: apparently, after I regained consciousness, after I got away from the fireball, I got hold of Marty Duane, and we went around and gathered up a few Port Authority police officers and positioned them at key locations in the mall to facilitate the evacuation. When I ran into Duane the second time, he was busily engaged in the evacuation.

I stood there for a couple of seconds talking to Marty, and from what I could see the evacuation was going well. There were hundreds of people moving through the mall from the area of building 1. The majority of the seventy-five stores in the mall had already been evacuated. They were practically empty.

But all that morning I don't think I really had a good understanding of what was going on. And whatever it was, it was bigger than us. I was outside now and looking up at the North Tower. I pulled my radio out of my back pocket and I contacted our police desk again and I told the police desk for the second time to evacuate the entire complex. After I made that radio transmission, I was thinking I would walk up Liberty Street past building 2. But I heard that voice in the back of my head again, which said, "Don't walk up Liberty Street." So I didn't. I walked that short block over, by the Greek Orthodox Church, and I started to walk north up that block.

No sooner had I cleared the church when I heard the same roar that I had heard earlier. I heard it again. And then, "Wham!" A tremendous explosion. That was the second plane coming in. And again, that voice in my head said, "Don't look up." I didn't look up, but I didn't have to. That explosion was something else. And the heat from it was like a wave, which just slapped me on the left side of my face, and knocked me sideways.

A security guard opened up one of the lobby entrances, I started running toward it, and I dove in. I don't know where two other guys came from, but there were three of us that hit the floor, inside the lobby. We weren't on the floor that long before I got up and spoke to the security guard. I said, "Look, is there another way out of this building?"

He said, "Yeah, there's a back street."

I said, "Take me to it." He led me through the building, and we went into a truck bay. There were other people in there, and as soon as they saw me in uniform, they went crazy. They started asking me a million and one questions. Obviously, I had no answers. The only thing I could tell them was "Look, just stay inside. Stay indoors. You're safe as long as you stay indoors. We're doing all we can do. But just stay inside."

So he led me through the crowd, to a door, and I walked out and I was on a side street, and I started to make my way up toward Broadway. I got to the corner of Broadway and Liberty when I ran into a co-worker, Barbara Reynolds, who was just beside herself. She was screaming at me that her female cousin worked in building 2. She wanted to go back there to look for her. I told her, "Barbara, you can't go back in. You just can't. It's too dangerous. We're doing all we can. Just stay away and get as far away from the complex as you can."

I think I was extremely lucky on September 11. I know God was on my side. I feel that God did me a favor, like with my blackouts. I feel that was God's way of telling my conscious mind that I should get busy and do his work. And his work that particular morning was to save as many people as possible. And that's exactly what we did. We got busy and we got thousands of people out of there. And in my judgment, as a thirty-year police officer who also had the benefit of eight and a half years as an airport fire crew chief, that's the only thing we could have done.

Four days a week, I used to stand in front of Banana Republic, probably for half an hour, between eight-thirty in the morning and nine. Literally, I kid you not, thousands of faces used to pass me by, coming from the New York City subway system and coming from the PATH, and coming from the downtown area, and coming from Battery Park City. In that half hour, I literally greeted people every morning, for four days a week, for twenty-eight months, thousands of people.

One thing that really bothers me is that I don't know what happened to all those many faces that I used to wave at. In the *Daily News* they ran spreads of photographs. And one of the things that really hurt me was that I recognized almost 80 percent of those people.

Brian Smith, right, and his son, Kevin.

BRIAN SMITH
24, Battalion 31, FDNY

"I FEEL LIKE THIS CHAPTER IN THE BOOK ISN'T OVER YET."

I am stationed in Brooklyn, at an EMS Command on the corner of North Portland and Park Avenue, maybe a mile or so from the Manhattan and Brooklyn Bridges. I had worked the night tour. So we didn't get back to the station until about eight-thirty or so. It was about eight-forty-five when my partner, Brian Gordon, and I were heading out to my car in the parking lot to go home, when we heard some kind of muffled explosion.

We just disregarded it as vehicular noise up on the BQE. We took a few more steps and looked out to the west, where you could see the Trade Center. And just at that point we saw the beginning of that plume of cloud from the plane driving into the North Tower. So we ran back inside. I spoke to the desk lieutenant, and I got changed back into my uniform, picked up radio equipment, and then we went outside, logged on, and called the dispatcher to let her know we were available as an extra unit if they needed us. And they dispatched us right away.

I didn't know lower Manhattan very well. But we got over the Brooklyn Bridge and we followed an undercover police car hoping to get somewhere near the staging area. We got down to Broadway and followed it to Dey. We took that to Church and then Church to Liberty. A police officer on the corner said that he didn't know where EMS was being staged, but he said there were a lot of injuries down at the 10 House. Not being familiar with the area, I had no idea where the guy was talking about. He said, "Just drive down Liberty. Engine 10 Ladder 10 is down on the left-hand side across the street from the South Tower. You can't miss it."

So that's what we did. We went down to the 10-10 House, backed the ambulance into the one of the engine bays, and asked the captain what he needed. He said there were a lot of injuries. At this point, things were just starting to happen. The South Tower was struck right then, and we got a whole bunch of new injuries. We called our dispatch to let them know we we were and told them that we were setting up triage.

Liberty Street was full of firefighters. All kinds of different debris were falling. I heard somebody outside was down, so we made our way west down Liberty Street toward West. The street was littered with debris. There were people that had jumped from the upper floors. The sidewalk was carpeted with body parts. We got down to maybe thirty feet from where this injured firefighter was, and some other firefighters just picked him up on a long board and started carrying him in the opposite direction. I could see from where I was that he was in pretty bad shape. I said, "The heck with it. Maybe they're taking him to a triage center around the corner. Maybe there is something already set up. Let's just get back into the firehouse. We're going to killed out here."

We started to make our way back to the 10 House. There was this little coffee stand, like a concession trailer. It was locked up, but I said, "Let's get whatever we can out of here, water, juice, things of that nature, and we'll set up a rehab center inside of 10 House." I figured we would be there for a good twenty-four hours before we got relieved.

We got one milk crate full, and a firefighter went back with it. And as we were filling up the second milk crate, it sounded like another plane was coming in. The firefighter and I just looked at each other and we dropped what we had and started to make our way back toward the firehouse, running down Liberty Street. The sound was deafening. I really thought that it was another plane coming. I thought it was a 747 looking to make a landing on Liberty Street.

So we ran into the firehouse. Most of the people weren't there anymore. The only guy who was in there was an Asian man named Fu. And because of the damage to his hip, he couldn't walk and he was trying to claw his way to the back of the building where the others were. So I stopped and grabbed him by a brace that we had put on him, and I dragged him to the back of the building.

The impact of the South Tower collapsing literally picked me up and threw me through the air. I landed facefirst on the ground and a wave of debris came blowing by me. Things were hitting me, smoke, dirt, dust, and who the hell knows what else. It was instant blackness, the thickest, most choking smoke you could imagine. And then I thought, "I'm in a firehouse. There must be packs around here somewhere." Both the Engine and the Ladder had been deployed. They had left earlier after the North Tower was struck. So they weren't even in the house, and there was basically nothing there to breathe with. So I just pulled my shirt over my face and tried to breathe.

My partner and I made a decision to stay in the 10 House and continue treating people. He and I were really the only medical people that were there. There were a lot of civilians, a lot of firefighters. There were people that were just picked up and blown around by the thing when it came down. There was a firefighter with a broken leg, people with all kinds of different injuries. So we just stayed and began to treat them. We splinted the guy's leg up, put him on a long board. Eventually, we got most of the firehouse completely evacuated through the back of the building because the front of it was completely covered in debris.

When the South Tower came down, I had gotten all kinds of injuries. Later on, when I went to the hospital, I found that I had a concussion, whiplash, smoke inhalation, cuts and bruises, and all kinds of stuff. And that was all just from the impact of the South Tower collapsing. But we stayed. We continued to treat people. We evacuated the building.

And just when we were getting ready to do our last run through the building, my partner, another firefighter, and I started to hear that sound again. It sounded like another plane coming in. At this point it just seemed like all these planes forgot where La Guardia Airport was. Everybody was looking to make a landing. I had no idea what had really happened. I just thought they were planes. I didn't know until after I left Manhattan that the towers even came down. I just thought that 747s were landing all over the place. I honestly thought that a plane landed on Liberty Street in front of the firehouse, and that by some miracle I survived it.

We were inside the engine bays of the 10 House, which is about a hundred feet across the street from the South Tower, to the left of it. So after the South Tower came down and while the North Tower was coming down, we made a beeline and ran into the bathroom and just crouched down on the floor in the corner of the bathroom. And we just waited for the end to come. And it didn't.

We got up and after a few more scares we were able to pick our way through the back of the firehouse. That's where Fu was. Three of us, including my partner and a volunteer firefighter who worked as an accountant in the towers, took turns carrying Fu on our shoulders. We carried him about two blocks south to Rector Street. Everything was on fire, smoke everywhere, and it was just complete bedlam. It looked like a war zone.

We made our way down to one of the office buildings in the vicinity. There was a crowd of people in the lobby. We couldn't carry Fu all the way back to

Brooklyn, so we put him down. It was a pretty big building. The guy said it was twenty-seven stories. He said that there were seven stories full of people still in it, a couple hundred people. So my partner and I went in there and started to evacuate the building. This was 2 Rector Street. Again, I don't know Manhattan. All I know is that this is an office building and it's tall, and there are planes. I know it's a common reaction to tell everybody to stay inside, under their desks, or whatever. But we started getting on the floors and yelling down hallways for everybody to get out.

"We're the fire department and you guys have to leave now."

And people were saying, "We were told this is the safest place to stay."

I remember yelling at these people, "Listen, you can stay here if you want. I'm not going to go in there and drag you out. But, you know, your blood is in your own hands. I'm telling you, if you want to go home and see your family you have to come with me now." We didn't get too many arguments after that. We evacuated anywhere from two hundred to two hundred fifty people.

We were in there for some time, but eventually we started to hear vehicular traffic outside. We went out and flagged down a police car, and we put Fu and another guy with a mangled foot in the back of the police car, and we told them to take these guys to the hospital because they needed to see a doctor immediately. And they drove away.

My partner and I then said, "All right, let's get out of here. We've done all we can do." And we left. We made our way down to Wall Street, and then down to the piers. We got a ride from an NYPD harbor patrol boat back over to the Brooklyn Navy Yard. From there, we got a security guard to take us over to our battalion. When we walked into the battalion, we were pretty much spent. People had to do a double take because they thought we were dead. They figured we were goners. So they were very surprised to see us walking in the door. We were pretty banged up, bloody, and covered with dust and everything else. My partner had badly twisted his ankle, so he couldn't really walk that well.

We went to Kings County Hospital and they started to treat us. From that point forward, the roles reversed. I went from taking care of patients to becoming one myself.

Right now, I have this stupid recurring thing. It's a condition called angioedema of the uvula. It means that the punching bag in the back of my throat swells up. It's pretty nasty. I've also developed a bleeding ulcer. The doctor says it's from stress, but I've never had it before. I'm twenty-four years old and I have a hole in my stomach. They have me on all kinds of medicine now to keep it from flaring up. Then they found that I have black spots on my lungs. I don't know if it's a temporary thing, but I haven't had as bad a cough as some of the other guys. I also have bad nightmares. It's hard to get a good night's sleep.

Anyway, so we were in Kings County Hospital, and it was about eight o'clock that night when I was able to get in touch with my family. Actually my mother-in-law called me. She said, "Are you okay?"

I said, "Yeah, I'll be fine. I'm just a little roughed up."

Then she asked me, "Has your father tried to get in touch with you?"

And I said, "No, he hasn't. Why would he try to get in touch with me? I don't even think he's working."

She said, "No, he was working."

I found out later that my father had been working overtime. But at that point, I said to my mother-in-law, "Nah, even if he was working, he wouldn't try to get in touch with me. He'd be busy working."

And she said, "Well, you know, he's been missing since nine o'clock this morning. No one's been able to find him. They don't know where he is."

I said, "I'm going to call over to his firehouse and find out what's going on." And I called over to his house and the guy on house watch answered. I said, "I'm calling to find out the status of Hazmat 1."

"Well, who's calling?"

I said, "This is Brian Smith. This is Kevin Smith's son." I explained to him that I was on the job, explained to him where I was, and the guy just started crying.

He said, "They're all gone. We haven't heard anything."

Being down there since and seeing everything up close firsthand, I kind of knew right away. I mean, there's no way that he was able to get out. To this day they still haven't made a recovery, so I'm hoping that maybe I'll get some kind of answer, but I haven't yet.

I've been digging. I still go down there to work. Not too often now, but I usually still try to go there on my days off. If they find anybody from Hazmat 1, they'll notify me and then I'll take my unit out of service and I'll go down there and we'll do the final removal. But I've been down there just basically digging through the debris and pulling out all kinds of people. We've pulled out firefighters and pieces of firefighters, so who knows? Maybe I already pulled him out and I'm just waiting for the DNA to come back. But there's been no positive ID yet.

Because they haven't made a recovery, it almost feels like it's not done yet, like that day still isn't over. It will make a difference if they find him. I know it will. At first I didn't think so. For the first month and a half I thought, Whatever, if they do or they don't, it doesn't matter. I know he's dead. I'm not one of those types of people that need to go to a cemetery to feel at peace. But as time has gone on, the thought of my dad buried out there somewhere is very unsettling to me, and that's part of the reason I go down there to work. When they do find him, I think it'll make a big difference. Right now, I feel like I'm in limbo just waiting for the whole episode to be over. I feel like this chapter in this book isn't over yet.

When things start to feel really heavy, I pray a lot. Sometimes I'll talk to my wife, or to my partner, especially my partner. He can relate. We were step-and-step almost the whole way through, so it's easy for us to talk to each other because we have pretty similar perspectives. I just keep busy, I pray, and I talk about it if it gets to be too much.

GARY SMILEY
38, Paramedic, Battalion 31, FDNY

"ONE YOUNG GUY THAT WORKS WITH MY STATION WANTED TO GO
ACROSS THE STREET AND TRY TO CATCH THE FALLING PEOPLE. I WAS
HOLDING ONTO HIM. I ALMOST HAD TO KNOCK HIM TO THE GROUND.
I SAID, 'YOU CAN'T. THEY'RE GOING TO KILL YOU.'"

On September 11, I was actually working an overtime tour in downtown Brooklyn. We responded as soon as we heard the initial radio call that the first plane
had hit the tower. We made it over the Brooklyn Bridge, through the traffic, to
Church Street between tower 1 and tower 2. We met three other ambulances
there and a couple of fire engines. I set up an initial triage area outside in the
street. By looking up, you could see that it was a pretty bad fire, but no one
expected what was going to occur in the next hour or so.

There was a lot of debris in the street. Victims were coming out from the concourse, from building 1, and from 5 World Trade Center. My partner, Danny
Rivera, went into the lobby to start directing people toward me. About ten minutes later I saw a hysterical woman coming out of the lobby. She had been cut up
really badly. So I went and grabbed her and as I was carrying her across Church
Street, she tugged on my turnout coat and started yelling, "Plane." I thought she
was just yelling that a plane had hit the tower. And she kept yelling, "Plane."

I looked up at that point, and that's when the second plane hit the South
Tower. The explosion was unbelievable. It was right above my head. You didn't
hear anything. People ask me sometimes, "What did you hear?" I heard nothing.

I ran with her as stuff came down. I didn't even make it three-quarters of the way across the street. I just threw her on the ground and threw myself on top of her. Parts of the building, parts of everything came down all around us. I got hit with some burning debris, which burned me a little on the back. It was chaos. Everybody was running around. Then it clicked in my head. I knew exactly what was going on. I was there in 1993 when they bombed the building. I ended up taking care of a hundred people across the street in the Millennium Hotel. So I knew this was an attack. That's what we started telling people, and that's what got them moving. We had them run toward Broadway because we figured it would be safer.

An enormous amount of debris began to fall out of the South Tower. People running out of buildings toward us were getting hit with stuff and killed. I remember one guy who ran up to me and he was holding onto a leg. I thought, My God, he's holding his own leg.

He was screaming, "Help me, help me." He was holding somebody else's leg. I'll never forget that guy. He was just standing there with this entire leg in his arms. He had lost all control of what was going on and was screaming.

And you know, when I got burned on my back, it was a human arm that hit me, and it was on fire. That's what burned my back. It was unbelievable, an absolute nightmare at that point—bodies everywhere, people falling out of the building.

I made a decision at that point that it was just too dangerous to be where we were. We took the truck around and we went down Vesey Street. It was already littered with bodies. It almost looked like a graveyard. Then we were on West Street with about twenty or thirty people. People were jumping out of the North Tower. At first, you didn't know what the heck they were doing, and then you realized when you saw one after the other after the other. Two people hit two separate firemen and killed them right before my eyes. One young guy that works with my station wanted to go across the street and try to catch the falling people. I was holding onto him. I almost had to knock him to the ground. I said, "You can't. They're going to kill you."

This went on and on, and I remember watching fourteen people jump, including a couple that must have jumped from at least the ninetieth floor. They held hands and jumped. That was the most sickening sight I've ever seen in my life, the most helpless feeling, watching these people who have no other choice but to leap from some ninety floors. At one point I had to turn away. I couldn't watch it any more.

Then, just as we were going into the North Tower, we heard a rumbling and people screamed that it was coming down. And we were, like, "What's coming down?" It was the South Tower. People went in every direction. You dropped whatever you had. We ran and ended up right next to the atrium in the AmEx building. We dove in there. Then you started to hear the Mayday calls from the radio, from different units that were trapped all over. Nobody really knew where anybody was. It was just "Mayday, Mayday." Then I heard my friends, EMTs Brian Smith and Brian Gordon, come on the radio and say, "31 Mary. We're trapped on Liberty Street." I looked at Danny and we knew what we had to do. We told the fire chief with us that we had to go get these guys. He said, "Listen, I can't make you go, but you gotta do what you gotta do."

We took whatever we could—trauma bags, IVs, a couple of portable stretchers—and off we went down West Street. We met a couple firemen and we asked if they knew where anybody was. They said, "No. We're looking ourselves. Just be careful."

The North Tower was still burning out of control. Even at that point, it wasn't on my mind that the other tower would come down. I never even thought about it. I was just focused on these guys. We got to the north pedestrian bridge and I remember hearing a noise like thunder. I hear it in my nightmares all the time. I never forget. I just looked up and you could see the antenna on top of the North Tower moving, and you knew it was coming down. There was no time to scream. If you hesitated, you were dead. There were about ten people in the area where we were. Only three of us made it out alive. I started running. I dropped everything I had. The gush of air that came down with the building picked me up and literally threw me through the air, almost like Peter Pan.

I landed not too far from the truck that I had responded in. Something told me to crawl underneath that truck. That's where I ended up. I couldn't hear anything. I remember screaming for Danny, and every time I'd breathe in it was as if my head was stuck in sand. And I remember thinking, I'm dead, and I got really angry. I've been a paramedic for seventeen years and I've never really gotten hurt. I've been in some pretty crazy situations. I've made a lot of lifesaving decisions in my life. But I got very angry because I have an eleven-year-old and an eighteen-year-old. My kids are just getting over the loss of my dad, who was killed three years ago during a random street robbery. My son was traumatized by that. He was unable to sleep. And now I was so angry that I was going to be leaving him with two horrible things to deal with.

My mind just switched at that point, and I think that's really what gave me a desire to get out of there. Something just clicked, and I thought, I know I'm not going to die today. I'm going to get out of here.

You know how people say, "God had other plans for you." I think it was my father who had other plans for me. He had to be looking out for me, and I just started digging. I don't know how long I was under the truck before I figured this out, but I started crawling my way out of there, digging through the rocks and the debris. Just as I got out, a fireman who had also been lodged in the debris had gotten himself out. Both of us staggered around. I don't know how long we walked for. We went in one direction, more and more toward the buildings, which was no good. We walked the other way, along a fence for quite a while.

We figured it had to lead somewhere. We ended up going all the way down West Street, across to Vesey, and up Vesey going toward North End Avenue, which is a small street one block toward the water.

People started calling out, "Is anybody out there?" We went toward their voices. It was a deli owner and his wife. They pulled us in their deli. About six or seven cops and some firemen were already in there, all variously injured and having a hard time breathing. They had taken a hose out of the kitchen to clean everybody off. I had first-degree burns on every part of my skin that was exposed. Stuff started exploding outside the store. One of the cops thought that it might be secondary explosions. When terrorists do this sort of thing, they'll put secondary bombs around to kill the rescue workers. That's an earmark of terrorism. And at that point you didn't know what to believe. Everybody had lost all concept of what was going on, and everything was up for grabs. For all we knew, they had attacked all of Manhattan.

The first few months I couldn't sleep at all. When I hear an airplane, I follow it in the sky until it's out of sight. Every time I hear a noise like that I have to look up. I will never get on an airplane again, at least that's the way I feel now.

I keep going to doctors and they keep doing blood work. I still have very severe muscle cramps. Everybody still has shortness of breath, and ear and mouth infections. I've actually lost a couple of teeth and they can't figure out why. I go to work because that's what I do. I've been doing this for seventeen years, and it's my life. Being a paramedic is the greatest job in the world for me. I would do it if I lost my limbs. I'd crawl. But I don't have the energy to do extra stuff. That's the hard part. Hopefully it will get better. But the doctors don't really have answers about what was inhaled that day. God knows what was in all that stuff, the levels of trace metals and asbestos and mercury, the gas from the air-conditioning units and mercury from the lightbulbs. Nobody really knows.

I told health services, "You know, I lost two teeth. They just fell out."

They said, "Well, you should see your dentist."

I said, "No, you don't understand. My teeth just fell out of my head. There's got to be a reason."

And there's no valid reason why Danny and I should be alive. There's a lot of guilt involved. There was this one emergency medical technician who had volunteered her services when we were still operating on Church Street. And she was thrown into the back of the ambulance when the second plane hit. When the South Tower collapsed, I lost sight of her. Danny and I checked the papers for faces. We thought that we had gotten her killed, and we felt very guilty.

Then a month and a half later we got redeployed into Manhattan. A scaffold had collapsed in lower Manhattan, and I worked that collapse. I went into the building, and it was one of the greatest feelings I had at the time because people were being pulled out alive. Afterward, I was dusting myself off out on the street when somebody grabbed me from behind. And it was that girl. She worked three blocks away and had heard about the crash and come down to help. It was the greatest feeling in the world knowing that she was alive. I had felt for sure that we had gotten her killed.

And, of course, Brian and Brian, the guys I was looking for when the building collapsed, and I are inseparable, like three brothers, at this point. I credit them with saving my life. If I hadn't gone to look for them, if Danny and I had stayed in the lobby of the AmEx building, we would certainly have been killed.

I go to a survivors group. There are some firefighters in there, a policeman and civilians with stories worse than mine. We just sit around and talk. It's hard to talk to people who weren't there at the time. They don't get it. We've had people ask us, "Oh, aren't you over it yet?" I'll never be over it. Two of my best friends still haven't been found. I knew about twenty firemen who were lost there. I knew the two paramedics who were killed. Death is something you never get over.

But I was doing what I was supposed to do. I was looking for the guys and I was looking for people. And if I had been killed with that debris when I first arrived there, well, that's where I was supposed to be: helping people.

ADA ROSARIO-DOLCH
46, Principal, High School for Leadership and Public Service

"AS EACH KID CAME OUT, I TOLD THEM, 'YOU HOLD HANDS. THIS IS LIKE KINDERGARTEN. FIND A PARTNER. DON'T BE ALONE. THIS IS A GOOD TIME TO MAKE A FRIEND.'"

It was a very exciting morning for us at the school because we had arrived at a new juncture: for the first time our building at 90 Trinity Place was being used as a voter center. The Wall Street neighborhood is a business neighborhood. But in the last couple of years, it has started to become a community where people live. So we were called by the League of Women Voters, and for the first time on September 11, primary day, we were a voting site.

I got to the school bright and early at six o'clock in the morning because I wanted to see it all start. We saw the first one or two politicians who showed up to vote. We got some signs up. I took a good look at the lobby in terms of security, because I didn't want outsiders commingling with my kids as they walked in.

At about eight-thirty, I said to my secretary, "You know what, I'm going to go downstairs and observe the voting and then I'm going to run to the World Trade Center to get a battery for my watch." I took five dollars and put it in my pocket. I took my walkie-talkie, which I never leave anywhere without, and my keys, and I went to the lobby.

All of a sudden the lights went out. We're a fourteen-story structure, so the kids use elevators to get upstairs. The entire building runs on one switch. So I'm thinking maybe somebody leaned on the switch. But I know the switch is not in an easy place to get at. So I looked toward the custodian's office and I noted that the door was locked. A few seconds later, the lights went back on. Then, maybe five seconds later, we heard this tremendous boom. I immediately thought it was a bomb.

I was in the lobby, trying to monitor what was going on, when I looked through the glass and saw the reflection of 1 Liberty Plaza. And in the reflection, I could see glass debris just falling out, spewing out, of the World Trade Center. One of my students came in, and she said, "Mrs. Dolch, a plane just hit the World Trade Center."

And I said, "Well, maybe a little Piper, maybe a helicopter."

And she said, "No, Mrs. Dolch, a real plane."

A bunch of people from the street just started pouring into the building lobby, and they were screaming, crying, and yelling, "It's a plane."

I contacted my assistant principal on an intercom and told him to call the superintendent's office, which is really our first line of communication, and tell him that something had happened at the World Trade Center. "Tell him it's close, but we're over here and the school is fine, everybody is fine."

I then got a call from my secretary, who said she had just gotten a call from a teacher on the fourteenth floor who said that the kids just watched a plane hit the World Trade Center. The superintendent's office called back, trying to get information from me, and I'm insisting, "I'm not leaving this lobby. I've got to protect the kids." We have about 550 kids, high school kids, ages fourteen to eighteen.

I called my secretary again. I said, "Make sure you call my husband."

Then a kid comes in and says, "Mrs. Dolch, a plane hit the tower."

I said, "Which tower?"

And she said, "The one with the antenna."

I became very concerned because my sister worked there. In '93, when the bomb hit the World Trade Center, we were frantic. And it turned out she had been shopping all day. So in '93, my sister was fine. This time I said a prayer for her. I said, "God, you really have to take care of her because I can't. I've got to take care of the kids." And in my mind, I thought, Maybe she's shopping again. And when people talk about the miracles of 9/11, I can honestly say that one of the first miracles was that I didn't think about my sister again for the rest of the day. She worked at Cantor Fitzgerald and she did die in the World Trade Center that day, but at the time all I could think about was the kids.

And then there was another horrendous bang, and the building shook. This time we felt the impact. That's when we found out that another plane had just hit the South Tower. You can't begin to imagine the chaos that was going on in my lobby. People were just in total hysteria. I threw people to the floor. "Sit down on the floor, don't stand." People were shaking. I got my hand around this woman and she was shaking uncontrollably, and I'm thinking, Oh, my God, my kids are upstairs. They're watching everything from the windows. They can see everything. And I immediately asked my A.P. to make an announcement to get everybody out of their classrooms and into the corridors. I had two concerns: Number 1, that the kids were watching this. And number 2, I was concerned that something could fly from the World Trade Center right into one of our windows.

People were running into our lobby, and I got very concerned that one of them could be a terrorist with a bomb on their body. And then I had this horrendous thought that maybe something would fall on the top of our building and start a fire. And I thought, I'm not going to die in a building like this. I'm not going to have a building burn and the kids burnt in stairwells. I had these horrible thoughts going through my mind, and I said, "We've got to get the kids out of here."

I had two girls in wheelchairs, one girl who had just come back from heart surgery and one girl who's 90 percent blind. I asked the elevator operators to go upstairs and get them, because we knew exactly where they were. When they brought them down I told all of them, "Start going toward Battery Park. Meet me at the corner." I then told my A.P. to go up to the fourteenth floor and start the evacuation, floor by floor. I wanted everybody out, custodial workers, kitchen workers, everybody. I mean, these people were phenomenal. Nobody panicked. They waited floor by floor, starting with 14, 13, 12, 11, 10. We got everybody out, and we went to Battery Park. In fire drills, we had never gone as far as Battery Park, but this time we knew we needed to go in that direction. We knew the problem was north. We needed to go south.

The two head security officers from the American Stock Exchange made sure that the street was clear and open, so that as the kids walked out they could walk out freely toward Battery Park. I waited by the exit door, and as each kid came out, I told them, "You hold hands. This is like kindergarten. Find a partner. Don't be alone. This is a good time to make a friend." Some kids were crying, some were shaking. There was a bit of panic, but everybody was pretty much under control. And as each teacher came down, I told them to make sure to gather their students at the park.

The last person down was my secretary. I said to my custodian, "Good luck. We're leaving," and we did. When I got to the next corner over, I turned around. And it felt like in the Bible when Lot's wife turns around and becomes a pillar of salt. I could not believe what I was observing. It was total destruction. I said to my assistant principal, "Do you see what I see?" And all you could see was the top of the two buildings just billowing fire and black smoke.

As we were nearing the park, we heard this noise. Some people call it a rumble. I heard snapping, a tremendous snapping. I looked back and all I could see was the tsunami wave of dust and debris that was just rolling, and it was going to get us in a second. And I said, "My God, where are all the kids?" I couldn't find them, and that's all I worried about. I said, "God, please take care of them."

The wave was just about to get my back. It was ashy, but it was thick. You felt like your face was getting cut. I remember seeing a fence. It had a bench in front of it. I was wearing heels (by the way, I don't wear heels anymore. I've changed my shoe wardrobe)—and I remember saying, "If I'm going to die, I'm not going to die by being trampled. I'm going to go by that tree." It was this big gigantic tree in Battery Park, and don't ask how, but I flew over this fence. Believe me, I am not an athletic person. So I don't know how I did it, but I found myself at the base of this tree with about fifteen women and men who were on their knees screaming, and praying. Everybody was praying, calling out to God.

Then I remember seeing a ray of sunshine coming through this dark haze, and I'm thinking, I'm not going to die. I'm going to be okay.

I used my walkie-talkie. "Can anybody read me? Where are you?" Some people responded. I said, "Keep talking. Tell me where you are." I found some people by the water. We hugged, we cried. I asked, "Where are the kids? Do we know?" And people said to me that a lot of kids had already gotten on boats and they had gone to Staten Island.

And then I heard another call through the walkie-talkie that a lot of kids were in a restaurant. I didn't even know there was a restaurant in Battery Park, but a lot of them were under the awning at the American Park Restaurant. I kept looking and sure enough, I found the awning and I found more people. Elation. No one was hurt, not one person. The blind girl stubbed her toe on a gigantic piece of wood, and a boy who had broken his ankle over the summer reinjured it because of the trauma of running and walking. But those were the only two injuries.

My girls in wheelchairs, Becky Zheng and Stephanie Sealy, their stories send chills down your spine. At one point, the paraprofessionals, the classroom assistants responsible for the two girls, literally took them off the wheelchairs because there was so much debris and so much garbage on the road that the wheels wouldn't turn. They simply put them on their backs and started running with them.

Once we were all safe in the restaurant, we were able to gather about 150 kids and some teachers, and we broke everybody up into boroughs. "Bronx, you go here. East Side, you're going here," and so on. I took the Brooklyn contingency, and we walked over the bridge and I ended up at 110 Livingston Street, the headquarters for the Board of Education. I got there with five girls, two boys, my secretary, and another teacher. I hugged all of them. My secretary and the teacher stayed with me all along. I pretty much collapsed at 110 Livingston. My husband picked me up. When I saw him, I said, "Oh, my God, what a day." I didn't say, "Oh, my God, you're here. I'm alive. I missed you. I love you." None of that. I just said to him, "Oh, my God, what a day."

By later that night, we still hadn't heard from my sister. Not an e-mail, not a phone call, nothing came through. Of course, I kept thinking, The phones don't work. Maybe we can't communicate. Maybe she's hurt. We kept hope alive for about two or three days. We went to every hospital. We went around with pictures. On about the third day, we didn't give up hope, but we decided that we better start believing she's not with us anymore. That's when the reality started to hit.

KENNETH MERLO
48, Executive Director, Chances for Children

～

"AND I THOUGHT OF ALL OF THOSE FOLKS, MY GOD, THE WAITERS,
THE WAIT STAFF, THE BARTENDERS, THE WINE PEOPLE, AND
SUDDENLY EVERYTHING STARTED TO SINK IN."

Chances for Children is a children's charity, founded by Sarah Ferguson, the Duchess of York. I run the New York branch and our offices had been on the 101st floor of the World Trade Center, building number 1, the North Tower, for the last two years up until 9/11. We had two private offices in the Cantor Fitzgerald offices. They underwrote our occupancy costs, so they paid for our rent, our phone, our postage. That was their contribution to the charity. We have a similar relationship with Cantor Fitzgerald in Milan.

It varies, but the duchess is here once or twice a month, and on September 11, she was in New York City just finishing up a live television interview with

Charles Gibson, on *Good Morning America*. I think she was on in connection with her spokesperson duties, maybe in behalf of Weight Watchers. When she's in town, I'm normally at the office by eight-fifteen or eight-thirty. I try to get there early when she's in town because the phone may ring and I may be required to answer some questions or get some material together.

I had planned to be at the office by eight o'clock that morning. But the evening before I received a voice mail on my cell phone from one of the supporters of the charity, Sharon Hoge. I had offered to help her with her computer, getting her laptop hooked up to AOL or something. So I knew I had her message on my cell phone.

My daughter goes to school on the Upper East Side. At seven-thirty on the eleventh I dropped her off at school. Then I got into the subway at Seventy-seventh Street and Lexington Avenue. I remembered that Sharon had called, and I said to myself, "Oh, shit, if I don't do it now, I know I'm going to promise to come by after work, because I live up on Eighty-sixth and Madison, and with all good intentions I'll agree to come up and help her but I know I'll never get to it."

So out of real guilt, I got out of the subway at Fifty-ninth Street and I called Sharon. She lives at Fifty-ninth Street and Park Avenue, and she said, "Oh, great. Come on over."

Naturally, I thought dealing with Sharon's computer would take only a few minutes, but it never takes a few minutes when you're dealing with computers. So I was working on Sharon's computer when my cell phone rang and someone screamed, "Ken, where are you?"

I was sort of taken aback. Who's calling me asking me where I am? I said, "Who is this?"

And she said, "It's Duchess." She calls herself Duchess.

But I said, "Who?" It was just total disconnect. So John O'Sullivan, her assistant, got on the phone and he said, "Ken, Ken, it's Johnny, with the duchess. Where are you?"

And immediately I thought, Oh, God, was I supposed to be somewhere? Was I supposed to be at a meeting that I forgot about? Why would they be calling me at nearly nine in the morning asking me where I was?

I said, "I'm at Sharon Hoge's. She's one of our supporters and I'm fixing her computer. What's up?"

And he said, "A plane just crashed into the World Trade Center. Turn on the television. We've got to go."

I asked Sharon if I could turn on the television and she said sure. She was getting ready to leave. The next thing I know, there's my building, the North Tower, in flames. I thought, I better call my wife. She'll be concerned. So will my daughter, who's twelve. I got through to my wife right away, and I said, "I'm fine. I'm at Sharon Hoge's." I felt funny telling my wife that I'm at this woman's apartment instead of being at the office. At this point Sharon is on another phone trying to get through to my daughter's school. I just wanted to let her know I was okay. My daughter has been to my office. She knew where I was headed. I had no idea what the school was going to do, whether they were going to announce what had happened, or just send the kids home. But my wife left her office and went to pick her up.

And I immediately started thinking of all the people upstairs, all the Cantor people I knew, all the people at Windows on the World. My daughter used to come from school and I would take her upstairs to eat at Windows on the World. We were on 101 and Windows was on 107, and my daughter and I used to walk up the stairs and go through the kitchen and meet my wife. I'd say, "We're not going to use the elevator. I'll show you a secret way up." And we'd walk up a fire escape from Cantor's 106th floor. My daughter loved looking at the kitchen. And I thought of all of those folks, my God, the waiters, the wait staff, the bartenders, the wine people, and suddenly everything started to sink in.

On Thursday night, the thirteenth, I got a call on my cell phone and the guy says, "Kenneth Merlo?"

I said, "Yes, who's calling?" And it was a fireman at Ground Zero, who said he had just found a box of my business cards. And my cell phone number is on my business cards.

He said, "We wanted to be sure that you're okay, so we just tried the number."

I said, "I'm fine, I didn't make it to the office that morning."

Then I heard him shout to his colleagues, "He's okay. He wasn't in that morning." And I heard a little cheer go up. These people were apparently rummaging through debris and they found my business cards. The duchess of York also had these little red dolls, called Little Red. It's for the charity and she sells them at F.A.O. Schwartz. It's a rag doll that looks like Raggedy Ann, a cute little thing. We sell them and the profits go to Chances for Children. And all of a sudden this doll pops up on a website on Friday. A photographer took a picture of the doll on top of rubble, with the wreckage behind it. I had, like, 150 of these dolls in two offices and somehow they survived. They had been blown out, only to lay on top of the debris. How the hell does this doll, of all things, make it out? We took it as a sign that we're meant to go on.

DAVID KRAVETTE
41, Broker, Cantor Fitzgerald

"THIS HUGE FIREBALL IS COMING RIGHT TOWARD ME.
PEOPLE GOT INCINERATED. AND I REMEMBER JUST LOOKING
AT THIS THING, NOT FEELING SCARED, BUT JUST SAD BECAUSE
I KNEW I WAS GOING TO DIE."

On the morning of September 11, I was on floor 105, tower 1. I had an 8 A.M. meeting set up with a client. He was bringing by some tech people to do some due diligence on our technology company called E-Speed. I get to work usually around seven, seven-fifteen. At eight, the client called to tell me they were running late. And I said fine. But I reminded him to bring photo ID. Ever since the last terrorist attack in '93, the building requires photo ID downstairs. He's been there before, so he knew the drill. He said, "Fine. No problem."

At 8:40, I get a phone call from the security desk downstairs, asking me if I'm expecting visitors. I said yes. "Well, they're here," they said. "But one of them forgot their ID."

I'm 105 flights up. The commute to get downstairs takes about five minutes, especially around that time. So I'm annoyed, obviously, because I have to go down now to sign these people in after I just told them to bring ID. I look at this desk assistant across from me, thinking maybe she'll help out and go down, but she's on the phone. She's also about eight months pregnant. She's a few weeks from maternity leave and she's on the phone talking to a friend and she's on a website looking at bassinets and cribs. A very nice girl expecting her first child. So how lazy am I? I decide to go myself.

I get up to go and the phone rings. I pick it up. It's my wife. She wants to cancel our newspaper delivery because she thinks our kids might end up in the street to fetch the paper every day, and it concerns her. I have a seven-and-a-half-year-old son and a five-year-old daughter.

I said, "Janice, I have to go. I have people waiting downstairs. I gotta pick them up. We'll talk later."

She goes, "No. I'm out all day. Let's just talk now."

I said, "Janice, it's rude, I'll talk to you tonight. This isn't that important." And we ended it like that. So I hang up with her and I take these two elevator rides down. I take the elevator from 105 to 78, change, and take the express down to the ground. I got down to the lobby. Our elevator banks actually face the visitors' gallery. And I started walking over to the visitors' gallery, I'd say it's about thirty yards, and they're standing there waiting for me. And I remember yelling, "Which one of you knuckleheads forgot your ID?"

And as I say this, you hear this really loud screeching sound. I turn around and it's kind of coming from the elevators. So I run away from it, like ten steps, and look back. And the elevators are free-falling. Then, from the middle elevator bank, not the one I came down on, but from the middle one, a huge fireball explodes in the lobby. This huge fireball is coming right toward me. People got incinerated. And I remember just looking at this thing, not feeling scared, but just sad because I knew I was going to die. But as quickly as it came toward me, it actually sucked back in on itself, and it was gone. It left a lot of smoke and everything was blown out, all the glass and revolving doors leading into the shopping area. All I felt was a big wave of heat come over me, like when you put your face too close to a fireplace. My customer and my general counsel and I just ran out. The three of us ran over the overpass to where the Financial Center is. We went down to where the marina is, where the yachts are. And that's when we found out what happened, that a plane had hit the building.

I looked up and saw this big gaping hole. I said, "What's that falling out the window?"

My general counsel looks at me like I'm nuts. And he says, "That's people jumping out."

Meanwhile, I'm trying to call my wife and none of the cell phones seemed to work. I didn't see the second plane hit. I just heard a noise and people yell. I saw the immediate aftermath. We started heading uptown. I was walking with my general counsel to his apartment, I think on Jane Street. None of the phones worked, and I was trying to reach my wife and I was praying she didn't know about any of this yet.

She was home. Everyone had called her, and she was watching. I couldn't reach her for an hour, hour and a half. I finally got through. I remember I just broke down crying on the phone, and I stepped into this freight loading dock to hide and talk quietly. I lost the connection after about thirty seconds. But I remember when I called, she was just filled with such joy that I was alive because she was convinced I was dead. And I was just crying. And this total stranger, this big guy, gives me a big bear hug and says, "You're okay now," and walks away. A total stranger.

Later on, a couple of weeks later, I spoke to the client. They were running late, obviously. They forgot their ID. But they also went to 2 World Trade Center first. They went into the wrong building and waited on line for five minutes, and discovered they were in the wrong building. Had they gone into the right building, I would have gone down, signed them in, and went back up with them. I would have either perished in the elevator, or we would have been back upstairs. Either way, I would have been dead.

Cantor Fitzgerald had four floors in the North Tower—101, 103, 104, and 105. Nobody got out on those floors. Everyone who was upstairs perished. There were a lot of phone calls to wives and husbands at around nine o'clock saying good-bye, as though they knew they were going to die.

Later that day, I walked up to the home of the chairman, Howard Lutnick, and a bunch of us just started calling families. "Have you heard from your husband or your wife?" And the only people who we knew were alive were the ones who were downstairs, or just going to work, or didn't go to work that day. Everyone who was there seemed gone. So it became clear as the days went on. They were all trapped up there. There was no way out and no way down. I heard stories about one guy who called his wife and said, "We're all in a circle on 104 and we're just praying. We're in a big circle holding hands." One friend of mine called his sister and his girlfriend just to say good-bye. You hear so many stories like that. It's heart-wrenching.

There were others like me who had come to work that day, but for some reason were not on the floors when the plane hit. At 8:15 Chris Pepe got a call from a customer at Goldman Sachs to come over and help with something. So he was already out of the building.

Harry Waizer was severely burned. He managed to get down to the lobby from 78 with burns on half his body. Ari Schoenberg helped him down. Lauren Manning was in the fireball in the lobby. It missed me, but it got her. She got burnt over 82 percent of her body. She was on the other side when she was lifted by that fireball, and was thrown out the windows.

I was on overdrive the first few days. I was surprised how together I was. It actually gets worse as time goes on. It sinks in more as life gets more normal. You look around, I'm working at a firm with a lot of new people. I've been there for ten years. I'm a partner there. You're constantly reminded about it: Cantor Fitzgerald, the epicenter of this attack. But you get home and you look at your kids, and you're just, like, "God, they're lucky. They still have me."

ROY BELL

47, Account Manager, Alliance Consulting

"WHEN I LEFT THE ELEVATOR, IT LOOKED LIKE SHEETS OF WHITE FIRE, THIN SHEETS OF FIRE. THE FLAME WAS COMING THROUGH THE ELEVATOR CAR DOORS FROM THE INSIDE OUT."

I worked on the 102nd floor of the World Trade Center, building 1, the North Tower. On September 11, I got there right at 8:45 for an 8:45 meeting. The meeting was originally scheduled for 8 A.M., but I had convinced my boss, Eric Bennett, to make it for 8:45. We were at the ball game the night before, a Yankees game. Roger Clemens was going for his twentieth win that night. The game got rained out, but we knew Clemens would pitch the following night and we were going to use the tickets again with the same customers. So I asked my boss to push the meeting back, and he did.

The next morning, I was on an elevator on the seventy-eighth floor, which is the Sky Lobby, when the plane hit the building. The elevator hadn't started yet. The doors hadn't closed. The doors were closing when the plane hit the building, and the doors stopped closing when they were about eighteen inches apart.

There was fire everywhere. And I ran. I just took off. I mean, I was knocked to my left. I was standing on the right side of the elevator car and I was knocked to my left. There were five people in there at the time, and I'm sure some were down on the floor. My recollection is pretty fuzzy. One woman who was in the elevator with me, who I later spoke with, is named Virginia. She couldn't recall what happened. Some people were knocked to the ground, but I was on my feet and I bolted out of there. I just took off. I had no idea what had happened. I thought it was an explosion. I thought it was perhaps a generator. I came out of the elevator by squeezing through the open doors. There was room to get through. Virginia got out too. The other three people died in there, all women.

The elevator had been knocked off its track and a fireball came from above the ceiling. As quickly as it came that's how quickly it left the car, like a backdraft, eating up all the oxygen. I can still hear those women screaming, freaking out. I ran. So did Virginia. I didn't know until later that the other three women didn't get out.

When I left the elevator, it looked like sheets of white fire, thin sheets of fire. The flame was coming through the elevator car doors from the inside out, shooting through the elevator shaft. Each elevator bank went right to the roof, so the plane had obviously passed through the shafts above us.

I ran into an office. It was a Port Authority office. There were flames on me and people patted them out. My shirt was on fire. My hair was burning. I had second-degree burns on my hands and first- and second-degree burns on my face.

Virginia stumbled into the room. She had third-degree burns. She was burned pretty badly. She must have been knocked down because she came into the room on her knees. She didn't look too good. But she made the trip down the stairs with us. And fortunately, because of our burns, once we got down to about the fiftieth floor, maybe the fortieth floor, there were firemen coming up, and the firefighters saw us with our burns and they made sure that we got out in front of everybody because right about that point it was getting real slow going down. It was a single-file situation moving down and people were merging at every landing. The firefighters were coming up on the inside, people were going down on the outside, and the injured people went down the middle. And because we were injured, we got out a lot quicker than everybody.

I exited through the parking garage at the Barclay Street exit. The second tower had already been hit, but I never felt it on the staircase of tower 1. There was a man down there who was taking injured people out through the garage. I didn't need assistance. I could walk on my own. The man said to me, "The building is not secure. Get far away from the building." So I ran my ass off, up the Barclay Street exit. As I was coming up the exit ramp to the street, someone saw me, pulled me into an ambulance and we went about four blocks north up to Murray Street and Church, where they attended to me.

They tended to a police officer who had gotten hit with some falling debris. He was watching people jumping out the building. His radio was going off and he refused any further treatment and he went back to the building. The guy driving the ambulance said he'd been told to go back down to West Street in front of the building where they had the triage area. And I really started to scream. I didn't want to go near the building again. They wanted to take me to the triage area and I refused. I got out of the ambulance at West Street and Murray. He moved the ambulance down toward the front of the building, and less than ten minutes later I watched the building fall down. I never found out what happened to the ambulance.

I actually consider myself really fortunate and blessed to have been able to come home that night, unlike the seven colleagues of mine from my office, those people in the elevator, and thousands of others. I was just very, very fortunate. My instincts were right on the money. I was lucky.

MICHAEL JACOBS
34, Investment Banker, May Davis Group

"I COULD STILL SEE THIS FAINT LIGHT COMING OUT.
AND I THOUGHT, I'M JUST GOING TO TRY TO OPEN THESE
DOORS AGAIN. SO I GET MY FINGERS IN BETWEEN THE ELEVATOR
DOORS, AND I OPEN THEM UP EVER SO SLIGHTLY. ALL OF A SUDDEN
I SEE THE LIGHT COME IN, LIKE THE LIGHT OF GOD."

I go to work every day at the same time. My office was in the North Tower, eighty-seventh floor. That day, I was a little late because I had to meet with some attorneys. I spoke to my partner-slash-boss, Owen May, before I got on the subway at Grand Central Station. I live at Forty-fourth Street and Second Avenue. It took ten or fifteen minutes to get down there. I went to the concierge desk of the North Tower, where I planned to wait for the attorney. I was a little early for our nine o'clock meeting. He worked in the building too, and we had decided to meet there and then walk over together to the meeting in the NASDAQ building, the glass building.

I thought to myself, I'm going to go upstairs to check a couple of e-mails and let everyone know I'll be in a little late today.

I just missed the first elevator. I said, "Hold it, hold it, hold it," but it just shut in my face. I don't think those people made it out.

I got into the next elevator. There were eight of us in there, I think, four women and four men, but I don't remember exactly. The door shut. The elevator went up about four or five flights, if that, and then it felt like the elevator cord snapped. And we fell back down, a slow drop kind of thing. We had no clue a plane had hit the building because we were at its base, unlike my office mates who were up on the eighty-seventh floor at that time. People say the building swayed twenty feet, something like that. That's not what happened down at the base. You don't hear a boom. You hear noise, but you don't hear a plane crashing.

I grew up in apartment buildings my whole life. I've been stuck in elevators. So I was pretty much the voice of reason. "Don't worry," I said. "This is the World Trade Center. People will come and get us."

There was white stuff coming in, not a lot, but it seemed like we were rubbing the side of the elevator shaft. And maybe some asbestos, or whatever they use for padding, came in. That's what I thought it was. So we slid back down and it was over in a couple of seconds.

I didn't know where we were. I thought maybe we went past the first floor. But I said to everyone, "Don't worry, read your paper. I'll drink my coffee." I always bring coffee with me. The ladies were crying. I had no clue who any of them were. Sometimes you recognize people's faces. I didn't know any of these people.

A half hour goes by. The alarm in the elevator is going off. Couldn't shut it off. Tried. Tried to open the elevator doors. Couldn't. I said, "You know what, let's have them come and get us." So everyone sits down. Now we're going crazy. This alarm is driving me nuts. I start getting all antsy. I have to shut this thing off. Everyone's telling me, "Mike, just leave it alone."

I start playing with the buttons, just to try to stop it. All of a sudden I press a button and the alarm stops. Then we could hear things. The alarm had drowned everything out. We had thought people were coming to get us and that they were working on opening the doors. And then we hear crashes. I later saw the CBS *9/11* tape and realized what those crashes were—people jumping. But when we first started hearing it, we were thinking, Okay, maybe there are problems in other elevators in the building too.

Another ten or fifteen minutes go by, and I'm saying to myself, "You know what, no one's coming to get us. Nobody has made contact with us. No one hears us." And if you saw the CBS tape, you would have seen why they didn't. There was all the commotion, the yelling, everyone talking. And they were not very close to our elevator bank.

At that point, I start flipping out, to myself. I didn't really want to get excited because I was supposed to be the voice of reason in there. The women were really going to get crazy if they saw me get excited. So I start pacing in the elevator. And then I look at the corner of the elevator, and there's a crack at the corner, and I could have sworn I saw a light, a faint, faint light. The people in the elevator say, "You're crazy. It's nothing."

I think, Maybe I am crazy. Maybe it's my eyes playing tricks on me. But I could still see this faint light coming out. And I thought, I'm just going to try to open these doors again. So I get my fingers in between the doors, and I open them up ever so slightly. All of a sudden I see the light come in, like the light of God. I was so stunned. We were on the first floor. The first words out of my mouth were "Holy shit, we're on the first fucking floor."

Everyone gets up. I eventually get those doors open, and then another set behind them. All of a sudden we see firemen, and they're just stunned, looking at us. We still don't know what's going on. And they're not even rushing over to help us out of the elevator. They're too stunned. Their mouths are open. And I get out of the elevator and start freaking out a little bit because I still don't know what's going on. The women are hysterical. All of a sudden, I notice that the West Side window's blown out. I yell, "What the fuck happened?" A fireman tells me to calm down.

But they wouldn't tell us what happened. They told us to go up through the World Financial Center to the overpass. I walk up the steps with one of the ladies from the elevator. We get to the top step, where the promenade is. You could see out the windows. I look over and I see a smear of blood and guts on the window. I've never seen blood and guts before. I couldn't believe what I was seeing: smushed, splattered bodies all over the place. I don't know if it was one, two, ten, or whatever. The lady with me falls to the floor.

I have my cell phone with me. It didn't work in the elevator. My buddy, who I grew up with in Queens, had moved down to Florida, but he happened to have been staying with me that week in my apartment on Forty-fourth Street. He calls me right then and says, "Dude, get out of the building. Two planes hit the buildings."

That's when I found out what had happened. I say, "Call my mother. Tell her I'm okay. I'm getting out now." He thought I was still upstairs.

I shut the phone, and the lady won't move. I smack her in the face to get her up. I had to hit her. It was a light tap, basically. I wouldn't say I whopped her. I got her attention, let's put it that way.

She knew I was serious, so she got up. I say, "Let's get out of here." I keep looking back in disbelief. I can't believe both of those buildings are burning. I know my people are up on the eighty-seventh floor, and I'm trying to count floors. But I can't count. I can't concentrate. I stop every couple of seconds, and try to count. I ask someone, "Do you think it's twenty floors down?" He says yes. And I think, Oh, my God, everyone's dead. They're all dead.

Then all of a sudden I hear the ground rumble, and I look at people's faces and I start to run. Carl Lewis was not catching me on his best day. I have red hair, and all you could see is a red streak go by. I run top speed for three blocks, all the way down to Stuyvesant High School. And I duck into a deli over there.

I later found out that everyone from my company got out but one, Harry Ramos, and he died a hero's death. Harry was the nicest guy you'd ever want to meet. I know people always say that about other people, but Harry was the biggest mensch on the face of the earth. He was helping my coworkers get down, and on the way, they came across an obese man who had given up. He was just sitting on the steps, moping. And Harry asked his name and said, "Let's go."

Harry and another of our workers, Hong Zhu, started down with him. They actually got into an elevator and went down a few flights. But they couldn't take it all the way. They got as far as thirty-something. I forget if it was 36 or 39, but the guy gave up again. The firemen yelled, "Come on, get up, get up." The firemen walking up the stairs told Hong and Harry, "If he won't go, you guys get the hell out of here."

Hong got scared. He said, "Come on, Harry, let's go."

And Harry said, "No, I'm going to stay with him." And he did. Hong got out. They haven't found Harry.

I'm definitely one of the lucky ones. I was trapped in an elevator.

ROBERT LEDER

29, Executive, SMW Trading Company

—◆—

"I FEAR DEATH NOW. . . . AND IF SOMETHING ELSE IS GOING TO HAPPEN, I FEEL IT WILL HAPPEN IN NEW YORK."

Our office is on the eighty-fifth floor of 1 World Trade Center. I was looking outside the window, facing the Empire State Building, when I saw the plane coming into the building. There was such a dramatic change of atmospheric pressure from the plane hitting. The building swayed from the impact, and it nearly knocked me off of my chair. Our ceiling imploded. Some of our walls began to implode. I saw people coming past the window. I don't think these were people who jumped. I think people must have been sucked out of the windows because of the pressure.

The first thing that came to my mind was to call my wife. I told her that the World Trade Center had just been hit by a plane. She didn't believe me, and she just went about her business. Right after I spoke to her, I opened a door to see what was going on and this black billowing smoke came straight at us. I shut the door right away. I wasn't sure what was going on in the hallway. The whole office reeked of jet fuel, or kerosene. I started to get really nervous because I wasn't sure if we were going to be able to get out. People wanted to stay in my office. They said, "Relax, everything's going to be fine."

And my exact words were, "I'm getting the fuck out of here, and I don't care what anybody else does."

I had no idea where the stairwell was. I just never thought of looking for one. We saturated our jackets with water, and people across the hall directed us to the stairwell. We started to go down and it was packed. But there was a quick pace and the stairwell wasn't smoky. Maybe there was a little bit of smoke, and there was a little bit of a stench of burning, but it wasn't that bad.

By the time we got down to the seventy-something floor, fires were coming out of where a wall used to be. It was almost like a scene out of a horror movie. But it was not as chaotic as I thought it was going to be. Everybody was orderly and well mannered. Everybody was staying on the right-hand side of the stairs and letting people that were severely hurt go down on the other side. And this was before we saw any firefighters or police officers coming up. As we got farther and farther down, people started to calm down more, thinking that we're getting out and everything was going to be okay.

At around the 50th floor, I got a cell phone call through to my wife. I told her everything was okay and I'd call her when I got out. This must have been a minute before the second plane hit. I never heard it. We had no idea that 2 World Trade was struck by a plane. Thank God we didn't know. If we had, there would have been panic.

It was around the thirtieth floor when firefighters started to come up. They were all running up on the left side and we were going down on the right side. One after another, just running up with all their gear. You saw each one of these young firefighters running up with all their gear, and they knew what was going on with the other World Trade Center building. But they never said a word. You couldn't even see it in their faces.

The smoke actually started to get thicker as we got farther and farther down. At the twenty-second floor, I stopped my friend Billy and we helped an elderly woman. She had this huge bag with her that was filled with things from her desk, and she looked like she was having trouble. I grabbed her bag and I walked in front of her. Billy walked behind her, and we walked slowly. People were now passing us. It must have taken us an extra ten to fifteen minutes to get outside.

Once there, I was almost fixated on the debris, the body parts and blood. My friend Billy had to snap me out of it and wake me up. We were walking between the Gap and the PATH train when people started to scream, "Run. Run. Run. Oh, my God." We had no clue what was happening. And then we felt this wave and started to hear a rumbling. And the next thing you knew it was darkness. I thought it was over. I thought we were dying. I didn't know what was happening, but we threw the elderly lady to the ground and all three of us got into a ball against a little wall and we prayed. I'm not a religious person, but I prayed to God, hoping that we would be okay.

I still did not know if I was alive or dead. My eyes were wide open and I couldn't see anything. It was blacker than black. I couldn't even cough or breathe because I had so much soot in my throat and in my mouth. And then it started to settle, and I realized I was alive.

I started to scream for some sort of a light. "Does anybody have a lighter?" Nobody answered me. My friend Billy finally said something. The lady was also okay. Finally, a huge floodlight went on, and then another, and I began to see all the EMS workers who were there with us. And they kept leading us out. I've never really noticed EMS workers, or police officers or firefighters. But I was there and now I know. These people are the most amazing people I've ever come across. They were not out for themselves. They stayed in there, making a light path for everybody else to find a way out.

When I finally got out, it looked like a nuclear winter. I was walking, but I was in shock. I still had no clue what was going on. I was walking down the street and looking down and seeing all the e-mails and pictures, and then seeing this white manila folder with the letter J on it from a law office or a doctor's office. This is after 2 World Trade Center collapsed, and it didn't even occur to me that it collapsed. I was still thinking, How did all this happen from a small plane hitting our building?

My life dramatically changed on that day. I'm not the same person. I don't feel safe anymore. I don't conduct myself in the same manner that I used to because I'm always on alert. I'm a quieter person now. I fear death now. I'm waiting for it to happen. I haven't had a restful sleep since this whole thing happened. I've been taking medication to help me sleep, but it doesn't work. I mean, there are days that I sleep because I'm so tired that my body has no other choice. But more often than not, I get maybe three hours of sleep a night. I'm a restless person, that's my nature. But I'm worse than I ever was, and it's not good. I feel myself just breaking down, my whole body. I've been getting help, but it doesn't seem to be doing much.

Obviously, time heals everything as you get further and further away. But the memory stays. I have nightmares. The visions I saw aren't going away. Seeing all that carnage sticks in my mind. Seeing the plane and feeling the plane hit was terrible. It was just a frightening experience. Now I carry a flashlight in my bag and an air filter mask that was given out at my exchange a week after the attacks. I'm waiting for something else to happen. And if something else is going to happen, I feel it will happen in New York. I didn't go to the World Series games because of the stress. My wife was frightened for me to go. My choice was letting her be frightened for the whole night, or just going home, which is what I ended up doing. I gave the tickets away. And these are things that I love, going to baseball games, going to football games. Now I avoid crowds. I won't do it. And that's very sad, but I don't see there ever being a remedy to it.

CHRISTOPHER WIENER

32, Bond Trader, Garban Intercapital

"I HAD JUST GOTTEN MARRIED ON AUGUST 11. SO I LEFT THAT
MORNING ON OUR ONE-MONTH ANNIVERSARY, WHICH WENT FROM
BEING THE HAPPIEST DAY OF MY LIFE TO THE SADDEST."

When the first plane hit tower 1, I didn't know what it was. I just knew it was a bad place to be. I was in tower 2, fifty-fifth floor. I thought maybe it was the generator or some sort of explosion. We saw a tidal wave of debris rush past our windows and panic ensued. Everybody started to run for the stairs, myself included.

We started going down in an orderly fashion. When I got to 54, I realized that I had forgotten all my personal belongings. I'm an asthmatic, so the thought of going down fifty-five flights was a little overwhelming. I didn't have any medication with me. I didn't have my oral inhaler. But I figured I would take my time and go down the stairs and I would be okay, and then I would be able to go back upstairs and get them when everything was over, when I was given the all-clear. So I continued down the stairs.

When I got down to about 30, a man came out with a transistor radio and his briefcase. He put one of the earpieces into his ear and tuned into one of the local radio stations, and he started giving us a blow-by-blow of what had happened. And he repeated the broadcast as it came over: a plane had hit tower 1. They're not sure what it was, whether it was an accident or whether it was deliberate. But they were evacuating tower 1 and tower 2 as a safety precaution.

At around the twenty-eighth floor, they made a statement over the PA system in tower 2 to remain where you were, or to go back to your office because the problem had been contained in tower 1. I decided that it was best to keep moving down the stairs. It took me about fifteen minutes to get to the bottom floor.

The lobby was a sea of people. I have never felt so alone in my whole life, because I didn't know a single person. All I knew is that a plane had hit tower 1 and I wanted to get as far away from that as possible. So I made my way up into one of the concourses in the mall and headed toward the south exit in tower 2, furthest from tower 1. And as I came out of the tower, the second plane hit my tower. I had just opened the door to go outside and there was an explosion that I'll never forget. It haunts my dreams to this day, and it was the most blood-curdling sound I've ever heard.

I thought I was going to die right then and there. I thought the building was coming down on me. I tried to get back into the building so I wouldn't get crushed by anything, or have anything fall on my head. I crawled along the side of the building and managed to make my way into a Sam Goody. There were about twenty other people in there and we tried to get out the mall's side doors, but they were locked. And just as we were about to break the door, somebody came running by with a key and opened it for us. Everybody started running through the mall toward tower 1, in one direction, so I followed.

We wound up on the plaza by Pace University, where we stopped for a while. We watched in horror and in awe of what was going on. We were just completely ignorant of the situation because we were all just talking amongst ourselves about how and when we would be able to get back up there and get our stuff. It never occurred to us that those towers were going to come down. As we stood there, someone came over with a bullhorn and informed us that a third plane was in the air and that this was not a safe place to be in because City Hall was right across the street and the Brooklyn Bridge was right there.

One of the people I was with knew someone who lived on Mulberry Street, so a group of four or five of us decided to run over there, to a safe haven. People on the street had TVs and radios tuned, and we heard the Pentagon had been attacked.

Someone else gave us misleading information that they had attacked Disney World. By the time we got to the apartment, the first tower, my tower, had come down. We watched the events unfold on TV for the rest of the day.

For days I couldn't tear myself away from the TV. I read everything that I could. I tried to put it into perspective, but I had nightmares about it. I still can't escape them. Every night it's the same thing, like a dream, but it's something that I actually lived through: it's me trying to get out and the explosions play out over and over again in my head. I sometimes wake up five or six times a night from the nightmares. In the days that followed, I started hallucinating and having daymares and imagining that planes were crashing. Every time I heard a plane fly overhead, I was almost paralyzed with fear. I can't even go on the subway or a train. The thought of going to Manhattan is difficult. I don't know if I'll ever be able to go work in a tall building again.

Everybody that I worked with, for the most part, went back to work and I haven't been able to get myself into a position where I can yet. I feel kind of guilty about it. You know, they're all back there and I have to struggle with the fact that I'm not.

Therapy is helpful, but it's only one component. My wife and my family are very supportive, and it's brought us closer together. I had just gotten married on August 11. So I left that morning on our one-month anniversary, which went from being the happiest day of my life to the saddest.

I don't know when I'm going to be able to go back. I know I need to. If I don't, it will have defeated me. And I need to get back there for my own sanity. But my life was pretty much perfect, as far as I was concerned, before that day. I had everything going for me. Now, I just feel like a part of my life has been taken away from me and I'll never be able to get it back.

RALPH BLASI
52, Director of Security, Brookfield Properties

"WE SAW COPS AND FIREMEN RUNNING INTO THE
LOBBY WHILE THE BUILDING WAS COMING DOWN."

I am a former homicide detective who did twenty-two years with the New York City Police Department. Brookfield is an owner/manager of the World Financial Center and 1 Liberty Plaza. I was in my office at the World Financial Center, which faces the Trade Center, when the first plane hit. I looked out my window, saw the fireball, and said to my property manager, Mike Bosso, "Mike, they just bombed." That was my initial reaction: "Mike, they just bombed the Trade Center."

As I looked back toward West Street, I saw cars swerving and looking to avoid what I thought at that moment to be dead dogs in the road. I saw two, then four, and a car swerved into one of the light poles down on West Street. Then it was twenty. But they weren't dead dogs. They turned out to be body parts falling from the North Tower.

We went to the North Pedestrian Bridge, which connects the Financial Center to the Trade Center, and we had an evacuation plan created several years ago, a comprehensive evacuation plan which involved all our major tenants and also the New York Mercantile Exchange and the Battery Park City authority. For the first time in the history of Manhattan, a partnership was created between the private sector and the city. And this plan was all of a sudden put into effect on September 11.

We responded to the North Pedestrian Bridge and started evacuating people out of the Trade Center. As we were doing that, the second plane hit, which was directly over our heads. A fire truck pulled up and a fireman got out. He had his helmet on, but he got hit with a piece of steel, a steel beam, and it killed him instantly. The whole North Bridge actually jumped and knocked us on our asses. But we continued the evacuation.

I have the greatest admiration for the private security officers, guys who are only making around twenty-five thousand dollars a year. We had often asked security guards, prior to 9/11, what they would do if a bomb went off and they saw a couple of dead bodies. The consensus was always that they would run. But on September 11, I had sixty guards working with me and not one ran. With the two towers burning, standing with bullhorns in the Winter Garden, keeping people moving out of the towers, they never blinked. Usually you wait for the cavalry—the cops and the firemen—to take over. But they were so preoccupied with what they were doing that we had to be really on that day. And we effected the evacuation of approximately forty-five thousand people, without an injury. It went as planned.

A lot of the people being evacuated were going onto the plaza, which is right along the Hudson River. There's a marina there and it's enough to hold about ten thousand. Then we pushed them north and south. As I walked down to the plaza after we concluded the evacuation of the North Bridge, I asked one of the security guards, "Oscar, why aren't these people being moved?"

He goes, "Mr. Blasi, look up." And as I looked up, I saw what everybody was looking at. We looked over the Winter Garden, which is about a 250-foot glass atrium, and we're looking at the North Tower burning, and we saw people out on the windowsills, and we could actually hear them screaming. From that distance we heard hundreds of people screaming. You could hear them faintly. And then we watched them jump. It could have been a dozen. It could have been dozens. The analogy is, I was in a couple of shootings as a detective and when they ask you how many shots you fired, you usually say one or two. And then, when they look at your gun, you shot all six. It goes that fast, and that's the norm: you think you shot one or two, but you emptied your gun. It's still clicking and you don't realize it. This was the same thing.

We were very reactive that day. The first plane hit. You run, you do what you have to do. The second plane hit and you know this is not a situation where you can sit around the table and discuss what you're going to do. So you just react, react, react. Plumes of smoke forced the cops into the emergency operations room, which is on the second floor of the American Express tower. I'm there with twenty seasoned cops—chiefs, captains, all kinds of brass. We're there for two minutes, saying, "Yeah, this is nice." There are plug-ins, TV, computer hookup. "Yeah, this is a nice place to operate from."

Well, we were there maybe two minutes when a young cop came running in and screamed, "Everybody get the fuck out!" He's screaming at the top of his lungs, "The building's coming down."

We thought he meant the American Express tower. So about two hundred years of experience started running like madmen. When we hit the street (we were on Vesey), it actually turned out to be the North Tower that was coming down. We were half a block away and we saw the antenna tilt, and then the tower came down. One thing I'll never forget, because my son's a cop, is that we saw cops and firemen running into the lobby while the building was coming down. I'll never forget that. I don't think they knew the building was coming down, at least not completely. Maybe just the top part of it, maybe just the antenna. I don't think they envisioned the entire building.

Everybody gave accolades to the cops and firemen, and they deserved it. But I have to talk about the unsung heroes. These are guys that took a job to be security guards, to stand in a lobby and just protect the building from vandalism or whatever. When a cop or fireman takes a job, it is with the knowledge that it's dangerous and can be life threatening. These guys don't. It's very unfortunate what happened. My son was out on the line for three weeks, sixteen hours a day, pulling body parts out. It's tragic, it truly is. However, I don't think enough attention or recognition has been given to the private sector, these guys who sign on to be security guards and no more. And they stood with me shoulder-to-shoulder throughout this whole ordeal. I ordered the older ones to get to the ferry, and they just refused. "I'm staying with the group," they said.

Again, I'm a twenty-two-year veteran of the police department. But my hat is off to these guys. They're unbelievable and they deserve all the recognition. They saved lives—forty-five thousand people were evacuated and there was no panic. It was the professionalism, experience, and training of the security guards. They kept people going in the direction they wanted them to go. I can't say enough about them. With all due respect to the emergency services, my hat is off to the unsung heroes, as well.

BILL MULLIGAN
58, President, Mulligan Security Corporation

⌐

"IF HE COULD HAVE WRITTEN THE SCRIPT OF HOW
HE WANTED TO MEET HIS BOSS, THAT'S HOW HE WOULD HAVE
WRITTEN IT, JUST THE WAY IT HAPPENED."

I was a New York City police officer for eleven years, a detective for nine years, and then I was a special agent with the Office of Labor Racketeering with the Department of Justice for about sixteen months before I started my own business in 1988. After sitting in on wiretaps and doing labor investigations, I decided it was time for me to go. My office is downtown, right by the Trade Center, and a month before September 11 I was walking along the promenade with my friend Ralph Blasi. He's the director of security for the World Financial Center and my former partner in Homicide.

We had just finished a sandwich, and as partners we had seen the worst and the best of life. And I said, "Ralph, look at where we wound up. We wound up in heaven." It's a beautiful place that was just becoming a neighborhood. And a month later, it was gone. The planes hit and it was finished. And one of the people it took out was Mychal Judge, chaplain of the New York City Fire Department. Blunt trauma on the back of the head. Michael was leaning over somebody, giving him last rites, when he was struck by something and killed.

My friend Mychal Judge was one of the finest people I ever knew in my life. I used to call him Saint Mychal. He fought wherever there was injustice. He stood up and took a stand. He had balls of steel and the compassion of a kind and loving nun. And he was just sent here to make this place better, and he knew it. He was one of those guys that was gifted with the ability to know why he was here. He was the happiest man I knew. He could not have been doing anything more that would have made him any happier than he was. He loved being a chaplain for the fire department. He just loved the challenge.

For example, Mychal recognized that AIDS was a serious problem, that it was something the Catholic Church should immediately dive into, administer assistance, and help people. But at the time he was getting flak, from somebody, I'm not sure who it was, but there was somebody up in the archdiocese who was saying to him, "Stay back. Don't touch this. This is not something we should be getting into yet."

But Mychal knew in his heart that this was the place to be. He said to me one time, "If Jesus came down here, where do you think he'd be? He'd be in Greenwich Village, he'd be in the hospitals, he'd be taking care of these people. He took care of the longshoreman in Jerusalem." And so Mychal fought. When he was told he couldn't do anything, he said, "I'm going to take them into the rectory here at St. Francis," and he started clearing out rooms, and he made beds and he started bringing out AIDS-infected people and tending to them. This did not go over too well with the church. That's how Mychal got that wing in St. Vincent's Hospital. They weren't going to put a wing in there until Mychal took a stand. I believe they were thinking, "Well, you know, this is one of those fag diseases, and you know, there's a message being sent here." Then, when the first kid got it from a blood transfusion, they said, "Oh, wait a minute. This may cost us something. Let's take care of these people."

If you ever saw Mychal and Cardinal O'Connor on the altar at a mass, they needed gloves. They just didn't get along. Mychal would have been a much better cardinal. We used to go to retreats together and Mychal would say, "All that's well in my life is rooted in love. All that's wrong in my life is rooted in fear. There is no right or wrong. There's no judgment. There's no sense in judging."

The last time I saw him was the Thursday before September 11. It was an uneventful Thursday. On the night of the eleventh, my friend John Kelly called me and said that Mychal had died. They put toe tags on DOAs, you know, when they find people. The tag they hung on Mychal's toe was number 1. He was considered the first casualty, so they gave him the first toe tag, for identification purposes. They took him right from there and they laid him on the altar of the church around the corner. I still speak to him. I go into the church and I speak to him. Mychal couldn't have gone to heaven any better way. If he could have written the script of how he wanted to meet his boss, that's how he would have written it, just the way it happened: administering to someone else, going out of the picture helping someone else, and especially at one of the biggest events that ever happened.

JOSE RODRIGUEZ
28, Officer, NYPD

—

"I said, 'We need a priest to give somebody last rites.'
"She asked, 'Are you Catholic?'
"I go, 'Yeah.'
"And she said, 'You can give last rites
if you want, in an emergency.'"

I'm in the Fifth Precinct, which is Chinatown. I'm usually assigned to Fifth Precinct patrol, Adam sector, which is the lower part of the precinct area and the court area and right above City Hall. On September 11, I was assigned to Election Day duty. My job that morning was to secure the area and to prevent electioneering and make sure that the election was going to go smoothly. I started around five-thirty in the morning. When you start off a little earlier, they also let you off a little earlier. So I was thinking that maybe I could get off that day at one o'clock.

I was in a polling place when I heard people outside screaming. I remember coming outside, and I saw a giant hole and smoke pouring out of the North Tower. And people were screaming about a plane going into the tower, but they weren't sure what kind of plane. Cars started shooting up the Bowery, which is where I was standing. And all the emergency vehicles were coming downtown. But there's a little side street, Bayard, which cars were trying to come out of. And with the emergency vehicles passing the red light, I got into the middle of the intersection at Bowery and Bayard and I began holding cars.

And then an unmarked car pulled up. And this lieutenant in the car said to me, "Hey, officer, get into the car. I need you." So I jumped into the car and he said, "I want you to hang out with this deputy commissioner of the fire department. Drive him around." I didn't have a clue who the guy was. I'm almost positive that he had FDNY plates. Later I went through the names of the firefighters who were killed, and he wasn't one of them.

We went down to the World Trade Center area, near Vesey and Broadway. I got out of the car with the deputy commissioner. We heard a buzzing noise, which sounded like a plane. I never saw it hit. From where we were standing at Vesey and Broadway, St. Paul's Church was right there, and the Millennium Hotel was right next to us. All I saw was this humongous explosion, and flames just pouring out of the building. And at that point there was complete chaos. People started running, screaming. I saw the engine of the plane shoot across, and parts of the building come down. When I first saw it, I thought that maybe part of the North Tower had fallen on the South Tower. But, and then I was, like, "Nah, I did hear the plane. It was another plane."

We were just telling people to run, to run, to run. We went down to Church and Vesey, where we saw all the emergency police and the firemen start walking toward the building. They were pulling people out. I saw a man walking out, I think he was a court officer, and there was a press lady holding his arm. Blood was shooting out of his arm. So I said, "Hold on a second," went underneath my vest, ripped off my T-shirt, then ripped it in half and wrapped his arm up and then used the other half to wrap around my face.

There were a whole bunch of cops around me, and we all started walking toward the North Tower. People had already jumped from the North Tower and you saw that EMS had already tried to cover up their bodies on the ground in the middle of the plaza with tarps.

I walked back out toward Vesey and Church and a truck showed up with two workers and a whole bunch of medical equipment. They had oxygen tanks. So I asked over the police radio, "I have oxygen tanks. Where should I send them?" They told me to send them over to the west side, to Vesey and West, because they were setting up a command center over there.

But I said, "I can't send them over to Vesey Street because there's stuff falling off the North Tower." I said, "We need to set something up on the east side." I started walking back down Church Street, back toward the plaza, and the South Tower started collapsing. I ran up Church Street, and the smoke and everything hit me, and I just hid inside a doorway at 30 Vesey Street. I covered my head up and I tried to keep from moving. I rolled around a little bit, and I was trying to get up but I couldn't breathe, I couldn't see. I kept trying to stand up and somebody would knock me down. It was very scary, very scary.

Finally, the smoke began clearing up a little bit, and now everything was gray. And then I walked back toward the North Tower, telling people to run. There were very few civilians left at all. Almost none.

As I walked back down Vesey Street, I turned around and saw a bunch of guys carrying a man in a chair. And they placed him by an ambulance, a burnt-out ambulance at the corner of Vesey and Church Street. The man was lying there, and I heard one police lieutenant screaming at the top of his voice, "Can somebody get this man a priest? Can somebody get this man a priest?"

And I ran over to him. I said, "Lieutenant, what's wrong? What's the matter? What do you need?"

He goes, "Can you get this guy a priest to give him last rites?"

I'm Catholic, so I knew that the closest church was one block up: St. Peter's, on Barclay and Church. At this point I had adrenaline running through me at a million miles an hour. With the South Tower collapsing, I had my eye on the North Tower. I thought if one was going to go, the other one's gotta go too.

I ran up the back stairs of St. Peter's and I went inside. I looked for a priest. There was a lady there. She was ripping up linen, cutting it into strips. And I turned around to her, and I said, "Are there any priests here? We need a priest for some guy dying outside. We have to give him last rites."

She turned around to me and said, "No. All the priests just went outside. They all left already."

I said, "We need a priest to give somebody last rites."

She spoke so calmly, which I thought was a little weird. She was a heavyset lady with blond hair, and she turned around to me and she asked, "Are you Catholic?"

I go, "Yeah."

And she said, "You can give last rites if you want, in an emergency."

I was pretty shocked to hear that. I ran back out to Lieutenant Billy Cosgrove from Manhattan Traffic. I knew his face since I work in the area, even though I had never actually met him before. I said, "Lieutenant, there's no priest here, but the lady inside the church said we could give last rites in an emergency." And I said, "Are you Catholic?" And he said yes. I said, "So am I."

We went over to the man. I saw police officers around him, and Lieutenant Cosgrove was there, so I figured he was a cop. I asked Lieutenant Cosgrove if the man was with the PD.

He said, "No. He's the fire department chaplain, Mychal Judge."

We knelt down. I grabbed Father Judge's hand. He was already dead. Lieutenant Cosgrove put his hand on Father Judge's head, and we said an "Our Father." Lieutenant Cosgrove then said something else, like "Glory be to the Father," and then something else, like "Ashes to ashes."

Lieutenant Cosgrove covered Father Judge's head with a black jacket, and he made sure that the jacket wouldn't come off. We both got back up. We put our hands on each other, me and Lieutenant Cosgrove, and we both went back toward the North Tower.

I kind of feel that maybe it was Father Judge who saved me. I don't know how else to put it. When I think about it, I consider myself extremely lucky. After we gave last rites to Father Judge, I went back to the North Tower. We were there when it began to collapse. How did I get out? There's no explanation. If the tower had fallen east instead of imploding on itself and falling west and north, I would have been killed. I now really think that it may have been Father Judge who protected me. I have an extreme connection now. I mean, I never knew the man. I had never heard of the man before.

I've talked to priests about it. I never got above the rank of altar boy. I didn't think a regular person could give last rites. And I've gotten so much conflicting information from different priests that I don't know who to believe. There was a bishop who was sent here from Rome as a special agent from the pope himself. He said that technically, it wasn't last rites because there has to be an absolution of sin, and a regular person can't do that. But the bishop said it was the greatest thing we could have done for him. All the priests say that.

I saw Lieutenant Cosgrove a couple of times after September 11, and we have a very tight connection now. We hug whenever we see each other. And he says, "Don't listen to that bishop of yours. I talked to Cardinal Egan and he said it was last rites."

I've tried to find out more about Father Judge since that situation. It definitely makes me wonder, Why me? I'm just a lowly cop. I'm just a regular guy. But he wasn't. I've now seen the work he's done with homeless outreach, with people suffering from AIDS, with Alcoholics Anonymous, and he wasn't just a regular person. You know, it wouldn't surprise me if they canonized him. Being the fire department chaplain is usually a job by itself. But on top of that he did a million other things. I feel very lucky to have crossed paths with a man like that. If I was any help to him or to his family, then that makes me feel really good.

CHRISTOPHER KEENAN
60, Chaplain, FDNY

"I THOUGHT, WHAT DO I HAVE TO WORRY ABOUT?
IT'S IN GOD'S HANDS. YOU LET GO OF THIS AND LET GOD HAVE IT.
WHAT'S HAPPENING IN THE AFTERMATH OF SEPTEMBER 11,
WHAT'S HAPPENING IN THE FIRE DEPARTMENT, I CAN'T CHANGE,
I CAN'T FIX. ALL I CAN DO IS BE PRESENT TO IT AS MYSELF,
AS A BROTHER TO MY OTHER BROTHERS AND SISTERS."

I'm on the church schedule at St. Francis of Assisi. In the Roman Catholic tradition, it means that on weekdays I have a liturgy or a mass in the mornings, and then an hour-and-a-half shift of confessions.

I never worked with the fire department before 9/11. I never had a fantasy, or even a thought, about wanting to be a fireman, even though Ladder 24, Engine 1 is across the street from the church on West Thirty-first. But I made a commitment after Mychal Judge was killed. He was at St. Francis too, and Engine 24, and he was one of the six that died from across the street. I made a commitment to go over to see them every day so they knew they weren't alone. And one thing led to another. I was commissioned as the fire department's chaplain on November 16.

On September 11, I was at St. Francis and I heard loud voices in the television room. I watched what happened. After the second building collapsed, I went down to St. Vincent's Hospital with Jim O'Connell, who's the chaplain at St. Vincent's, Miguel Loredo, a Cuban Franciscan, and a fellow named Robert Gavin. We went to give what assistance we could. We felt it was the best place to be because it was the hospital closest to the site. And from late in the morning until five-thirty at night, 260 people were treated at St. Vincent's. Then there was a trickle, and then it stopped. I had to come back to St. Francis because I was on duty at six. As I walked out of the hospital, I looked back. There were hundreds of doctors and nurses with stretchers standing there, you know, waiting for the people that never came. All throughout New York and New Jersey, everyone was waiting for all the people that never came.

I had sensed that Mychal wouldn't make it. I knew he'd be at the center of things, and I couldn't imagine how he'd live through that. A lot of firemen were in and out of the hospital, and I kept saying, "I live with Mike Judge. Do you know anything about him?" And they just kept saying no, but of course they knew.

The last part of the *9/11* documentary by those two French filmmakers was Mychal's death. It's about as close to an eyewitness account as anything. You can't see, with the dust and everything, but you get shadows. They are trying to revive him. You see his leg on the film as they pick him up. Then there's a pan shot of them carrying his body through the doors and out into the plaza.

When I got back to St. Francis, I went over to the firehouse and they whispered, "His body is in the back." They had initially brought Mychal's body to St. Peter's Church on Barclay Street, and laid it in front of the altar and covered him. But then the pastor called the chancery office and said, "We have to evacuate the church. We think the building next to us is coming down. There's a dead priest in the sanctuary." They knew it was Mychal, so the bishop called St. Francis. Peter Brophy and Ed Coughlin put on their Franciscan habits and went across to Ladder 24. They got a ride down to Battalion 7, on Nineteenth Street and Seventh Avenue. Then they got an escort into St. Peter's and brought the body back.

The firefighters set up a place for him. They brought a bed down from their dormitory and put his body bag on it. Then they roped the area off and covered it with their blue bedsheets to have a sacred space for him. I stayed with his body, a lot of us did, until they removed it and sent it to the coroner. Firefighters and other friars were there. And when they came to remove his body to the morgue, we gathered and said a prayer, the St. Francis Prayer: "Lord, make me an instrument of peace."

You've seen the picture of Mychal being carried away from the scene in a chair. It's fascinating: There are two firefighters, two policemen, the person from the Office of Emergency Management, and a civilian. It's like Mary at the foot of the cross holding Jesus in her arms. There are all these people that Mychal worked with, carrying his body out. His is the only recognizable body that we see. He was the fire department's chaplain and they wouldn't leave him. It's kind of awesome how all of that really emerged. He became a primary integrating focus. He's one of the few that were found.

The *9/11* film has a very long close-up of Mychal's face. It pans from him to two firefighters against the wall. You can see the terror on people's faces as the film proceeds. But everything looks normal in the lobby, and in the mezzanine and in the background people are coming down the escalators in an orderly way. They don't come out the front of the building because of the falling bodies, which you can hear in the background. They go out the mezzanine and in the other direction, and everything looks fine. And then all of a sudden, you can hear the building collapse and see the dust.

Apparently, Mychal had just gone up the escalator to attend to some of the falling bodies on the mezzanine. The camera is still running, and they use its light to find their way. And there's a body—Mychal's. They try to revive him, but he is gone.

I was commissioned as the new fire department chaplain on November 16. The initial thought was overwhelming. How could I be possibly be present to this impossible situation? Maybe the best way to put it is that part of my own spirituality is a twelve-step spirituality that is a core part of my own life. And there's an eleventh step that says, "We seek through prayer and meditation to improve our conscious contact with the God of our understanding, praying only for the knowledge of God's will for us and the power to carry it out." Well, I've been living that, and the more I prayed and listened, particularly to my fellow staff persons, the anxiety and fear moved to serenity and peace, and then I knew it was God's will for me to do this, and not my ego.

I thought, What do I have to worry about? It's in God's hands. You let go of this and let God have it. What's happening in the aftermath of September 11, what's happening in the fire department, I can't change, I can't fix. All I can do is be present to it as myself, as a brother to my other brothers and sisters.

One time, Mychal said to me, "You know, Chris, it's like IBM. Just show up, be on time, and be ready to play." And that's my thumbnail sketch of it. And if Mychal were to expand on that now, he'd say, "Chris, show up, be yourself, just listen to the people, and be open to God's will each day. Keep praying, keep meditating and listening. Keep being open to God's will, knowing you have the power to carry it out. And enjoy these wonderful people as much as I did, and have a wonderful life."

When I look at the ministry now, it's a lot of wakes, funerals, wives, kids, family members left behind, Ground Zero, burn units, the morgue, hospitals, detoxes, rehab programs, all the post-traumatic stress issues and so many issues yet to come. And through it all the firefighters continually ask me how I'm doing. And my answer to them simply is "How could someone like me have it any better than with being with people like you?"

CATHY PAVELEC
52, Freedom of Information Administrator, Port Authority

"I'VE ALWAYS CONSIDERED MYSELF A PRETTY OPTIMISTIC PERSON, BUT SINCE SEPTEMBER 11, I KNOW THAT EVERY SINGLE DAY I HAVE UNTIL THE DAY I DIE IS A GIFT FROM GOD."

I worked in 1 World Trade Center, on the sixty-seventh floor. I had a window office that faced north. I just glanced out the window and I saw the plane. It was a little bit over to my right and I noticed that it was very low. But I had worked in the World Trade Center since before it officially opened, and we'd seen a million things over the years. But as I watched the plane get closer and closer and closer, I was in complete disbelief. I just sat there and watched as it crashed into the building over my head. I saw the blunt nose of the plane, over my head, and I watched the fuselage disappear into the building.

I ran around the floor yelling to everybody, "A plane just crashed into the building. We have to get out of here. We have to get out of here." I ran all around the floor and told everybody. And then, as I was running back to where I sit, some of the people caught me and said, "Calm down, calm down."

And I'm saying, "Calm down? A plane just crashed into the building."

But, interestingly, they told me to calm down, so I calmed down and I went back to my office, and I got my pocketbook and then I walked out.

Our lobby on 67 had already filled up with smoke, so we went right into a stairwell and we walked down. The lights were on in the stairwell. Everything was very calm. There was no panic. Everybody was very polite. I was mostly with Port Authority people, and we walked and we walked and we walked. Then the firemen started to come up. As they walked past us—both of my brothers are firemen in New Jersey—I was very careful to say, "Hello. Thank you, God bless you" to every single one of them. They were all in their full gear. They were carrying hoses. They were just so brave. They were huffing and puffing, and these were big strong guys.

Everybody started to get a little uncomfortable because there was a very odd smell in the stairwell, which I realized afterward was the jet fuel. But nobody realized that then. We just kept walking and walking. I came out of the stairwell on the mezzanine and walked out the door and all of a sudden everything in the world changed. I don't remember what I saw, but I remember that it was awful. I know from speaking with people after that day that there were body parts and torsos and pieces of the plane, but I did not process any of that. I just knew that I had to get out of there.

I came to Church Street where I met up with people I had walked down the stairs with. We all crossed over by St. Paul's Chapel and we turned around to look at the building. At this point, both buildings were in flames. We stopped and we prayed for a minute, and then I just said to everybody, "We've just gotta get away from here." So I walked over to Broadway and then I started to walk over on Park Place, on my way to Pace University. I had graduated from Pace, and I thought maybe there would be a phone I could use. I didn't cry. I wasn't upset, but I was completely in fight-or-flight mode. I knew I had to keep moving, or I was going to die. And I just knew that I had to be completely on my toes.

I went to Pace, but I couldn't get even near a phone. Then I ran into a woman that I knew from my office. Her name is Denise, and people were telling us to go over the Brooklyn Bridge. We started up the ramp to go to the Brooklyn Bridge, but then I saw all these fighter planes and I didn't know if they were ours or not. We really didn't know what was happening.

So I said to Denise, "We can't go on a bridge. We can't go on a landmark." I really thought the planes belonged to somebody other than us. We turned around to get off of the Brooklyn Bridge ramp, and we're walking back west, toward the World Trade Center, and we heard a noise and we looked up and we saw tower 2 explode and collapse. We just stood there for a minute and then the cloud started to come after us. For the first time that day I really thought we were doing to die.

We started running north and the cloud is after us, after us, after us, and I just kept seeing this monster, chasing us. It was big, it was roiling, it was ugly, it was angry, and it wanted to kill me. I thought it was going to suffocate us. I thought we were going to get caught in it and we wouldn't be able to breathe and that was going to be the end of us. So we were trying to outrun it.

We're running north, in that area between the Brooklyn Bridge and the Municipal Building, near what my husband calls a snow fence, which is one of those fences that they use to keep the snow from falling onto the roadway. Apparently, they're very sturdy. Denise and I are trying to break this fence down, and we couldn't do it. I said, "Put your jacket over your head." We put our jackets over our heads and just at this point the cloud hits us. By the time it got to us, all of the big particles were out of it, but it was full of powder and little pieces of stuff. It's getting in our noses, our ears, our eyes. And we're trying to get over this fence. Denise got over it, but I couldn't get over it. She came back and dragged me over it.

Once we were over the fence we were able to cross all of those roadways in front of the Municipal Building. Of course, all of this time we're in this cloud. We finally got through it. We're in front of the Municipal Building, the cloud is gone and it was now silent. And we're just holding hands, walking, and one of us just started to say, "Our Father, who art in heaven, hallowed be Thy name," and we just walked and prayed.

I've always considered myself a pretty optimistic person, but since September 11, I know that every single day I have until the day I die is a gift from God. When we ultimately got to midtown that day, I went into St. Francis Church, on Thirty-first Street, which is the church where Father Judge was from. I didn't know him, but I do go to that church. My husband and I support it. They have a bread line, and that's our one special charity that he and I always support. I went into the church and there's a big crucifix in the back. I got down on my knees in front of that crucifix and I thanked God because I know it was a miracle that I lived. I know that if that plane had been any lower, I would have died. But that didn't happen. I am the luckiest woman in the world and I know it. There were so many people that I knew who died, I can't even begin to tell you. One of the things I said to my therapist is that I am no longer afraid of death. I have been to his house and he doesn't scare me anymore. I mean, we all looked death in the face, and he can't scare me anymore.

Sean Crowley, right, with Bernard B. Kerik at Ground Zero

In Frank Capra's much-loved 1946 movie *It's a Wonderful Life*, George Bailey, as played by James Stewart, is given a chance to see what the world around him would have been like had he never been born.

In one of the more memorable scenes, George's guardian angel, Clarence (Henry Travers), walks George into the town cemetery, where they come upon the gravestone of George's younger brother, Harry. The inscription on the stone reads IN MEMORY OF OUR BELOVED SON—HARRY BAILEY—1911–1919.

Clarence says to George, "Your brother, Harry Bailey, broke through the ice and was drowned at the age of nine."

"That's a lie," yells George. "Harry Bailey went to war. He got the Congressional Medal of Honor. He saved the lives of every man on that transport."

"Every man on that transport died," says Clarence. "Harry wasn't there to save them because you weren't there to save Harry."

On September 11, similar stories occurred in which people who were saved by one person later went on to save others.

Tim McGinn, right, with his father, Raymond.

TIM McGINN
44, Retired Lieutenant, NYPD

—

"IN MY TWENTY YEARS OF SERVICE, I'VE RESPONDED TO
MANY EMERGENCIES. IN THIS ONE, YOU WERE EITHER DEAD OR
YOU WERE ALIVE. THERE WAS NO IN BETWEEN."

I joined the department in January of '82 and I retired in January of '02. For my last nine years, I was a commanding officer in Barriers, which are those blue barriers used for parades and street fairs. We also respond to anything that has to do with crowd control, building collapses, fires, presidential visits, almost anything. We work out of Pier 40, which is at West Houston Street and the Hudson River. I normally leave my house from Staten Island at eight-thirty in the morning. On September 11, I felt great. I had just had two days off, had a good night's sleep. I was all fresh and relaxed. I couldn't believe what a beautiful day it was: not a cloud in the sky, and maybe a quiet day for the Barriers section.

Every morning during my commute I listen to 1010-WINS, not just for the traffic report, but also, you know, for anything that might have happened the night before. If a building collapses, or there's a bad fire scene, Barriers needs to go to that scene. So the first account comes on WINS that the North Tower was struck. I immediately got on my cell phone. I got through to my office at 8:51, according to my phone records, and I tell Sergeant Jerry Jones to get the trucks and every available man down there, and I'd meet them there.

All I had was the bubble light that I slapped on top of my car. I got through because I managed to piggyback with the emergency vehicles and the ambulances that were responding. I got into the middle of a caravan.

My wife is a deputy chief in the police department. This didn't dawn on me until about a week later, but I passed her that morning on the lower level of the Verrazano Bridge. I remember waving to her and she waved back to me. And then I was able to jump in with the caravan. She works in Brooklyn with the detectives and that's where she was going.

With all the lights and sirens going, I never heard that the second tower was struck. It wasn't until I arrived at the scene and parked my car that I saw it. I looked up and I saw the second tower was struck. I said, "Oh, my God. We're in deep shit here."

I'm in plain clothes, work boots, dungarees, and a golf shirt—normal clothes for the pier. When I exited my car, as I'm walking to the southwest corner outside 1 World Financial Center, I look to the right and I noticed that except for the sirens on the emergency vehicles there was an eerie quiet. You could actually hear the towers burning. There's a parking lot on the southeast corner of Liberty and West, and I see four or five cars and trucks on fire, just exploding. I've spent my entire career in Manhattan South. You see one car or one truck on fire, that's a big thing. But on September 11, I watched five cars and trucks burning and exploding and nobody paid any attention.

When I arrive outside 1 World Financial Center, I meet Officer Pete Moog. I've known Pete for twenty years. We started together in the police department. A lot of debris was coming down, and then all of a sudden somebody says, "Oh, my God, look." And I look up and the bodies started coming. The whole experience was awful, but what was even worse was actually watching people jump. You're helpless, just standing there with these people's lives being taken in front of you. A lot of people. I couldn't give you a number. One couple came down hand in hand. We weren't close enough to see the bodies striking, but you could hear them and it was like a loud firecracker, like a cherry bomb going off when they hit.

But as gruesome as that was, maybe things happen for a purpose. This one particular man jumped and his body struck a fireman on the ground. The fireman's partners picked him up and removed him to the hospital. They thought their buddy was still alive. They thought they could save his life. He died, but the other firemen who carried him off all lived. Because they were trying to save him, they didn't go into the building. The person who jumped died. The fireman he landed on died. But the lives of his buddies were saved. If people weren't jumping, I would have been ten feet closer than I was because we were using the south pedestrian overpass as protection from the falling bodies. Those people jumping saved a lot of lives, that's how I look at it. They didn't die in vain. There was a purpose. Unfortunately, it cost them their lives.

So Moog and myself and a lot of others were setting up emergency command points when we heard that the Pentagon had been hit. I thought, We're really in for it now. Then I remember someone screaming, "Run for your life. The building is coming down."

I turned around and ran. We made it approximately twenty feet, to an alcove at 1 World Financial Center. I got down on my hands and knees. This may sound a little silly, but I went to Catholic grammar school years ago, and in the sixties we would practice air-raid drills because of the Russians. We'd run out into the hall, get on our hands and knees, and pull our sports coats over our heads. So I got down on my hands and knees. I didn't have a coat on, but I put my hands over my head. I was up against what turned out to be a glass window. Everyone came in behind me and they started piling on top of me. I guess they followed me. But now I'm suffocating, and I'm saying to myself, "My God, I'm going to die like in a soccer stampede. I can't believe this." I'm up against the glass and then everything hit us. Everything went black. I mean, pitch black. It was like being in a tub of ink. Not gray, not hazy, just black. And people were screaming, "We're going to die. We're going to die." Then somebody screamed, "Break the windows. Break the windows." We were banging on the windows with our hands and nothing happened. I was starting to lose consciousness, and I said, "I can't believe this. I work twenty years and I'm gonna die like this." I knew I was dying. No Hollywood ending. My life didn't flash before my eyes. But one thing I do remember saying was "Well, at least it doesn't hurt." And just as I'm losing consciousness, I remember almost yelling to myself, "What the fuck is wrong with you? Shoot out the window."

I had my gun in my fanny pack. I opened it, took the gun out and my first thought was, My God, what if there's somebody on the other side of this window? And I then I said to myself, "Well, everyone's going to die if you don't shoot out this window. Just pull the trigger." The first shot collapsed the window from my waist down. But now I was afraid that if we tried to go under it, the rest of the window would come down and decapitate us. So I reached up high and shot off another round. I smacked out the remaining shards of glass and we all piled into the lobby. There was little relief in the lobby because everything came in behind us, the debris and the blackness, like razor blades in your throat. It was better than outside, but still difficult to breathe. You could see nothing in front of you. Now I was afraid of falling down. I felt that if I fell, I would be trampled and I'd never get up.

So I'm walking with my hands out, feeling for something, a door, anything. I'm moving around and I find a door handle. I pull it. It's a door to outside, but everything hit me like a blast furnace and I couldn't breathe again. I got away from the door and I started telling myself to just calm down and don't hyperventilate. The only thing you could see at this point was anything that was on fire. You could see the fire through the haze and the smoke. People are still screaming, "We gotta get out of here, we gotta get out of here. We're gonna die." I just put my hands out and I keep walking until I feel another pane of glass. And this time I didn't even hesitate. I just aimed higher and shot another round and the whole thing dropped. I shot out this window and a bunch of us piled out.

In my twenty years of service, I've responded to many emergencies. In this one, you were either dead or you were alive. There was no in between. We were all choking and couldn't see. I'm walking around now, trying to get my bearings, trying to think of what I'm going to do next, and I hear a woman call from my left. She says, "Come in here, come in here. We have water." So I go into the room, which turns out to be an office for VIP yacht cruises. A fireman was bleeding from the head. He was in real bad shape. So we laid him down and his buddies stayed with him. The woman walked me into a storeroom where they kept supplies for the boats. Napkins, tablecloths, bottles of soda, bottles of water, a slop sink. I turn the slop sink on and stuck my head under it. I threw a case of water into a milk crate, grabbed a bunch of napkins, soaked them under the slop sink, and threw them into the milk crate. And I went running back outside.

When I got outside with the milk crate, I looked up. The North Tower was still burning and the South Tower was gone. I was standing there for a couple of seconds thinking, Where the fuck is the tower? I simply couldn't comprehend it. One tower is on fire and the other is gone. And I'm saying, "Where the fuck is the tower? Where the fuck is the tower?" Then I told myself, "Snap out of it. Come on."

I'm familiar with the area. I know there's a North Cove Harbor and a South Cove Harbor. I wasn't in uniform, but in my mind, my shield was around me. So I tell the women and the firemen, "Guys, listen, I'm Lieutenant McGinn. We can't stay here if the other tower drops. There's a South Cove Harbor. I know the area. We have to go down there."

So everyone grabs napkins and more water and we start making our way southbound on the esplanade. All of a sudden here comes that train again, but even louder than the first time. I couldn't believe it was possible. We all just started running. The thought occurred to me to just jump off the esplanade and into the river, but then I saw somebody out of the corner of my left eye running into a building. I just screamed, "Follow me." We ran into what turned out to be a restaurant-bar on the esplanade. It was already filled with a lot of civilians, a lot of women and children. A blind woman, a pregnant woman, an elderly woman with a dog. I'm assuming they sought shelter there after the first collapse. People were crying, screaming. The last person in must have left the door open because everything came in again, the air, the smoke. Two women were giving out water. I told them, "Turn the taps on. Soak the napkins." You couldn't see six inches in front of you. The explosions, the noise, the rumble was making people hysterical. When the smoke and the ash cleared, I told everybody again, "We're going to evacuate. As soon as you come out the door, we make a left and continue south on the esplanade to the South Cove Harbor."

So the firemen and the cops got everybody together and when we came outside, it was like a miracle. There were two police vans and a golf cart belonging to the Battery Park City Authority. And like a scene out of movie where everyone says, "Women and children first," we just loaded the vans, the two vans and the golf cart, with the women and the children, and we sent them on their way down to the boats and to New Jersey.

A woman's cell phone was working. I said, "Please, I need to use your cell phone. I have to get in touch with my wife." She was still in Brooklyn, with the detectives from her unit. If you weren't going to be hands-on with the rescue operation at the World Trade Center, you were instructed to remain at your current command, which is where she stayed. I got through to her and I told her, "I'm okay. Call my parents."

She said, "What do you mean, you're okay?"

I said, "I'm here."

And she said, "You were able to get through?" She had seen the traffic that morning and never thought for a second that I would have been able to get there.

My great-uncle, Jack Hogan, started on the force in 1927. My father did thirty years, from 1950 to 1980. Except for the gap of my father retiring in '80 to my coming in in '82, my family has served the police department for seventy-five years. I was a little melancholy about retiring, but working all these hours, all these holidays, took a toll on my private life. I felt that I paid my dues, and hopefully it's not too late for me to be spending more time with my family.

After September 11, when people were congratulating me for what I had done that day, I was, like, "No, no, no, I'm not a hero." But truthfully, I've gotten to where I feel more comfortable now just saying thank you. I hope civilians don't misunderstand what I'm about to say, but I felt better knowing that the thirty to forty people I saved were almost all emergency service workers— police, fire, or ambulance. To save their lives means more to me because of the ripple effect. I'm not only saving their lives, but hopefully they are going to go on and save other people's lives.

A perfect example of this came one month later when my wife woke me up and said, "You're never gonna believe what happened. A plane just went down in Rockaway."

I thought, Here we go again. So I jumped in my car and at the scene I run into a female lieutenant, Terri Tobin. I hadn't seen her in a while. Later on, at nine or ten o'clock at night after everything is contained, we're having a cup of coffee and I ask her how she's doing. She says, "Well, this is my first day back to work. I got hurt on 9/11." I hadn't heard. And she begins to tell me the story of how she's on the northwest corner of Liberty and West. Her skull was caved in by a piece of concrete. A shard of glass had embedded itself from one of her shoulder blades to the other. She broke her ankle. And she says, "If it wasn't for Pete Moog, I would be dead."

Pete Moog is one of the fellows I saved. There's that ripple effect. Pete was able to rescue her after he escaped from the lobby with me.

PETER MOOG
41, Officer, NYPD

"THIRTY OR SO OF US WERE STACKED UP IN THAT CORNER LIKE TRAPPED RATS. . . . I THOUGHT WE WERE DONE FOR."

I'm a police officer assigned to the technical assistance and response unit, TARU. That Tuesday started off like any Tuesday when I work the four-to-twelve. I dropped my kids off at school and I went to my local coffee shop to get a coffee and the paper. And when I got the paper, my beeper went off. When I called in, I was told that a plane had hit the World Trade Center and we were on alert.

Five minutes later, I got another page telling me to report to Vesey and West Streets. I immediately called my partner, Ed Gardner, and I picked him up on the way into Manhattan. I think the second plane hit while we were in the Battery Tunnel. We felt some vibrations and we heard a loud noise, but we weren't sure what or where it was. After we parked, I saw some emergency service personnel that I knew from working on hostage jobs, and I asked whether they had seen anyone from our unit. They said there were some people here earlier, but they weren't sure where they went. So we waited to get more instruction. As we waited, I started seeing some of the most horrific things I've ever seen. I was actually watching the people jumping from both towers. I basically stopped counting at twelve.

I did see one jumper actually hit a fireman on the corner near Vesey and West. I later found out that the fireman was Danny Suhr. He played for the fire department football team. I coach our team, and I've played, so I knew Danny. He was one of the first firemen to get killed. When he got hit by the jumper, I saw it but I didn't even know it was him because we were across the street.

Then somebody said that the TARU guys were down at the end of the block. I saw my friend Tommy Dowd, who works in emergency services, and they were all about to go into the North Tower. They were concerned about a secondary attack, a possible ground attack, so they were ordered to get on their heavy vests and helmets and large heavy weapons. So they ended up doing an about-face.

Ed and I went to our location, which was actually 1 World Financial Center. Our job there was to establish a temporary headquarters and document the event with film and video. Police headquarters was having difficulty with communications, so we pulled phone lines out of the basement of 1 World Financial and set them up outside on Liberty Street. We were getting a flashlight for somebody downstairs, out of our command vehicle, which was basically a Suburban loaded with equipment, when one of the guys said that the South Tower had exploded. So we ran. I thought we were running from an explosion and some debris. It turned out we were running from the collapsing building. We ran behind some pillars and into a corner, which I thought was a doorway, but it turned out to be a dead end.

Thirty or so of us were stacked up in that corner like trapped rats. We tried to break a fifty-foot window, which is made to resist being broken. We pounded on it with helmets and flashlights and everything else. I thought we were done for. I was pretty close to suffocating. I found out later that Tim McGinn shot out the window, which enabled us to get into the building and away from the debris.

Once we were in the building we tried to get a head count to see who was with us. Timmy also shot out the back window of the building so we could get out to South End Avenue. Then we realized we were missing people, so John Malic, Pat Lynch, the PBA president, myself, and some other guys formed a search party, and we returned back out onto West Street. Malic and I found a couple of people under debris. Ambulances a couple of feet away from us burst into flames. The rubble was eight feet high in some spots. We dug with our hands to free people. Then Malic yelled, "Run, the second one's coming down."

It was a stampede. Everybody was running in different directions. The only presence of mind I had told me to run back to where I had come from, through the window that Timmy had shot out and then back through the other window onto South End Avenue. Ralph Cefarello, the guy who drives Chief Esposito, was running with me out on South End Avenue. Ralphie's a little older than me and neither one of us are fleet of foot. But we could see that this black cloud of something was catching up to us. Nobody had any idea what it was, whether it was all metal, whether it was all rock, but it was something that was wiping people out. And it was catching up to us.

Across South End Avenue, there was a parking garage, a Gateway Plaza parking garage. The concussion, or air, or whatever it was, caught up to us, and it almost knocked both of us through two parked cars. Both cars had substantial damage. It was pitch black in the garage. I spent at least twenty minutes in complete darkness. We took a head count. There were seven people in there, including us. They were mostly EMS workers. They had some medical supplies and some water. Ralphie and I moved some light debris and said, "Okay, we can get out. Let's head toward the water. There have got to be some boats coming."

At that moment, I heard some lady yell, "Help, TARU." She had read the shirt I had on which said "TARU" on the back. She was a lieutenant I knew, Terri Tobin, and she had a huge piece of rock embedded in her head and two very large jagged pieces of glass in her back, both left and right of her spine. And she was lying on the ground.

I carried her down to the water. Ralphie and I got her on a boat down by the North Cove Marina. There were one or two fireboats and some civilian boats that people were being loaded onto. One of our harbor boats pulled in, and I knew a guy on it, Keith Duvall. He said, "Grab a sledgehammer. We'll break into one of these yachts and take it." There were about a thousand people there, all waiting to get the hell off the island.

Keith and I broke into a boat. I said, "Rich people always leave the keys in the boat." So we ended up finding the keys and Keith got the boat started. I think he made about ten trips back and forth to Jersey, with this big boat taking about a hundred people a trip.

And while evacuating people off the island, I heard this jet roaring in. I had no idea what it was. I thought it was another part of the attack. I squatted down behind a garbage can with my little pea-shooter nine-millimeter pointing up at the jet. And everybody was looking at me and thinking, What are you doing?

And I'm like, I'm not going without a fight. But it turned out to be our fighter pilots. I thought, Thank God. But I mean, I had had enough.

I don't remember whether it was day three or four, but we were now meeting with the emergency services personnel, and they assigned us a camera guy and a sound guy. I don't know if they were called FEMA teams, but it was search and rescue. I remember waiting to be assigned. It was as though it was the first sporting event I ever played in my life. I was so nervous. I paced up and down. I went to the bathroom nine times in less than an hour. I couldn't keep enough water in my mouth. I was so dry-mouthed. But I knew if I didn't go back down there at that point that I would be whipped for the rest of my life and I would twitch at every loud noise I heard. I didn't want to go down, and I told the guys I didn't want to go down, but I knew I had to go down. It was a tough thing to get over. And, you know, the guys who weren't there were like, "Hang in there, Pete." But some guys never came back to work. They never went back down there, or they couldn't. It's no fault of theirs, but for me, with the way I am, I just had to go back down there.

Terri Tobin, left, with Peter Moog.

TERRI TOBIN
40, Public Information Office, NYPD

"THE FORCE OF THE COLLAPSE LIFTED ME UP AND THREW
ME FROM THE EAST SIDE OF WEST STREET TO THE WEST SIDE OF
WEST STREET. I WAS LITERALLY BLOWN OUT OF MY SHOES."

I'm a lieutenant assigned to the deputy commissioner of public information. It's kind of a misnomer because we mostly deal with the press. It's really a press information office. On September 11, in the morning, I had to review the schedule of the events that we would have to cover. And I was meeting with the deputy commissioner. Someone came in and said a plane just hit the World Trade Center. The deputy commissioner immediately sent myself and another sergeant over to the World Trade Center. My beeper went off, alerting me that the police department was mobilized to Church and Vesey. The first deputy commissioner there, Joe Dunn, grabbed me and told me to get a helmet from the emergency service truck. So I hopped on the truck, and we got two helmets. They were the heavy, ballistic-type helmets. The reason why I'm making the distinction here is because it's the thing that wound up saving my life. They're bulletproof. They're made of Kevlar.

As the second plane hit the South Tower, I went into the North Tower. Every five feet there was an officer directing someone to safety, and it was moving along really well. So I moved over to the South Tower. A photographer over there was taking photos of people coming down the escalator. Obviously, he was in a frozen zone and shouldn't have been there. So I grabbed him and told him that he'd have to leave the building, that we were trying to evacuate people. I walked him out, and there was a uniform officer standing outside the tower, and I handed the photographer off to him and asked him to escort him outside of the frozen zone.

I thought I was really close to my car, which was parked on the corner of West and Liberty, and I thought, It's going to be a long day. Maybe I should put my sneakers on. So I started to walk toward my car from the South Tower and I heard rumbling. The first thing that came into my mind was the trains. I knew that the A and the C and the PATH train pulled into the World Trade Center. So I turned around and walked back to the South Tower. And as I got there people were running toward me saying, "Get out of here. It's coming down." Obviously, it was the building rumbling. Before I even had a chance to figure out what was happening, the force of the collapse lifted me up and threw me from the east side of West Street to the west side of West Street. I was literally blown out of my shoes, and I landed on a patch of grass outside the Financial Center. The sprinkler system had just gone off, so it was very soft. And after I landed, maybe a minute, I got smacked on the back of my head, and I feel the blood running down the back of my neck. The helmet I had on literally split in half. I reach back, and there was a piece of cement embedded in the back of my skull.

At this point, I had no perspective as to where I was. It's extremely dark. It's really difficult to breathe. And cement is embedded in the back of my head. I'm just laying there, and I was in shock. I mean, it was some blow to the head. For a minute, I thought maybe I was knocked unconscious. And then I was thinking that I wouldn't be thinking how black it was if I were unconscious.

Stuff was continuing to fall on top of me, and I couldn't get air into my lungs. And all I heard were extremely loud explosions. I thought we were being bombed. As the smoke began to clear, I saw an opening. A firefighter had lit a flashlight, and I could see the silhouette of his helmet. He said, "Stay down, and try to cover your mouth and your nose with a shirt." I heard someone moaning off to my left. I reached out. It wasn't like I had much mobility, but I reached out and I grabbed fingers and I grabbed a hold of a hand, and I said, "I'm with the NYPD." And basically, I just repeated the same instructions the firefighter had given me.

After maybe a minute, I said to this person, "I'm going to try to get up, but I'm not going to let go of your hand." There was the sense that if you let go of something, you weren't going to get it back. I was pulling, pulling, pulling, and then all of a sudden the hand just came up, and I looked down: I had a hand and an arm and no one was attached to it. I tried to scurry over and climb and go through the rubble, but I could not find the body of this person.

And I got up. The firefighter was not too far from me, and two EMS workers were there. So the firefighter grabs the two EMS workers and says, "Wrap her head." And they did. As the four of us were standing there, it was eerily silent. But we heard calls for help and we pulled three people out from the rubble.

After we got the third person out, people were running south now, toward us on West Street. And people are screaming, "The second one's coming down. Get out of here." The best thing was to run toward the water, so I started to run. I cut through Battery Park City, and as I'm running, and I thought I was running really fast, but I didn't realize I had fractured my ankle.

I took a hard hit to my back, and it knocked me from my feet right down to my knees. I turned around and I saw the black cloud coming, approaching very quickly. I knew I wasn't going to make it to the water. So I got up and I ran into an apartment building. I wanted to get away from the glass facade, so I walked toward the lobby. It was dark, but the emergency lights in those yellow cages were lit. But then the smoke started to come into the elevator shaft, so I went into the stairwell. Residents of the building were there, and I don't know how long they had been there, or what they were doing there, so I waited a few minutes and then I opened up the door and the smoke was manageable in the lobby. So I said to them, "Come out and go into the lobby, but stay away from the windows.

I got them out of the stairwell, and then I walked back to the door that I had come in through, and I see two guys with NYPD shirts on through the window across the street. So I opened the door and I called to them. One of them was Pete Moog, who knew me. So he came over and I said, "Listen, there's all these people in this building."

And he tells me that he's heard over the police radio that they're evacuating people to New Jersey. I said, "Well, all right, then let's start getting these people out."

And then he said—he was a real cutie—he said, "I think I should carry you down to the water."

I responded, "Pete, that's okay. I saw EMS. They wrapped my head."

He said, "No." He said, "Through your blouse, between your shoulder blades, there's a shard of glass just sticking out of your back." Obviously, that was the hit that caused me to go down.

I said, "Well, just leave it." We're taught that if anyone's stabbed, you leave it in.

So we went down to the slip, and a line of people were waiting to get on the boat. Then an NYPD harbor boat pulled up and the captain (who I knew), hopped out and he saw me. He said, "You need to go to a hospital." But I couldn't get on the boat with a shard of glass in my back because they were afraid that if it rocked, it would just cause more damage. So he called over two EMS workers, and as I held onto a railing, they put their feet up against the railing, and then the two of them ripped this glass out of my back and compressed it. They poured peroxide on it. It was rather deep. It was in my back and I didn't see it, and it was deep enough to be embedded the whole time.

We were taken over to Ellis Island, and from there I was taken to a medical center. When I got to the hospital, they immediately did a chest X ray. And then a doctor came in and said, "Well, we have some good news and we have some bad news for you."

I said, "Okay, what is it?"

And he said, "Well, we have a surgeon here, and obviously you need to see a surgeon. The bad news is that because of your head trauma, we can't give you any anesthesia."

They did my head first. I was lucky. The cement had dented my skull, but not fractured it. They cut my hair and then they cut the cement out. It was on the outside of my skull, but totally embedded into the skin. They stitched underneath it, across the back of my head. I didn't count, but I think I had forty stitches in my head and another forty stitches in my back.

When I left the hospital, I had on green surgeon's pants, a blue paper top, and booties. And I had this turban on my head. My back was wrapped. There was an officer there that had come over with someone else who was injured, and he needed to get back. He asked my brother and me, "Can I jump into the car with you?"

We said, "Sure." So we made our way back into Manhattan, and we went back down to the World Trade Center site and dropped him off. My brother brought me to headquarters because I needed to tell everyone that I was all right. I worked for a couple of hours, and then people started to say to me, "You know, one of your pupils is bigger than the other." You hear all these horror stories of people that have been hit in the head. So we went out to North Shore Hospital and I got my CAT scan. My brother then brought me to my sister's on Long Island, where I stayed and recuperated. And, you know, as injured as I was, there was still a sense of "I'm really lucky."

RALPH CEFARELLO
50, Detective, NYPD

—

"ONE GUY IN FRONT OF ME WAS DRIVING A
LITTLE SLOWER THAN I WAS. HE COST ME FOUR OR
FIVE SECONDS, AND THAT PROBABLY SAVED MY LIFE."

I was home when I found out what happened. When the first plane hit, my wife called me from work and told me I'd better get to work because, obviously, Chief Esposito would need me. I am one of his aides. In the car, on the way there, I found out that the second plane had hit.

I guess I was moving kind of quickly. They weren't letting anyone over the bridge except for emergency vehicles from Staten Island, so I got through at a high rate of speed. One guy in front of me was driving a little slower than I was. He cost me four or five seconds, and that probably saved my life.

When I got through the tunnel, I saw my old boss, Captain George Duke, and he was standing near his car on West Street. I asked him if he'd seen Chief Esposito or any of the other guys from my office. He said he hadn't seen Chief Esposito, but he'd seen Chief Sal Carcaterra, another chief and a close personal friend of mine. Chief Duke pointed down toward the towers and said Sal was up there, near the bridge that crosses West Street. So I pulled up as close as I could get, which was across from Morton's Steakhouse. I was on that service road there. As I went to get out of the car, I heard a tremendous rumble and I saw people running toward me. The next thing I know, the building was coming down on top of us. The chief is one of the guys who is always telling me to put my seat belt on, and considering the fact that I was doing well over a hundred miles an hour on the way there, I had put it on. When the stuff was coming down and debris was hitting my car, I tried to get the belt off so I could get out, but I couldn't. I said to myself, "I'm dead," and I ducked my head down.

I still had the window open from talking to the captain, and everything came in the car. I was finding it hard to breathe. I couldn't see. I had thought I was going to be running up and down the steps of the building, pulling people out of the smoke, like in '93, so I'd brought an extra shirt with me. I reached over and grabbed the shirt and put it over my face so I could breathe. I got the window up and tried to catch my breath.

I tried to relax myself and realized, Okay, I'm still alive, so let me see what I can do. I climbed over the seat, and I have this big flashlight in the back of my trunk and I grabbed that. And not being all that bright, instead of taking a helmet, I took a baseball cap that said CHIEF OF DEPARTMENT. I guess I needed people to know who I was. I guess I wasn't thinking that well at the moment.

I pushed the door open. I wasn't buried. There was probably a foot of stuff on top of my car, parts of the building and everything, but somehow—and I don't understand it myself because some of the cars around me were crushed—my car wasn't crushed. I think the building that Morton's was in probably shielded me somewhat.

I walked toward where I thought Sal was, yelling his name. When I didn't see him, I started to go into fire trucks and whatever was in front of me, seeing if there was anybody that I could pull out. I heard a woman yelling for help, and I tried to find out where she was. It was very quiet except for that woman. I kept yelling to the woman to yell, so I could find where she was. At one point she stopped, and I couldn't find her. I looked, but I just couldn't find her.

I said to this guy next to me, who I'm pretty sure was a lieutenant from the Seventy-second Precinct, "Do you hear that? Do you hear that?"

He said, "Yeah, I hear it." But we just couldn't find her.

Anyway, it's a little blurry how everything went. I was trying to help whoever I could. I ran into Pete Moog, who is a friend of mine, and I said, "Have you seen Sal?"

And he said, "He was standing here with me, and that's the last I've seen of him."

I asked Pete, "Did he get away from the building?"

He said, "I think so." So we looked for him some more and started yelling his name. And then as we were walking, I ran into another guy who had a broken leg, and he said, "You better get out of here. This building is coming down too." So as we looked for Sal, Pete and I picked this guy up and left him with some firemen. Then we heard another rumble, which sounded like the first one, so Pete and I started running. And as we were running, we found an opening in a garage and we ran in. It got dark again and I couldn't see, couldn't breathe. I started yelling for Pete, "Are you all right? Are you all right?" I heard him say yeah. I told him, "Walk toward the light."

He asked, "What light?" I had a flashlight, but he couldn't see it. And he was only about five feet from me. I told him to keep talking, and I reached out, grabbed him, and pulled him to me.

When we got back out into the street, there were other people. We saw a man carrying his kid, a little girl, and his wife, and he started running toward where we had come from, which I knew was a bad idea, so I tried to stop him. And he's yelling and screaming, "I've got to get to lower ground."

And I'm telling him, "Listen, you have to turn around and go toward the water. Go the other way." And he was fighting me. Pete and I stayed in front of him, and we wouldn't let him go.

His wife finally told him, "Listen to them, listen to them," and they turned around. There was a building there, and there had to be thirty or forty people in there and they looked like they were in shock. They were just standing there, behind this glass. So I started hitting the glass with a helmet that Pete gave me, and saying, "Get out, get out." And they came out. And we led them down toward the water. And that's where Sal was. Eddie Aswad knew we were looking for Sal, and at the water he yelled to me, "Ralph, Ralph, Sal's on one of the launches."

I thought about that guy who was going slower than me in the tunnel, the guy who I think probably saved me. Had he not been there, I probably would have gotten out of the car. I would have been a little earlier, and been walking, and who knows, maybe I would've gotten hit by something. Maybe the car saved me.

When I did finally get back to my car, it was covered with stuff but seemed drivable. I wanted to take it out of there, but they wouldn't let me. When I got home, I went to my backyard. My wife came out, brought me some clothes. I undressed back there, threw the other clothes into a black plastic bag. Then I took a shower and just sat there. I couldn't sleep.

SEAN CROWLEY
36, Captain, NYPD

—◆—

"WE ACTUALLY SAW CARS FLYING THROUGH THE AIR.
WE SAW I BEAMS, EIGHT-TON I BEAMS COMING AT US END
OVER END LIKE TOOTHPICKS. WE SAW AIR-CONDITIONING DUCTS.
WE SAW PARTS OF BUILDINGS, AND NEWSPAPERS AND DEBRIS,
ALL IN A DUST BALL AND COMING AT US."

At the time of the incident I was assigned to the police commissioner's office as the head of security for Police Commissioner Bernard Kerik. I've been a police officer since 1986.

On September 11 at about 8:15 A.M., I dropped my son Sean Jr. off at the bus stop. It was his first day of school. The bus came at eight-twenty. He got on and I began my drive into Manhattan, to 1 Police Plaza and the commissioner's office. I was on Highland Boulevard, in front of the 122nd Precinct, when I heard this radio transmission that a plane had just struck the World Trade Center. Having been at the first World Trade Center bombing, and in emergency service for four years, I knew this would be a big job that would require the police commissioner, the mayor, and other elected officials to respond. I immediately turned on my lights and sirens. I went down Hylan, then over the Verrazano Bridge to the Gowanus Expressway.

As I was going into the Brooklyn-Battery Tunnel, I heard the second transmission that a second plane had struck the building. I knew it was terrorism at this point, but I didn't know how they were accomplishing their mission of hitting these buildings. My gut reaction was that they had taken control of the plane, almost like in *Die Hard 2*, when the pilots had no control and computers overrode what the automatic pilot was doing, which made them crash. As we found out later, that was incorrect. The planes were hijacked.

I was in the bus lane heading into the tunnel when that second plane hit. There were probably more than fifteen police cars and unmarked cars behind me. I was leading the way through. We made it maybe 80 percent through the tunnel when we got stuck in traffic. We couldn't move. Knowing that terrorism was probably to blame for the two planes hitting the Trade Center it wasn't a comfortable feeling sitting in that tunnel waiting for the traffic to clear. The lights and sirens were still on, but nothing was moving in front of us, so I got out of my car. Chief Sal Carcaterra was in a Jeep right behind me. He saw me, and he said, "Sean, what's going on?"

I said, "It looks like it's all backed up from the fire trucks trying to get out in front of us." As I'm talking to him, the traffic cleared in front of me. I jumped back into the car and I pulled out of the tunnel, right at the south tip of West Street. I made a right turn toward the Trade Center, and as I'm driving up West Street I saw the fire engines, ambulances, police cars, emergency service trucks, the police emergency service unit, all different city official cars parked and double-parked in the middle of the road. I made it up to Liberty and West, which is were the South Tower is located. I pulled up to that intersection and Captain Eddie Aswad pulled up next to me. Where he came from I have no idea, but he ended up being right next to me in a car. So I rolled down my windows, he rolled down his, and we agreed to make the left turn onto Liberty, away from the Trade Center, to keep out of the way of emergency vehicles. I forget whether it was Eddie or me who said, "Let's pull it onto the sidewalk so we'll be out of the way and we won't be blocked in case we have to use the cars again to get out of here." There's a little grassy knoll directly in front of 3 World Financial Center, which is the southwest corner of Liberty and West. So we pulled the cars up there and we parked underneath a pedestrian crossover.

We got out of the cars and immediately talked about setting up a temporary command center for Police Commissioner Kerik, the mayor, and the fire commissioner. Was it safe to bring them down there? Could we fly a helicopter in and out of this area? Could we get a harbor launch in and out of this area? Could we get out by car if the whole of West Street gets shut down? The answer to all the questions ended up being yes.

I went into the lobby of 3 World Financial Center and it did afford us some protection from all the elements outside and in case another plane crashed into the Trade Center. So we determined that this may be a good spot, if they wanted it, for a command post. You could still get a full visual of the whole Trade Center, West Street, and Liberty Street. The only thing we didn't see was the northeast side of the complex, which is actually where the mayor and the police commissioner were, in 75 Barclay, when the building came down.

I saw some pretty disturbing things as we were setting up the temporary headquarters. I was on the SWAT and Rescue team, and I've seen people jump off buildings in front of me. I've cleaned up people run over by trains. But probably one of the most disturbing things I saw that day were those people jumping from the towers. And it wasn't just one person jumping, or the sound of one person hitting. It was the sound of three and four and five of them holding hands together and jumping together. And the sight of seeing five people holding hands and jumping from a hundred stories up, and them hitting the ground and just disintegrating. These were regular, happy-go-lucky people. They weren't trying to commit suicide. They weren't psychos, or drug addicts who were so high they thought they could fly. They were people like me and you, people who worked hard every day, people from Cantor Fitzgerald and stockbrokers making a lot of money. And whether they made a dollar a year or a million a year, they were of sound mind when they went to work that morning, and now they were jumping out of windows a hundred stories in the air.

At this point Eddie Aswad and I were talking to Sal Carcaterra and Patty Lynch, who was the PBA president. We were all on that same corner, pretty much deciding that this was probably a safe spot, as safe as any, to bring the commissioner and the mayor down.

I'm walking forward with Patty Lynch and I see Glen Pettit, a cop we had used many times in the past to shoot video for us, for the police commissioner, for training, for pretty much anything we needed in the way of police department filming. We called Glen for everything. He always got the shot and he didn't miss much.

We're talking to Glen at the intersection of Liberty and West, in front of the Vista Hotel, when we hear a rumble, the sound of the building crumbling, and it was extremely loud. Eddie looked up at the building and saw it coming down and falling. My initial reaction was to run back toward the hotel, which would have made sense if it had been another plane hitting the tower. But I was looking away from the building, toward Eddie's eyes. I saw his face, and he goes, "Fucking run," or something like that. He turned around and ran toward where our cars were parked, which were right in front of 3 World Financial Center underneath the walkway.

I never saw Glen again. From what we know based on where he was found, he ran right to the Vista and then along the building line. He was found right at the building line of the Vista, between the South Tower and the Vista, which is exactly where we thought he would've been.

Eddie ran up West Street. I said, "Eddie, go in the cars." I think his response was, "Fuck the cars. Keep running." So I ran past my car and he ran behind a pillar that was holding up the overhang to a building. Right in front of us were our cars, so we got protection from that pedestrian walkover directly above our heads. We got protection from our two cars that were parked in front of the pillars, and the pillars that we hid behind. It was almost like the movie *Twister*. We actually saw cars flying through the air. We saw I beams, eight-ton I beams coming at us end over end like toothpicks. We saw air-conditioning ducts. We saw parts of buildings, and newspapers and debris, all in a dust ball and coming at us.

You really didn't have time to think about being scared when that building came down because you were running for your life and it happened so quickly. You know, it happened in fifteen seconds. I remember seeing this person, a civilian, carrying five or six bags, like knapsacks and garment bags, and he's running toward us. And all of sudden he dove to the ground, and I'm going, "What the fuck? Why is he diving to the ground?" It was like he was sliding into second base, only he's sliding fifty to sixty feet on concrete. A week later, I bumped into somebody who got 150 stitches from getting hit with a piece of air-conditioning duct. When she told me she got picked up and thrown across West Street from the plume, I realized that that's what had to have happened to the guy with the bags. There's no way you can slide sixty feet on concrete.

A couple of other cops made it in behind us. An EMT fireman made it to where we were, and his partner made it in next to him but he wasn't covered totally. He was killed when an I beam hit him. I mean, that's how close a difference it was. An EMT guy next to me makes it and his partner next to him doesn't. Glen Pettit ran the other way and was killed.

I'll try to describe what happened in those fifteen seconds. It went totally pitch black. My hands went over my face, my eyes. I closed my eyes and started coughing immediately. Picture taking a handful of flour and sticking it up your nose and in your mouth. That's what breathing was like. So I immediately started to cough. I tried not to cough, not breathe, not do anything and I tried to hold my breath. At the same time I'm feeling all the debris hitting me up the sides of my legs, hitting my ankles, hearing it pile up above me. I'm thinking to myself, I'm either going to die by getting crushed to death, or I'm going to suffocate to death. Which one is it going to be?

I'm not dead, but I can't breathe, and I'm thinking about my little son Nicky, who at the time was only sixteen months old. I thought he was never even going to know me. He's just going to know that he had a father and he died. And then I thought about my older guy, the five-year-old I just dropped off at school. I thought he would miss me and he's going to remember me. And as I'm thinking that to myself, I realize, Shit, I'm still alive. This is good. I didn't die yet.

I've never heard screaming like I did on that day. I didn't hear one woman. It was all men. Not to say that there weren't women firemen or women policemen there, but I just didn't see any around where I was. It was all grown men. It was just unbelievable screaming. I guess these were the people who were getting taken out by the I beams and the air-conditioning ducts. And as they're screaming, I'm thinking about how I'm probably going to die, and about my kids.

I had the occasional nightmare after September 11, but nothing major. Really, the only thing that plays into my mind when I'm sleeping is the sound of the building crumbling. The nightmares I get from time to time entail planes crashing, buildings collapsing.

It was probably ten, thirteen days after, on a Saturday night, when I got off around 7 P.M., and my two boys were up when I got home. It was the first time since the eleventh that I got to actually play with them for a length of time. I stopped having nightmares once that happened. It was like therapy. And I didn't have a nightmare again until the day they found Glen Pettit. The day they found Glen they called me to tell me they found him. And they found him right where I thought he would be. That's when I had a couple of nightmares again.

But I'm not ready to leave the police department. I'm going to get my retirement, which could be in four years, or I can get out in two years when I'm thirty-eight. I'll make that decision when the time comes. I don't look at this like I have to get away from the police department now. I still love this department. I still love this city.

EDWARD J. ASWAD JR.

46, Special Assistant to Police Commissioner Bernard B. Kerik, NYPD

"I DON'T HAVE NIGHTMARES, BUT SEPTEMBER 11
IS CONSTANTLY ON MY MIND. LIVING IN THE CITY,
YOU'RE ALWAYS REMINDED OF IT."

The commissioner gave me an assignment to do on the morning of 9/11 that I couldn't complete because the number and address he gave me were incorrect. So I called him and explained to him what happened. And he was just silent. He didn't communicate. Usually he asks me what's going on, and it was just complete silence. I'm explaining about the assignment and he's not acknowledging me. And then a split second later he says, "Ed, I don't know what the hell hit the Twin Towers. I'll see you in a few minutes."

I was in an unmarked police car and I put on my radio SOD channel, lights, siren, and I headed into the city. I'm approaching the Brooklyn-Battery Tunnel and it's getting gridlocked. All these emergency vehicles were trying to get through. The police who oversee the Battery Tunnel were trying to get the civilian vehicles off to the side so all the emergency vehicles could get through. We were stopped and we weren't moving.

I was trying to get into radio communication with Sean Crowley, but it was very bad reception. As I headed through the tunnel, just as I was getting on West Street, I heard another explosion. That must have been when the second plane hit. I tried looking up on West Street, but it was pretty hard because of the angle. And I see all these sheets, napkins, all over the West Side Highway. It was sporadic, but they were pretty much perfectly laid down. I didn't understand why they were there. And I was just maneuvering around these sheets and the debris all over the street. I finally got in touch with Sean—you know, solid communications—and we more or less said we would rendezvous at Liberty Street. So as I was making a left on Liberty, I had my window open and I just happened to catch a glimpse of something. It seemed like a piece of roast beef. It wasn't charred. It was just, like, cooked. Then I realized it was some type of human body part. And I realized that's what the sheets were for. I guess as the emergency people were coming to the scene, they were seeing body parts and they were just covering them.

I parked the car on Liberty and I met Sean. We parked the cars underneath this walkway. And then started trying to communicate with the commissioner and mayor's detail, because they were together at that time. We went into 3 World Financial Center to set up a command post.

We were able to get hard-line phones in that building. Sean was able to go in the back and ascertain that he could get harbor and helicopter to land in the back of the building, if needed. Firemen were just forming up, putting their equipment on and basically saying, "Hey, we're going in. We're going to go put a fire out."

We started seeing people jumping out of buildings. I realized they were desperate, but I got angry. I said to Sean, "What they hell are they doing? Why don't they wait for help?" I honestly thought we should be able to help them. I thought we were in control. There was no panic at this point. You didn't see people running around. You saw the emergency people pulling up to the building, getting out of their vehicles, firemen were putting on their oxygen tanks. You knew there were casualties, but there seemed to be plenty of assistance.

Then Glen Pettit said, "I'm going to get a little closer."

So I turned to him and I said, "Glen, you have to be careful. Debris is coming down."

And he says, "I'll be careful."

Then I said, "Glen," to get his attention, but he didn't turn around to acknowledge. He just said, "Yeah, I'll be careful," and kept going.

So I'm looking at the building, and Sean's facing me. And the next thing you hear is, "It's going." The loud rumble sounded like a jet engine. I look up and I just see like this black cloud of smoke. People are running toward us, so we just turned around and we started running.

The next thing I know we're pinned up against this panel of glass. I thought we were going to die. I thought about my children and family. I'm trying to gasp for air, but something is hitting me. It's other people, and whatever's hitting them is vibrating through them to me. I feel stuff going up my legs, the soot and the debris. I had a suit on, with very thin pants, so I felt like something was just riding up my leg. I was gasping for air. Then I hear someone say, "Break the window. Break the window." I was just pinned against the glass. I had brought two weapons with me that day, my Glock and a revolver. I couldn't get to my Glock. It was on my side, on my belt. But I had my revolver on my ankle. And with bodies pinned against me I was bent down. My arm was locked because I was pinned sideways. My hand was down where I was able to get my revolver, but I wasn't getting it so I could shoot it. I was thinking that I could use the revolver to bang out the window, but I could hardly even move. Finally, you could hear rounds go off, so someone shot the window. At some point, I was able to bring my arm up and I shot one round. I don't know which way it went. The way the gun was pointed toward the glass. I don't know if I penetrated it, but the glass went.

You couldn't see anything in the building. I was just choking, trying to get my breath. It was like a dry heave when nothing's coming up. Then I bumped into Sean. And he just said, "Let's get the F out of here." So we just started walking, hand in hand. We were doing little slide steps because of the debris. And we went sideways. Then we went around a revolving door. We just started spinning and then we were out. And Sean got frantic. He goes, "Eddie, we must be in another part of the building."

I said, "What do you want to do, go back in there and go around again?"

The next thing he says is, "We're still inside. We're still inside." With that, maybe a moment later, he falls off the curb. We're outside. He tripped and I stumbled into him. And we were choking, gasping for air. And still, we didn't see anybody. We just keep walking and walking and we come across water bubbling out of the ground. So I go toward it. I said, "I need some water."

He says, "Eddie, you don't know what that is."

I said, "Sean, I need something. I gotta clean my throat out, my eyes." So I bend down and just start cupping the water with my palms. It was a little pond, like a decorative pond, with a waterfall, in front of a building. I wasn't actually drinking it. I was just putting it in my mouth and gurgling it.

Then we came across the marina. We got on a boat, or we were trying to get on a boat. There was this one particular boat. It was all sided with glass. I guess it was like a sightseeing boat. There were no chairs on it. It was just wide open with these glass panels around it. We were still bending over, trying to catch our breath. Sean keeps saying he needs water, and I'm rummaging through this boat. There was this silver cabinet, like a cooler, and I opened it and there was water and beer. So we start getting bottles of water and we're just pouring it all over our faces, our heads, taking our jackets off. We're looking for maybe a phone line, anything on the boat, and there's nothing. There were cameras and all kinds of other stuff there, but nothing we could use to help us. But we got our bearings. And then we started seeing people walking toward the harbor. And then we saw a police harbor boat and firemen crawling, and people just injured and shocked and walking around like it was *The Twilight Zone*. From there, we assisted people on the boat.

From that day on, we lived at Ground Zero. The commissioner paired everybody up and Sean and I were paired together for the next two weeks. We just went out and did whatever we needed to do. They talk of how it wasn't healthy down there, and we never really had any masks or eye protection. They gave them out, but we really never used them because everybody was telling us it was okay.

After that, it was just going to funeral after funeral. I cry. I get teary-eyed. I get upset. I knew a lot of people in those buildings. I knew a young woman. She was a secretary. She was going to be getting married, and she died.

I don't have nightmares, but September 11 is constantly on my mind. Living in the city, you're always reminded of it. It's in the papers and it's always there. And if I had done the assignment the commissioner asked me to do, I wouldn't have even been in the city. I would have been nowhere near that place. So maybe fate helped me save a life or two. Maybe it would have been different for Sean if I hadn't been there. We really got tight that day. And who knows, if I wasn't there that day and he had gotten back into the car, maybe he would have been killed. You think back and you see the decisions we made. We made good decisions. We were protected. I know a lot of those people who were in back of me that didn't make it. We were very fortunate.

GREGORY FRIED
55, Executive Chief Surgeon, NYPD

"The harbor boat is ready to take off and I notice that they don't have a packed load. I say, 'Wait a second. There're more people.' And Jimmy says, 'Doc, there's nobody here. They're all dead.'"

My wife works locally in a hospital and on the morning of September 11, I dropped her off at work and then took the Long Island Expressway to my office in Elmhurst. Over the radio I heard them announce that the World Trade Center had just been hit by a plane. I turned on the police radio, which I usually keep off because it's noisy. There was a suspicion of mass casualties, so I turned on the siren and hit the express lane of the expressway. You could already see the smoke billowing up and it was pouring into Queens.

I was there in '93 when the Trade Center was attacked. I knew there would be a real need for authorities in positions, and I can do what's required in that kind of situation. I can tell cops what to do. I can tell other doctors what to do. I can evacuate. I can do all those things. So I was there to assist at the triage. I wasn't going down there to perform surgery, but rather to create some sort of order in what I knew would be pandemonium. So I parked on lower Broadway and started walking. From there it's west and sort of down. And as I was walking, I immediately saw an emergency service van, with police officers, and I have identification so I hitched a ride with them. I got out near West and Liberty and took a helmet from one of the van guys. And as I was walking, there were bodies coming out of the building. You'd hear this *whoosh*, and then it would go, *crash*. And then all of a sudden you'd hear a *splat*.

One of the cops said to me, "What was that?"

I looked at him and said, "That was a person." A woman came down out of one of the upper floors and as she hit the ground she literally disintegrated. She looked like a bug on a windshield, but her arm came off.

I saw Charles Hirsch, the New York City medical examiner, and we just sort of stared at each other. I continued walking and I saw Mychal Judge, the fire chaplain, who's a friend of mine, or was a friend of mine, and I just said, "Father, be careful."

And he said, "God bless," because he always said, "God bless." Then he headed right and I went left.

I saw a guy on the ground, probably a firefighter, in a brown jumpsuit. It must have been a firefighter. Anyway, he was bleeding to death from his armpit. He had been hit by flying glass. And my thought was to stop the bleeding, throw him into a van, and get him to a hospital. But from a distance of maybe ten to fifteen feet away, somebody yells, "The building's going down." I turn and I look up. I had to look almost straight up, and the thing explodes and it starts coming down at me, literally. It couldn't have been more than fifty feet over my head when I realized what was really happening. It was like in the movies. It was like slow motion. It was big. And it was incredible. Your brain couldn't adjust to the concept of the World Trade Center coming down on you. I remember thinking to myself, Those aren't feathers, and in a remote way, You're dead.

I rolled into a ball and hit the ground. I put my hands over my head and waited. The first thing I felt was a tremendous slap, like a crash. And the rumble was incredible. I can't even give you an analogy. I guess if you were standing by a jet plane, that's what it would sound like. And all of a sudden I was hit and I heard crashing and smashing and I knew I was hurt.

Then it turned completely black. First it was cold. Then it got very hot. And I was lying there waiting to be killed. I figured I would get chopped in half, or I'd lose a leg. I can't tell you how long I was down, but then it stopped. I wasn't dead. But I was really hurting a lot.

I was looking around trying to find the firefighter, and he's gone. There was nobody around, just a few bodies and a couple of body parts. I remember seeing a leg. And I said, "Where is everybody?" in my head. And then I decided, if the building is to my right I better get up and go to my left. And I did. I squirmed to my feet, and I guess the rubble was about shoulder-high in certain areas. My head was fairly well out of it, but I felt my right buttock, my right cheek. That was where all the pain really was. It was swelling, so I knew I was bleeding. I took my belt and wrapped it around and started heading to the Hudson.

I saw Sean Crowley at the water, and I said to him, "Where's the police commissioner?"

He said, "He's okay. We got him out."

Sean was gray, but not as gray as I was. I asked, "Are you okay?" He said that I looked terrible and he wanted to get me out of there. I said, "Sean, we've got all these people who are going to be killed and injured. We have to stay here."

He said, "No, we gotta get you out of here." And then Eddie Aswad comes along, because the two of them were pretty much together, and he says to me, "We're going to get you out of here."

And I said, "Guys, there's nowhere to go. The rubble down there is waist high. We can't get anywhere. The fire engines and ambulances were all destroyed. We have to stay here and help people."

Eddie insists, "No. We're getting you out of here." So Sean radios to the harbor guys, to the scuba guys, to the boat, and suddenly they were right there, nosing up against the seawall. Jimmy Cowan takes a ladder out of the boat and puts it over the seawall. It floats up and down with the waves. I get on the ladder and crawl backward into the boat. If you asked me to do it today, I'd probably faint.

So they get me on the harbor boat and I lie backward. Now I don't remember telling Jimmy this, but he tells me nowadays that all I wanted to do was to stay and help people. I have no recollection of that. They're ready to take off and I notice that they don't have a packed load. I say, "Wait a second. There're more people."

And Jimmy says, "Doc, there's nobody here. They're all dead. We're going to take off and get you over to the hospital."

I remember lying on my back in the harbor boat. I love the harbor boat. I've been on it a million times. And I lie down and a very good feeling comes over me. I realize that if anyone can help me make it, it'd be these guys. I mean, who better than the cops?

So they say, "We're heading to Jersey."

I say, "Whatever you want." I'm lying there feeling my pulse when all of a sudden it disappears. I knew my pulse was fast. I mean, my blood pressure and pulse were going a mile a minute. Then my blood pressure stops. I knew things were pretty bad, and I was dizzy, and I remember hanging on for dear life.

We get over to Jersey where a couple of the paramedics start attending to me. One of them sticks an IV into my arm. I'm a trauma surgeon. I know what to do. So I say, "Guys, you won't get a line in. I have no blood pressure any longer."

One of them goes, "You're right. His blood pressure is sixty. We have to get him out of here." So they throw me on a stretcher and they head to the hospital.

I wasn't willing to die over this. I didn't want to trade my life for this. I was there that day because that's what you do. Ask Sean or Eddie. They won't tell you they're heroes. They're not heroes. They were doing their jobs. It's in their blood. It's in my blood. I've been in shoot-outs. I've been with cops who are dying. When someone says, "He's a hero," we listen and we shrug. You know, heroes, shmeroes. It doesn't matter. It probably would have been a lot easier to stay home that day, or to hide or to find four reasons not to go. But if it happened today, I'd go again. That's the way it is. Look, I don't want to die. I don't think anybody really wants to die. But so what? Eventually you're going to die anyway.

I felt terrible that day. When I got to the hospital, they asked me, "Where are you injured?" I described most of my injuries. And then they said, "Well, aren't you bleeding from your leg?"

"No. Why?"

"Well, you know, your pants are all full of blood." And I looked down and I realized that my pants had that firefighter's blood all over them.

JAMES COWAN
39, Harbor Unit Scuba Team, NYPD

—◆—

"IT WAS SOME FORM OF ARROGANCE THAT WE REALLY
THOUGHT WE WERE PREPARED TO HANDLE EVERYTHING. . . .
NOW NOTHING IS BEYOND THE REALM OF POSSIBILITY.
ANYTHING CAN HAPPEN NOW, ANYTHING AND EVERYTHING."

We are based in the Brooklyn Army Terminal in New York Harbor. On September 11, we received a call over the VHF radio from a passing tugboat saying that a plane had struck the World Trade Center, and that the World Trade Center was on fire.

We headed over there right away and arrived in about three or four minutes. It was just a pretty unbelievable sight. There were already dozens of people jumping from the upper floors. And the heat coming off the building was incredible. We could hear the emergency services officers who were going upstairs. We were on the same frequency, a citywide frequency, and you could hear how much trouble they were having from the volume of fire, the volume of heat, and the volume of people they were removing from the building.

A little while later we heard a sound that we thought was one of our fighter jets. And that was the plane that struck the South Tower.

We were on the seawall, right next to the World Financial Center, which I guess would be about a half block over from the South Tower. In our unit, we keep three divers on the boat and two divers in the helicopter at all times. So the helicopter was evaluating whether they could do a rooftop rescue when the second plane was coming in. And the second plane came in so tight on them that the pilot took evasive action and pulled up, and the plane actually flew underneath them before striking the building.

We set up a triage center to remove injured people to New Jersey, figuring we could see the amount of debris that was already falling off the buildings. Everybody theorized that there were going to be thousands of injuries. We thought possibly there could be other planes coming in. We got on the VHF radio and got in touch with the ferry that takes people over to Liberty Island. We asked if they had dropped anybody off yet at the Statue of Liberty, and they said no. I said, "Don't bring anyone there." We were sure a third plane was coming, and if it wasn't going to go to the Statue of Liberty, it could have been headed for the UN, which was being evacuated simultaneously. We also had ambulances waiting on Ellis Island. In the harbor unit, we had about six or seven boats at that time transporting injured people back and forth. People kept coming down to the seawall just looking to get away, not knowing what was coming next.

We were right near the North Cove Marina, looking to set up the triage area, when the first tower collapsed. It was like watching an avalanche from a mountain. It looked exactly like an avalanche coming down the street at you. There were hundreds of people running toward us. We were sure that people were going to jump in the water. I think that's probably what I would have done. We were yelling for people in the water to answer us. There were dozens of people in the water. Luckily, a New York City fireboat was tied up on the seawall. Most of the people were able to get over to the fireboat, where some fellows with ladders and ropes were pulling people up. We picked people up on our boat, but we were reluctant to transport anyone that was not injured.

We made between a dozen and twenty trips. We came up to the seawall one time and Sean Crowley and Eddie Aswad had come down there with Chief Surgeon Dr. Fried, who looked really horrible. Eddie and Sean didn't look too good either. They were covered with debris, but they weren't seriously injured. Dr. Fried was bleeding from his nose and mouth and he was covered in what looked like cookie dough. We brought them on board, and we were bringing on others—one woman with a two-week-old baby, and a lot of other children and their parents. After the second building collapsed, we backed away from the seawall and we brought people over to Jersey City.

But the thousands of injuries we expected didn't come. They just didn't come. It was unbelievable. I've spent six and a half years in emergency and nineteen years in the police department. I've been at six major airline crashes. I spent two and a half months out at TWA Flight 800. I thought I had seen everything. But it was nothing compared to this. We had the equipment there to help people, and we had the capability to do it, but in this instance there was really nothing you could do. It was some form of arrogance that we really thought we were prepared to handle everything. We really thought that as the police department, we were capable of anything. We did an outstanding job that day. But we never expected, nor did anyone else in the world expect, that a plane loaded with civilians would be used as a weapon. I don't think anybody ever thought that was a possibility.

Now nothing is beyond the realm of possibility. Anything can happen now, anything and everything.

And this is not one of those things that nobody wants to talk about. We've talked about it nonstop for months. What could we have done differently? What should we have done? What could we have done better? The thing that bothers everybody the most, obviously, is the people who were jumping from the windows. From our vantage point you could see hundreds of people up there, and there was no way anyone was going to get to them. The aviation guys wanted desperately to get to that roof. It just wasn't going to happen. Nobody was on the roof, which I think bothered aviation more than anything. I think if there were people on the roof, they would have found a way to make it happen. But it was just total helplessness, a position none of us ever gets used to.

ROGER PARRINO
40, Lieutenant Commander of Detectives, NYPD

"AND THEN ALL OF A SUDDEN I FELT LIKE I WAS
COVERED IN BLANKETS. AND THEN IN ONE SPLIT SECOND,
I BEGAN TO SUFFOCATE."

When I first found out that a plane had hit tower 1, I was on Thirty-third Street dropping my children off at school. My wife was with me. I told her that I needed to respond. Now, in May of 2001, I had had a problem with Commissioner Kerik for not being dressed properly when I responded off-duty to the Carnegie Deli triple homicide. My wife mentions this to me. I'm wearing just jeans and a shirt. So I actually go home, as ironic as this sounds, to put a suit on to go to the World Trade Center. Under Kerik, you always dressed, no matter what the emergency was.

When I came out of our building, the second plane hit. My wife was waiting for me downstairs, and she was crying. At that point, we both got back in the car, and I drove downtown. She was originally supposed to go to the World Trade Center that morning for a three-day seminar, but she had had an argument with her boss the night before. He had wanted her to go, but she said she felt uncomfortable and didn't want to. Of course, we had an argument about it, and I'm telling her that she's being ridiculous and overly sensitive. But she didn't go, and that was the best thing that happened that day, as far as I'm concerned.

Now I'm responding to the World Trade Center and she's in the passenger seat next to me crying, and I'm not really showing much sympathy. I drop her off at the foot of the Brooklyn Bridge, so she could walk across and go to work at Metrotech. I park my car opposite 7 Dey Street, which is less than seventy-five yards from the South Tower.

I went into my investigative mode. I had no idea that the planes had been hijacked. I just started walking around inspecting airplane parts for serial numbers. It was 9:25 A.M., and I'm marking off in my notebook where all the airplane parts are. I had no desire to enter the towers. I've been a police officer for twenty years, and when we were trained in the academy we were told you never enter a building once the fire department is there. So that training really hit home. All you do is get in their way and then they end up saving you instead of saving other people who need the help.

So I ended up walking on Liberty and marking off these airplane parts. Then I came up West Street and I ran into a temporary fire headquarters. I introduced myself as a ranking police officer with the Detectives Bureau. I called my office and told them to send me more detectives. I was trying to reach Chief William Allee's office when I felt a vibration coming through my legs. I thought it was the subway. My first reaction was, "I better tell him to shut down the subway because it's still running."

But then the vibration just got tremendous, and then the phone started going across my desk, the desk I'm sitting at. I still didn't realize what was happening. All of a sudden, *boom*! Everybody was screaming and yelling and what we thought was smoke, but what was really soot, dust and shit, was coming into the building and getting worse. I ended up running into a sergeant, Mike Kosowski, and he told me the building was falling. I thought he was overexaggerating. I mean, obviously I knew something happened.

The dust was taking over the different sections of the building, so we ended up retreating to the back end, a group of us together. I identified myself, telling everybody who I was. And I said, "Unless anybody's got a better idea, we're not going to do anything separately. We're going to do everything together."

I don't know how many people were with us. I say eight. Mike says thirteen.

But one of the guys with us was the head of security for Merrill Lynch. I never knew his last name, but his first name was Rich, and he knew the building. So I said, "We're going to follow him. Nobody does anything independently."

Rich took us to four exits and all of them were sealed shut. We couldn't get out, so we made our way back to the security room where there were closed-circuit cameras. We looked at the cameras and there was nobody else in the building, which made me feel comfortable because I was afraid that if there were other people, we'd have to go search for them. Then the cameras went dead. Rich ended up breaking open a locker, and he handed out security radios and flashlights.

And then Mike said, "Listen, we can't get out of any of these other exits. Let's go into the worst part of it and see if we can get out the front of the building," which is where all the soot and trash was coming from. Mike took the lead, and we ended up in the lobby of the building. And once we're in the lobby, we were pretty good to go because the whole front of the building was gone.

I came out of the building and I said to Mike, "This is not the place we came in."

He said, "Yeah, it is."

I said, "But the building, the tower, is not here."

And he said, "Roger, the building fell. The building is gone."

We had been trapped in the Liberty building for twenty minutes. I don't remember this at all. I don't know why I don't remember it. But Mike says we helped a couple of firemen. That's something I should remember. But for the life of me, I don't remember it. Mike moved the majority of the debris, and then I went back in and got everybody and brought them out. And once we were out, Mike said we helped a couple of the firemen. I must have been in a state of shock. I just remember going into the fire headquarters and picking up fire department equipment and hearing the fire chief say, "Big guy, just leave that shit and go north." I guess I was at a loss for what I was supposed to be doing. At some point, I figured, Okay, there's not much me for me to do.

So I'm walking north and I had just gotten to Vesey when I saw ten or fifteen EMS workers lined up with hard hats on. So I went up to the captain and I asked him, "Are you guys going into the building that fell?"

He said, "Absolutely."

I was so taken back by their courage that I figured, Fuck it, I might as well go with them. I asked this ambulance if they had an extra helmet. They said no. I went to the center of the intersection at West and Vesey. There was another ambulance parked over there, and I asked them if they had a helmet. And I didn't get a chance to get an answer because just as I said that somebody yelled that tower 1 was coming down. I remember just taking off. But while I was running, I turned around and I looked up. And what I saw I haven't really seen on video. I saw the flames kick out, like if you turn the flame up on a stove. And then I saw the flames coming closer to me. In reality, what I think I actually saw was those top floors landing on the fire, which kicked the fire out.

I started feeling like the wind was pushing me like a concussion. I've been in a hurricane, and that's what it feels like. Big things were flying by me. So I dove into the curb right at Vesey and West, and this tremendous wind was blowing over me.

In the Marine Corps, they taught me to put my feet toward the explosion and my head away from the explosion. But I couldn't remember what the Marine Corps told me to do with my hands. It's kind of funny, because at first I covered my balls. Then I said, "No, that doesn't make sense," and so I covered my face. I'm six feet, 240 pounds, and I'm trying to hide in a six-inch curb, which is pretty funny.

I have no memory of any noise. I didn't even hear anything landing near me. I could see shit landing near me, but I couldn't believe I wasn't being hit. I saw stuff hit. I saw a car flip. And then all of a sudden I felt like I was covered in blankets. That's the only way to describe it. It was really super soft and basically very comfortable. I felt like it was twenty blankets. And then in one split second, I began to suffocate.

I had to get up on my knees and reach in my mouth to pull out the crap that I had swallowed. I started dry-heaving. I was still trying to keep my head low. But now I'm pissed off at myself that I wasn't smart enough to hold my breath. All these things went through my head, I don't know why. I was undisciplined in turning around. I was undisciplined in not holding my breath. Then I was undisciplined getting onto my knees. I started to puke, and then all of a sudden it went black.

I had my sunglasses on, so I figured, Oh, that's why it's fucking black. And then I remember putting my sunglasses up on my forehead, and I still couldn't see.

I crawled over to what I thought was a fence. I put my hands on the fence, and I couldn't see my hands. I couldn't see the fence. On my knees I start going hand over hand. I refused to let go of the fence because it was the only way I knew where I was.

I came across a body. I actually punched him a couple of times to see if he was alive. And he responded. I said, "Relax. I know where we are. Put your hand on my shoulder. I know where we're going. We're going north." I couldn't see him and he couldn't see me. I tried to make light, like I'm trying to make conversation. So I asked him if he was a news reporter. And he answers me, "Yeah, yeah," like he was slurring. I said, "Boy, this guy's groggy. He doesn't even know who he is."

Eventually, we got to the point to where we could see each other, and he was a fucking fireman. He definitely was not there when I dove for the curb. I'm not trying to say I saved his life. That's not what I'm getting at at all. I'm just trying to say he was not there when I dove. And then he was there, and he didn't know how he got there.

HECTOR SANTIAGO
41, Detective, NYPD

—

"I SAW THE MAYOR AND THE POLICE COMMISSIONER
WHEN THEY WERE TIRED, WHEN THEY WERE BEATEN UP,
AND THEY NEVER LET NEW YORK KNOW THAT, EVER."

On the day of September 11, I was assigned to Police Commissioner Kerik's bodyguard detail. I was sitting at my desk in his office on the fourteenth floor, having breakfast, and I'll never forget this: I had just thrown my plate away when I heard a muffled *phoom,* a very low *phoom.* The Brooklyn Bridge is right outside, so I thought absolutely nothing of it.

Within seconds, I hear screaming. An emergency service cop is screaming on the radio, "Central, send everybody. We have a plane." He describes the plane: "It's a commercial airliner, and it just hit the World Trade Center."

And I yell, "Bobby, Bobby. Go, go," to Bobby Picciano, who's the advance for the police commissioner. His job is to get to places and make sure that everybody is in place for the arrival of the commissioner. Bobby runs out the door. I say to the driver, "Go downstairs. We've got an accident." I have a Nextel, which I keep on speaker. A personal friend of mine is screaming in the radio, "Hector, pick up. Hector, pick up. Pick up, pick up, pick up."

I pick up the Nextel. I tell him, "Howie, I got it, I got it, I got it."

Sergeant Lenny Lemer, who's in the NYPD, calls me screaming, "Hector, I'm on the highway. I'm watching it. I just watched the plane hit the World Trade Center." I ask him what kind of plane. He says it's a commercial airliner.

I run to the back, to the office. I knock on the door. The commissioner does not answer. I use my key to get into the main office. Now I hear he's in the back taking a shower. He's just finished working out. I knock on the door. He doesn't hear me. So I kick the door, really hard. And the commissioner opens the door and he looks at me, like, What are you doing, kicking my door? But he realized, This is Hector, so it's gotta be something.

I go, "Boss, a plane just hit the building." He thinks it's probably a small Cessna.

His chief of staff turns around and says, "It's probably a boiler."

I say, "No, boss, it's a big plane. It's on the ninetieth floor. There are no boilers on the ninetieth floor."

We run over to the window and the boss just goes, "Oh, my God. Get me the mayor."

I get on the phone and as I'm trying to reach the mayor, his office reaches me on the other phone. "Hector, this Patty. The mayor wants to speak to the commissioner." They have their conversation. They discuss where they're going to go, what they're going to do. The commissioner runs to the back and within two minutes he's outside dressed, his tie is on, the elevator's waiting for us, we shoot right down in the car from police headquarters with lights and sirens, and we get there.

We're standing on the north side of the building, on the corner of Vesey, and we're right underneath the building, a half a block away from the tower. I say, "Boss, look at the debris." But it's not debris. It's people jumping. I look at the commissioner and he looks at me, like, What can we do? I count. And then I just have to stop, at about seventeen people. I say, "I'm not counting anymore. That's it."

There's a coffee stand every morning on the corner of Vesey. A black gentleman screams, "Oh, my Lord. My cart. They're jumping in my cart."

The commissioner turns and goes, "Relax. You gotta calm down. You can't get like this."

The guy says, "But look what's happening."

I say, "Guy, you gotta calm down. We're going to do something. We don't know what to do, but we're going to do something."

All of a sudden there's a secondary explosion: *Boom!* And you see the fire coming out of the building. And we're like deer in the headlights, just standing there and thinking, Holy shit. What was that?

The boss thinks it might have been a bomb. Now you think terrorist, and now he's getting into the groove. We had no idea that it was the second plane because we're on the north side of the building. Then the debris, water, glass, or whatever, starts to rain on us. I grab the commissioner. I push him and he's running. We start to run away, but for some reason some of the debris caught up with me before it caught up with him. "Bobby," I say, "Get the boss, get the boss." And they run off. I can't keep up with them because I'm getting hit with debris, so I run into a garage. The commissioner's car, car 1, as we refer to it, driven by Detective Craig Taylor, jumps right into the garage. I see a piece of the plane coming. I see debris bouncing. I put myself against the wall and I get nicked by a piece of debris.

We run back out and I see the commissioner. At this point, he meets up with the mayor. We go from Vesey onto the West Side Highway and we go over to where the fire department had their temporary headquarters. We see the firemen, Father Mychal Judge, everyone, and the mayor is shaking hands and saying, "God bless you guys."

Now I hear there's a third plane en route. I say, "Boss, we gotta get out of here. We gotta get the mayor out of here." They start talking about going to City Hall, and I say, "Boss, you can't let them go to City Hall. We don't know what the targets are." He's listening, but he's not listening. Finally, I grab him. I yell, "Boss, we have to go. There's a third plane coming. We're underneath the building. We have to go."

He turns to the mayor and says, "Mayor, we have to get out of here now," and he just goes into cop mode. And getting out of there saved our lives.

We decide to go over to 75 Barclay Street. The commissioner says, "Hector, shut down the airspace." I call our central radio dispatcher: "Central, you have to shut down the airspace. Notify the military." All of a sudden the mayor and his staff say that the Pentagon has been hit. I get on the phone. I'm supposed to be calling for some other things, but I just have to do this: I get on the phone and I call my mother. I say, "Ma, get dressed. You're going to my house."

She's like, "No. I'm staying. I'm staying."

I insist, "Ma, please just go to my house." I hang up, I call my mother-in-law and she's crying. I say, "You have to get dressed. You gotta go get my daughter and you have to go to Westchester. I will talk to you later."

Now I'm starting to do police work again when a gentleman I'll never forget—white, about thirty-something—yells, "Everybody, hit the deck! Hit the deck!"

And all of a sudden a rumbling builds up, almost like an earthquake. I grab the commissioner. The mayor's guys grab the mayor. I say, "Out the back. Everybody out the back." And just then, the windows bust out, a huge cloud of gray smoke overtakes us all. There's debris everywhere and I'm saying to myself, "We can't die in here. We cannot die in here." And as I'm going out the back, there's this little Asian-American girl, Chinese maybe. She's under the desk on all fours and she's hiding. I said, "Sweetheart, you can't stay here." I reach out to her and

I say, "Come with us, come with us." I just couldn't leave her there. She comes with us. And we run out of the back and I take a whiff and I realize it's debris. Debris has a certain smell.

All the doors downstairs are locked electronically, and it's dark. The only way they open is if the fire alarm goes off, and the fire alarm does not go off because it's debris, not smoke. We don't know what to do. I see two maintenance guys and say, "You gotta get us out of here. I got the mayor and the police commissioner. You gotta help us."

They take us through a maze of tunnels and we come out on Church Street and all you can see is gray ash everywhere. I remember saying to a sergeant with me, "Donny, whatever happens here, we have to take care of the boss and the mayor. We have to do this. Even if it means us dying, you know, we gotta do what we're supposed to do."

And Donny goes, "You got it, kid."

When we finally get outside, we see what everybody else saw: the building is down. Everything is covered with ash and people are walking around like zombies.

We make our way up to a firehouse. On the way, people are saying to the mayor and the police commissioner, "Help us, help us." And the mayor and the police commissioner are telling everybody, "Just keep walking. Just keep walking." Just before we get to a firehouse, the second building comes down, and you see that big smoke cloud again.

We break into the firehouse with a knife. We're assuming we're safe now, but we don't know what's happening. The boss makes a command decision. "Okay, we're going to establish a command center. We're not going to let anybody know. I don't want it over the radio. We don't know what's happening. We don't want them to know where we're all going to be."

Then we got together a bunch of cars very discreetly, a motorcade of about fifty cars. I remember going up to a captain and saying, "Uh, sir, I need your car."

He goes, "This is my car. You can't take my car."

I say, "The mayor of New York City wants your car."

He says, "Well, if you put it that way."

So we confiscated a bunch of cars and motorcaded all the way up to the police academy, where we regrouped.

They called us heroes. After September 11, people would say, "We love you." But I saw things I've never seen before. I saw New Yorkers, I saw people from all over the United States, I saw everybody come together in such an unbelievable way. As Mayor Giuliani was saying, as tragic as September 11 was, they thought they were going to break our backs, and they never did. What they did was unite us more than ever.

To see cops from the sheriff's office and the Los Angeles Sheriff's Department sleeping in the back of their cars, to see fire department guys sleeping in their cars with their dirty boots on top of the roof, made me think, Wow, look at these guys. It made me want to be in the pile. I wanted to dig for the officers, for my brothers. But you know, I have just as important a job. I have to make sure the commissioner and the mayor are well taken care of. From the time Giuliani got on the phone, he never stopped. I read Mark Green saying during his mayoral campaign that anybody would have done the job. He said, "I could have done just as good a job." That's bullshit. I saw these two men every morning. I saw them every night and every day. I saw the mayor and the police commissioner when they were tired, when they were beaten up, and they never let New York know that, ever.

BERNARD B. KERIK

47, Former Police Commissioner, NYPD

"I'VE BEEN IN THIS BUSINESS FOR TWENTY-SIX YEARS AND I'VE
DONE EVERYTHING UNDER THE SUN. I'VE BEEN INVOLVED IN GUN
BATTLES. I HAD PARTNERS THAT WERE KILLED. . . . BUT I'VE NEVER
FELT AS HELPLESS AS I DID ON THAT MORNING."

I was in my office that morning. I had just finished exercising. I had a workout room in the back of my office, and I went in the back to take a shower. I'd locked the outside door to my inner office, and all of a sudden I heard this banging on the door. You know, kicking, banging, people yelling. So I ran out and opened the door. I had a towel wrapped around me. Hector Santiago and John Picciano, my chief of staff, were there and they were yelling at me that a plane had just hit tower 1.

I said, "All right. Shut up. Calm down." They were screaming, and I said, "Relax. It's okay." In my mind, I was thinking that it was a small plane flying up the Hudson. You know, we deal with tragedy every day in this city—and accidents, major accidents and the like.

But they kept saying, "No, you don't understand. It's the whole top of the building. It's enormous."

I said, "All right, get out of the way." So I walked out into my office with a towel draped around me. I walked through my personnel office and into my conference room. When I got in front of the TV, I was stunned by what I saw. I turned around and replied, "Who the hell said this was a plane?"

They said, "Well, that's what they're yelling over the radio." So I ran back to my desk and I called the mayor. He was uptown at a breakfast. I spoke to him and said, "Look, something has just happened at the towers. I'm heading down there. I'll meet you at the command center," which was the Office of Emergency Management in 7 World Trade.

I was dressed within minutes. I got in my car with Hector and Craig Taylor. We got to West Broadway between Barclay and Vesey, and I said, "Stop the car." I got out and I looked up at the tower. I could see the smoke and the debris, and then I saw these things coming from the top of the building. It was so high up. I thought it was debris. But as it got closer to the ground I realized that people were jumping from the building. I've been in this business for twenty-six years and I've done everything under the sun. I've been involved in gun battles. I had partners that were killed. Hector and I were in a shooting. He got shot. But I've never felt as helpless as I did on that morning. You couldn't yell to these people and ask them to stop, or make them stop. I guess they had a choice: stay within a two-thousand-degree inferno, or jump. And they were jumping.

I told the guys to back the car away from the building. We were only about a half-block from the towers. They backed the car up Barclay Street. I was talking on the radio, telling the guys to bring in resources, activating rapid mobilizations from around the city, calling in cops from every precinct.

I turned around to say something to Hector when there was this enormous explosion. I looked up and the other building, building 2, was sort of exploding and igniting above. And I thought, Now what's happened? How did that building ignite this other building? I don't know what was going through my head, but all of a sudden somebody yelled, "Run." And Hector grabbed me by the shirt, and we started running up West Broadway. Debris and body parts and the plane and the building, it was all coming down right on top of us. Hector got hit in the back of the leg with a piston or some piece of the plane. We ducked behind the post office behind 7 World Trade and waited for the entire thing to stop.

I looked back out. I saw the damage. At that point, I could hear aviation and the pilots yelling on the radio that it was a commercial airliner. I realized at that minute that we were under attack. I yelled to John to get on the telephone to call headquarters, but there was no phone service. The cell phones were down, so we're calling on the radio. I'm yelling for them to get aviation to close down the airspace. We needed air support, and I'm screaming at these guys to get me air support.

They're looking at me, like "Is there a fucking number to call for an F-16?" Like "Who do we call? How do we do that?"

But aviation had taken care of that and closed down the airspace. They had called in the military. I ordered the entire city to be shut down at that point. All bridges and tunnels closed. No entry. No exit. My main concern at that point was that there could be other secondary attacks set up on the ground. They're hitting us from above, did they do anything on the ground? Are they on the ground? My other concern was who the hell they were. Who are they? You know, as all of these events were unfolding, you're trying to put it all together. You're trying to think of so many things at once.

Then I thought about other targets—police headquarters, City Hall, the U.N., the Empire State Building. That's what was running through my mind. And as I thought of each target, I would tell my staff to start evacuating these buildings.

Within three or four minutes after the second plane hit, the mayor pulled up. I ran up the block and I stopped his car just north of Barclay. He got out of the car. He stood there with me. We were looking at the building and I was telling him what had just happened.

He made a comment to me, some kind of comment, like "We're in uncharted territory. The city has never experienced anything like this." I forget exactly how he said it, but it was something to that effect. And then he asked where the command posts were going to be, and I told him they were going to have to set one up on West Street or on the west side of the towers.

He said, "All right, let's go around to West Street. We'll go down West and we'll look at the damage from the other side of the building and see what they are doing there."

So we walked west on Barclay and then south on West Street. We stopped and met with First Deputy Commissioner Bill Feehan from the fire department; Chief Peter Ganci; ESU Sergeant John Coglin; Mychal Judge, the chaplain; and Ray Downey. They were setting up their staging area right across from tower 1. My guys kept pushing me to get into a command center, and I was telling the mayor, "Look, we have to go back north on West Street. We've got to get out of here."

The mayor wanted to talk to the White House. I said, "We've got to get you out of here and into a command center. You can call the White House from there." So we said good-bye to everybody and started walking. Mychal Judge grabbed the mayor and said, "Be careful and God bless you."

So we all went into 75 Barclay with the mayor; his chief of staff, Tony Carbonetti; Joe Lhota, the deputy mayor of operations; Steve Fishner, the criminal justice coordinator; and Sunny Mindel, the mayor's press secretary. The mayor got on the phone. They got through to the White House. As he was talking on the phone, somebody's pager said that the Pentagon had been hit. I've known the mayor for about eleven or twelve years, and I've never seen him look as worried or concerned about anything as much as he did when he was on the phone with the White House. He put the phone down and he said, "Well, that's not good at all. They've hit the Pentagon and they're evacuating the White House." It was a clear signal that this was no longer just about New York City. It was about the United States.

Then all of a sudden somebody slammed the door open in this office where we were standing and yelled to hit the deck. And just as they said it, the whole damned building started to shake. I started walking to the door to look outside and all the windows outside in that outer hallway of 75 Barclay started to shatter. Then there was this gush of smoke and soot, like this black dust. Hector grabbed me by the middle of my back and started pushing me to the back of the building. And everybody sort of followed. We didn't know what was going on. I didn't know if 75 Barclay was coming down, if another building was hit.

We went out through a back door and wound up in this maze of hallways. And every exit door was locked. We couldn't get out of this building, and it was filling up with smoke and debris. I remember thinking, All the shit I've been through in my entire life and I'm going to suffocate in this damn building.

Then in one of the basement areas we saw two maintenance guys. I don't know where they were coming from. I don't know what they were doing, but they were definitely as surprised to see us as we were to see them. We said, "We need to get out of here. We need to get as far away from the towers as possible. Can you open these doors?"

One of them said, "Yeah, absolutely." So he opened the doors, and we were in the lobby, I think, of 100 Church Street. The front of the lobby had these huge glass windows, and outside was solid pure white. You couldn't see anything. As we were standing there, in walked a guy covered in this white stuff from head to toe. His eyes were totally red and bloodshot. And it was my deputy commissioner of administration, Tibor Kerekes. We were in Korea together. We were in Saudi Arabia two different times together. He worked for me in New Jersey. He's my best friend. He walked in the door and his eyes were solid bloodred. He had been outside when the building fell and he ducked into one of those little three-foot openings in the side of the post office building. He stood there as all this debris came down around him. And now he was running into us. The mayor and I took him to the side. We were pouring water on his face and cleaning out his eyes.

We regrouped and started walking north on Church. We walked into the Tribeca Grand Hotel thinking we'd take the place over and set up the government in there. The advance people were up there, and they were running all over the building, getting phones, doing all this stuff. The mayor and I walked into the lobby. We looked around, and when we looked up, we saw that the entire ceiling was glass. There was an instantaneous feeling of being uncomfortable. I looked at the mayor, he looked at me, and we just walked right out the door. We didn't say anything. We just kept walking and everybody followed us right out of the building. We got back on Church Street and kept walking north.

We got to a firehouse. Everybody was gone. The firehouse was locked up. We had to break in. We broke in the door and then started making some phone calls and started putting together some mobilization plans. We needed to create a command center for city government. I said, "Let's go to the police academy. We can run the city from there." And that's what we did. We set up an enormous conference room in the police academy where the mayor and the fire commissioner and myself were able to call in all the other agencies and start working on a response to the attack.

I don't remember where we were when tower 1 came down. But I can remember the look on Tommy Von Essen's face. He knew that a lot of his guys were in those buildings. I can just remember seeing him at the academy. He was in a daze. We all were in a daze.

As for the mayor, I guess you'd have to know him to understand this. If there was a major tragedy on December 31, if something had happened on the afternoon of the 31st, his last day in office, he would have reacted no differently than he did in September. I made a comment to him, I guess it was around December 20, a week or so away from the end of his term. He used to have daily staff meetings at eight o'clock every day. And Tommy and I used to joke about it, because before September 11 we didn't go to the dailies. We went once a week. Now we were going to dailies and it was a week away from the end of his term, and I said, "Why do we have to have a daily? Next week we're outta here." I was joking.

And the mayor said, "Why? Because you're the police commissioner and I'm the mayor until December 31, that's why."

It was just another lesson in dealing with the mayor and working with him, and witnessing his work ethic and his integrity and what he did and how he did it. He set the tone on September 11. We didn't do anything that we hadn't done before. It was just far more enormous and far bigger than anything we had ever one, imagined, and two, experienced. I mean, I was a really active cop. I'm probably the highest decorated police commissioner that's ever served this city. I was awarded the Medal of Valor. I'd been involved in gun battles. I knew. I'd been around. And yet to witness this, and to be there, was like nothing that I would have ever imagined.

JOE ESPOSITO
52, Chief of Police, NYPD

"**When I entered the building, it was daylight, bright and sunny. When I walked out the door, it was pitch black.**"

I was pulling up to police headquarters, on my way to work, with Sergeant Michael McGovern, one of my aides. We went up to the checkpoint at Avenue of the Finest, and as we slow up, we could see that the officer on post was very excited and talking into his radio as he's looking up toward the Twin Towers. I heard him say, "A plane just hit the Twin Towers." I looked over my shoulder and I saw the building exploding. I guess I pulled up the minute the plane had hit.

But I wanted to be sure before I put anything out over the radio. I'm the chief of department. When I talk, people usually listen. I wanted to make sure I had accurate facts. I jumped out of the car, ran over to the officer, and I asked, "What did you just say?"

And he repeated that a plane hit the Twin Towers. I saw the explosion, but I still had to make sure this was accurate. So I'm saying, "Tell me exactly what you saw."

And he actually gave me the number of the plane. It turns out what he saw was accurate, naturally. I felt I had the right information. So I got back in the car, made a U-turn, and put it over the radio that a plane has just hit one of the Twin Towers. We drove there. It's only two blocks from 1 Police Plaza. As we got close to the location, at the mouth of the Battery Tunnel, we couldn't go any further. Debris was still coming down from the tower. So we just stopped traffic and tried to evacuate some of the people. Again, I went over the radio, telling what we had just seen. I called for mobilization. I needed more officers. I needed hospitals to be notified. We had drilled for this type of thing—nothing of this magnitude, but we've drilled for disasters—so we started putting those things into effect. At this point, everyone's thinking, A plane hit the tower. Okay, we have an accident.

An ESU truck pulls up, a response unit is there. I get on the running board of the rig and I tell my sergeant, Mike McGovern, that I'm going off to the scene. We make a right turn on Vesey, which is right adjacent to the North Tower. As we're on that block, the recorder who's in the passenger seat of the emergency service truck starts yelling, "Another plane, another plane." And at that point, we hear the explosion.

I was on the running board, so I didn't see it immediately. I said, "What happened?"

And he said, "Another plane just hit the other tower." We look up and we see all the debris coming down on us. We are in a really dangerous situation at that point. The plane is coming down on us, parts of the building, and everything imaginable was coming down on us. Luckily, it's one hundred floors up, so we had time to react. We drove under the pedestrian bridge that goes to building 7, and we waited for all the debris to stop. That walkway protected us. Everything was coming down all around us.

Now this was clearly not an accident. I determined that we were under attack. I let the dispatchers know that a second plane had just hit the South Tower. I ordered every borough commander to put their disaster plans into work. I ordered the city shut down. I asked for special attention or directed patrol at susceptible locations. We didn't know if another shoe was going to drop.

Then we had to find out where everybody was. We wanted to get together and make sure that our response was coordinated with the other agencies: fire, EMTs. We had to make sure there was a coordinated effort going on. We wanted to make sure the mayor was safe. We wanted to inform him of exactly what we were doing to address the attack.

At one point I was ordered to meet the mayor's group at West Street, which is where the fire department was organizing their response. I started heading in that direction, as did First Deputy Commissioner Joseph Dunn and Police Commissioner Bernard Kerik.

Before I got there I was rerouted to the Barclay Street location. We entered the building and we were trying to get on the phone with the Pentagon when it was suddenly attacked. We hear that there's a plane still in the air, the one over Pennsylvania. The mayor is on the phone with the White House. They're coordinating air support for the city. We're trying to see what the scope of this attack is. We're concerned about key locations in our city. We're sure those key locations are covered. We're in touch with some of the bureau commanders making sure that no one is allowed in or out of the city. We're worried about a follow-up, possible truck bombs. We'd just been attacked and now everything is running through our minds to stop the next hostile attack from happening.

While we're doing that, we hear this rumble all of a sudden. I'm in the Barclay building with the first deputy commissioner, the police commissioner, the mayor, and a lot of his staff. His deputy mayors were all there trying to get a handle on what's going on, and to respond to it in the right way. Actually, I think the mayor was on the phone with the vice president when we heard this rumble.

The rumble gets louder and louder. The lights start to flicker and go out. I make it to the front door to see what's going on, and as I'm going out, a fellow running in is saying, "The building is collapsing. The building's collapsing." We're all assuming, rightfully, that it's the building that was hit by the plane.

When I had entered the building, it was daylight, bright and sunny. When I walked out that door, it was pitch black. So I knew something horrible had just happened. I grabbed the fellow and I said, "What happened?"

And he said, "The tower just collapsed. The tower collapsed."

He didn't think it was the whole tower, maybe the top slid off, maybe a piece of the tower fell. So many people said that who were close. The closer you were, the less you knew. So I go back in the building and tell everyone, "We gotta evacuate," and we tried to orchestrate an organized evacuation of that building. We didn't know how vulnerable we were at that location. All we know is that the debris is all around us.

We got the mayor, his staff, the police commissioner, to safety. The mayor and the police commissioner went northbound and ultimately decided to regroup at the police academy, while myself, Commissioner Dunn, and Deputy Commissioner of Operations Gary McCarthy stayed on the scene trying to evaluate what had just happened. And when we looked up, it appeared that the whole South Tower was now gone. It was just unimaginable.

We're standing on the corner of Church Street trying to evacuate people from the area when the rumbling starts again. We look up and the North Tower just melts. We were so helpless. We're trying to pull people out, and we're thinking, Okay, where are we going to go now? We talked about going to City Hall and stopping there to see if we could organize or regroup. Our worse nightmare came true before our eyes. As we stood on the corner of the intersection and just watched helplessly, the second tower collapsed.

A lot of us ran toward the building to help get people, but by then we knew what the effect was going to be—that debris was going to take over the streets.

So we were telling people, "Come on, get indoors." We were just pushing people into any open doorway, any building they could get into. The best way I can describe it would be that it looked like the mushroom cloud from the atomic bomb, upside down. That's exactly what it was. That same effect, but upside down. And you just watched it roll toward you like a tidal wave. I felt helpless. We knew we were going to be choked by it, so we just pushed everyone into buildings and waited for that smoke cloud to clear.

And then your thoughts go to all of your workers, your staff. My entire staff was down at Ground Zero. Because 1 Police Plaza is so close, we all responded. I saw these towers come down, and I said to my sergeant, "We just lost a lot of people. The city lost a lot of civilians and every agency out there just lost a good number of our forces." I remember saying to him, "If we lost under a hundred, it'll be a miracle." And it was a miracle. We lost twenty-three, which is still an outrageous number, but that's a miracle. Under the worse conditions possible, it was a very well-run evacuation. People conducted themselves professionally, as calm as can be for the most part in those conditions. To have that many people get out of there and survive was unbelievable.

Equally unbelievable is what it's been like since 9/11. There is not one waking moment, and few of my sleeping moments, that aren't consumed with this department and this city. What can we do? What are we missing? After the eleventh, you say, "Okay, we have to make sure this doesn't happen again. How do we that? What am I forgetting?" You'll see me ask people all the time, "What more can we do? What have we forgotten? What have we overlooked? What can we do better? How can we be better equipped?" And that's what we're in the process of doing. That's been the driving force after the eleventh. It was with Bernie Kerik, and it clearly is with Commissioner Ray Kelly.

But there is guilt that I have. Could we have prevented this? And, you know, I don't have the answer to that. As the NYPD, I don't think we could have prevented it. This is way out of the realm of our responsibility. This is international stuff. Now we have a joint terrorist task force, but I'm wondering, if we had been more vigorous earlier, could we have prevented this? There's a little bit of guilt about that. Again, I don't know. I don't know if it could have been prevented. You hear about threats against this country, but there's only so much we can do to prevent them. How does the NYPD stop somebody from hijacking a plane in a different city and coming to this city? Maybe by knowing about it ahead of time and having informants with wiretaps, having investigations up and running, maybe then you can short-circuit these things. That's what everyone is trying to do now.

One other result of September 11 is that everyone in my immediate office has been to some type of counseling, including myself. We mandated it citywide for the whole police department. And we did it to remove that stigma: "Oh, you had to go for help? What the matter, you're not macho? You're not that big tough cop?"

We're going to remove that negative image of somebody going for counseling. Everyone goes, from myself on down. If I see somebody who is having some kind of stress and they're not dealing with it in the right way, we will deal with it and we'll get them as much help as we can. All the commanders we talk to, every line supervisor, we're getting them to recognize it right away. There is no doubt about it: this was the most dramatic thing that has happened to anybody in the NYPD to this day. So we know it's going to have effects, and it has already. And we're trying to deal with it the best we can.

ERROL ANDERSON
47, Recruiter, FDNY

—◆—

"I THOUGHT I WAS EITHER DEAD AND WAS IN ANOTHER WORLD, OR I WAS THE ONLY ONE ALIVE."

I've been with the fire department for over nineteen years. That morning, I was in the office at Metrotech headquarters in downtown Brooklyn. I had to interview someone who was interested in joining our cadet program. After the interview, I received the news that a plane had hit tower 1 at the World Trade Center. Lieutenant Sheldon Wright and myself looked out the window and saw it. And while in Lieutenant Wright's office I saw the second plane hit. Excuse my words, but I said, "Oh, shit. A plane just flew into the World Trade Center." That's when we realized something really was up.

I got up and I said, "We have to go over there. Are you coming?"

He said, "Yeah. I'll meet you there." I ran out of the office and took five cadets with me. These are cadets who are trained. They're in a transitional period, on their way to becoming EMTs and firefighters. We jumped into my fire department Suburban, drove across the Manhattan Bridge, picked up a few firefighters from Brooklyn, and made a left turn on Broadway. There were about eleven or twelve of us, all piled into the Suburban.

The firefighters had their equipment. I didn't have my equipment and neither did the cadets. We were just going over there on instinct, to see what we can do to help. We were there in a matter of minutes. I parked my Suburban on the corner of Broadway and Cortlandt Street. We set up a triage station, an emergency medical station. Who knows where the firefighters went, but the cadets I was responsible for. They set up a triage station right there on Broadway and Cortlandt, and they attended to people who needed medical attention.

I eventually ventured down to Church and Cortlandt Street, with no equipment or anything. I saw where they had a fire command station set up. The only reason I did not go to that fire command station was because I did not have my helmet, or what we call our bunker gear, turnout coat. So while walking over there, I realized I didn't have my bunker gear, my helmet, or anything, so I turned around I started to walk back toward Cortlandt Street. This lady came out of the subway station and she was gasping for air and saying, "Please help me, please help me." She fell down right then and there. I started to comfort her and work with her, and that's when I heard a rumbling. I thought it was the subway station, not even thinking that the subways had stopped running. I heard some more rumblings. When I looked up, I saw the cloud of dust coming down toward us. I grabbed the lady, and we both started running from Church and Cortlandt toward Broadway and Cortlandt, which is up the hill. We were right up by Century 21. I pushed her into an ambulance that was right on the corner of Broadway and Cortlandt, and I started to run. By the time that happened, I became engulfed in all this dust. I figured, You know what, I'm dead. There's no need for me to run, why even bother? And then I realized, Hey, I'm still alive.

I started yelling to anyone that could hear me. "Can anyone hear me? Can anyone hear me?" I couldn't see anything. For a couple of minutes I heard nothing. I thought I was either dead and was in another world, or I was the only one alive. I became nervous and panicky, not knowing what to do, because I couldn't see. And with no mask I swallowed enough of the soot and I started spitting all this stuff up. All kinds of debris started going in my eyes. I was rubbing them. I should have known better, but I did it anyway.

About four or five minutes later, while I was still trying to find my way around, I heard the voice of a young lady. She was crying and saying, "Please, Lord, don't let me die. Don't let me die."

I was so happy to hear this lady's voice. I said, "Keep talking, keep talking. I'm a firefighter. I'll find you by the response of where you are." Eventually we met up with each other and basically we ran into each other's arms without even knowing it. I told her, "Calm down. We're going to find our way out of here."

What I wanted her to do was to hold onto my belt, the belt that held up my pants. I would try to find my way out by feeling. While doing this, we picked up about four or five more people and we basically formed a chain. The first time I could physically see was out on Water Street. By that time we were all covered up with soot. We proceeded toward the Brooklyn Bridge. A lot of people were going across the Brooklyn Bridge. And this first young lady was hugging and holding onto me so tight and crying. When we approached the Brooklyn Bridge, there was a police officer there directing people across. I told him to get these people across the bridge. I had to go back.

And this young lady said to me, "Please, don't let me go. Can't you take me home?"

I said, "You'll be safe with this police officer. But I have to go back and help others." She really didn't want to let me go, so it took me a while to really comfort her to where she was comfortable enough to leave me alone. I eventually turned around and started to go back, and I didn't really realize how bad I looked. A couple of civilians approaching the Brooklyn Bridge saw how bad I was and they gave me bottles of water to wash my head and face off, and even my uniform a little bit, just to look presentable. I drank some of the water to clear out my mouth and I proceeded back.

While going back toward the site, the second tower came down. Needless to say, now I'm really going crazy. I thought, What the hell is going on here? I sought refuge on Fulton Street. I think it was 111 Fulton. I ran into that building and stayed there for a few minutes. I still had to come back out because I knew I had to find the cadets that I took over there because I'm responsible for them. I found them all by around 1 P.M., all except one. The last cadet, eventually I came to find out, was at home. She got home on her own. You could imagine how I felt knowing we were all down there still looking for her and she was home. We spoke later and I was happy she was all right.

I didn't realize until later how important that early-morning interview would be in my life. Interviewing that particular cadet caused me to miss being down there earlier. I have regular meetings with the department of youth, on Williams Street. Prior to those meetings, which are held once a month, I usually go to the World Trade Center for breakfast. But I didn't go because of the interview, which Lieutenant Wright had set up for me. And that morning, after the interview, I stopped to talk to Lieutenant Wright because I had to give him an update of what had happened with the young lady I had interviewed.

And that's how he and I wound up speaking and together at the time the first tower was hit. If I didn't meet up with him, more than likely I would have been on my way over there, or I would have been in the first tower having breakfast like I normally do prior to my monthly meeting.

Needless to say, I called that young lady a couple of days later to thank her for having the interview with me at that time. When I scheduled the meeting with her, I said, "I hope you don't mind having an early meeting because I'm an early person."

She said, "I don't mind. I want to get into the program that badly. I'll come over early."

So that's basically what saved me—Michelle Steplight. She was accepted into the program. And looking back on that particular morning, if it wasn't for her, there's nothing that would have kept me out of that building.

JOSEPH TORRILLO
46, Director of Fire Safety Education, FDNY

"I HAD A FRACTURED SKULL, ALL MY RIBS WERE BROKEN,
MY ARM WAS BROKEN, I COULDN'T SEE, AND I COULD HARDLY
MOVE. . . . AND I KNEW THAT IF I DIDN'T TRY TO GET MYSELF
OUT, I MIGHT BURN RIGHT THERE."

I had gotten to work very early because I had a meeting at Rockefeller Center. That was the morning we were going to introduce Billy Blazes, a new fire rescue hero that we developed with Fisher-Price toys. I had been working on this project for about a year and a half. We had planned a "911 Day," and we were going to introduce Billy Blazes on 9/11, at the learning center in the heart of Rockefeller Center, with all the TV cameras there. Of course, Fisher-Price developed this rescue hero based on New York City firemen not knowing what was going to happen that day.

So I was ready to leave for the meeting. I was walking out the door with three fire cadets—young kids, college kids—who wanted to join the fire department. As I walked out, one of them came running up to me and said, "A plane just hit the World Trade Center." As a firefighter I had spent fifteen years in Engine 10, Ladder 10, right across the street from the World Trade Center. I was there in '93. I said to the cadets, "Hurry up, get downstairs to my car. I want to get over the Brooklyn Bridge."

We were there in about two minutes. I was driving a fire department vehicle. A battalion chief and a ladder company were headed over the bridge in front of me. As I raced over the Brooklyn Bridge behind Ladder 110 and the 31st Battalion, I said, "The heck with the meeting at Rockefeller Center. This is a catastrophe." I told the cadets, "A lot of people are going to die today." I knew right away.

I got to my old firehouse, Engine 10, Ladder 10, which is on Liberty Street directly across from the World Trade Center. I parked the car on the sidewalk in the back of the firehouse. We got out of the car and ran around the corner to the firehouse, and with that the second jet came right over our heads and slammed into the building. At that point, there were people lying all over the street. There was debris, pandemonium. Civilians were lying all over the floor of the firehouse, people with broken bones. In order to even get into the firehouse you literally had to hopscotch and jump over all these people.

I grabbed some gear and I left the cadets inside the firehouse to help the people with some minor first aid. I ran down Liberty Street, toward West Street. I wanted to find Engine 10, my old company. And I found them on Vesey and West. One of my old friends was with the fire engine. I asked him to give me his air mask, which is normally kept on the fire engine. He said, "Somebody took it." I said, "What do you mean, 'Somebody took it'?"

He said, "A fireman came by and took my mask and went into the building."

I needed that mask because I was going to try to make it up to the floor where the fire was in the North Tower. But as it turned out, there were no extra masks around and there would have been no way for me to make it up the North Tower without a mask. I would have been wasting my time.

A lot of ambulances were coming out of the Brooklyn-Battery Tunnel. When the bombing occurred in 1993, the emergency vehicles that were left all over the place blocking each other were a big problem. So I ran down West Street toward Liberty Street, and I prevented all the ambulance personnel from parking in front of the World Trade Center complex because I knew that within a couple of hours, the tops of the buildings would start to come down. I didn't think the whole building would. I knew the amount of the fire would cause the tops of the buildings to twist and buckle. I figured it might happen around one or two o'clock in the afternoon, enough time to get out as many people as we possibly could. So I kept the ambulances parked on West Street, going back toward the Brooklyn-Battery Tunnel, away from the front of the World Trade Center complex. I had them park very orderly, and I left a lane free and clear for all emergency vehicles going north. In '93, some ambulances couldn't go anywhere because they were all blocking each other, and nobody knew where all the ambulance crews were. Many of them were freelancing. Also, I didn't want the crews in the lobby of the buildings because I knew it was dangerous. I wanted to keep them away and use only one ambulance at a time, as we needed them.

That's what I was doing when I heard a rumble and a roar. I looked up and there came the building.

I was standing right over by the Marriott Hotel, a short distance from the South Tower. I turned around and I knew I was going to get hit. I took about twenty steps and the pressure of the building coming down, the air pressure, threw me to the ground and the next thing I knew I was covered with all parts of the building.

It turned dark as midnight. I couldn't breathe. And I was bleeding. I had a fractured skull, all my ribs were broken, my arm was broken, I couldn't see, and I could hardly move. I was in so much pain. And I knew that if I didn't try to get myself out, I might burn right there. I don't know how I crawled, but I just started crawling because I couldn't stand. I couldn't get up. I kept crawling and crawling, aimlessly. Then all of a sudden I heard people screaming, "Over here, over here." The next thing I know, two people were dragging me by my coat into 1 World Financial Center. They tried to pick me up, but I just collapsed to the floor. I told them to leave me and just get out. They said, "No, we're not going to leave you behind." They said they were going to get me to a hospital.

And I'm saying to myself, "That's impossible. No way they can get me to a hospital now." I kind of gave up. I didn't think I was going to survive it.

But then they said there was a boat on the river in the back of 1 World Financial Center. What I didn't know, obviously, was that New Jersey state troopers had come over with boats, with the idea of taking possible victims over the water to Jersey hospitals. So they were able to get me on a stretcher, and I remember them running with me. The next thing I know I'm on the deck of a boat and I'm strapped down onto a long spine board.

Then all of a sudden I heard people screaming, "Here comes the other building."

Well, everybody jumped off the boat and left me on the deck of the boat. They all just started jumping because the other building was coming down. They didn't have time to take me. They just left me there. I couldn't see, but I realized what was happening. And I was stuck because I was tied down tight to the stretcher and I couldn't move. I don't know how I released it, but there's a seat belt that holds you down to the stretcher. Somehow my finger hit the release button. Pieces of the building and glass were hitting the deck of the boat. I heard crackling on the deck. It sounded like hail.

So I got myself loose. I was able to rip the tape that had my neck taped to the stretcher, and I felt a staircase and a door and a doorway. I dove headfirst down the staircase and I ended up in the engine room of the boat. Alone. And I'm thinking, "This thing could go under water." My whole head is wide open. I can't stand because all my ribs are broken. My arm is broken. I can't breathe and I'm bleeding internally.

I don't know how long it took, but after a while I heard people jumping back onto the boat again. And I heard somebody say, "Hey, I think there's a fireman down here." And I remember somebody came running down the stairs, and they looked at me and said, "Holy shit, this guy's hurt bad. We better get him out of here."

All of a sudden, the motors revved up and we started skipping across the water. And I was still lying in the engine room. They couldn't get me out. Then the boat was stopping someplace and I heard a whole bunch of commotion. Someone got me onto another spine board and they lifted me out. The next thing I know, I'm in the emergency room of a hospital, I have no idea where, and they're cutting all my clothes off. They get me stripped naked and put tubes in every part of my body. They're giving me morphine, shaving my head, bringing me for X rays and CAT scans.

They had me down as missing until the following day. I was in the hospital for five days, and as soon as I got out I made friends of mine take me back to Ground Zero. I had to see it.

Billy Blazes turned out to be the biggest-selling toy of the year. Because of

September 11, it became a collector's item. I think only one hundred thousand were made and you couldn't get your hands on them. And it was launched that day, September 11, and in stores that day. The only thing that was canceled was the press conference.

JOHN ABRUZZO
43, Staff Accountant, Port Authority

"THE PEOPLE WHO HELPED ME WEREN'T EMERGENCY
EVACUATION PERSONNEL. THEY WERE ACCOUNTANTS. . . .
IT'S IMPOSSIBLE TO DESCRIBE WHAT THEY DID FOR ME.
IT WAS A TREMENDOUS THING."

I worked on the sixty-ninth floor of the North Tower. I usually get to my desk around eight-thirty every morning, but on September 11 I was running early, so I stopped in at Duane Reade, the twenty-four-hour drugstore downstairs, and I picked up a few things. My receipt said 7:30 A.M., which is when I left the store.

I deal with the Port Authority's E-Z Pass system, which involves the tolls at bridges and tunnels. We more or less account for the moneys coming in and out, the shifting of funds and who owes what to whom.

So after I finished shopping, I went upstairs. I said hello to the people in my area, my supervisor and the people at the different desks surrounding me, and I got down to the business at hand. A lot of my work is done on the computer, and the entire floor is an open space divided by cubicles that are usually eight feet by eight feet.

My cubicle is a little larger because I'm in a wheelchair. I'm a C5-C6 quadri-plegic. I broke my neck in a swimming accident when I was fourteen. I can type. I have limited motions in my hands. I can use a pencil, or a computer, or an adding machine. So I'm able to function and get around on my wheelchair.

My desk faces north. I can see over my partition out the north windows. I don't remember hearing any sound, or an explosion. But I do remember that the building suddenly swayed, and that it swayed in one direction only. I thought the building was going to collapse right then and there. We've been in storms, you know, where the building sways back and forth, but that's nothing. An engineer once told me, "If you ever hear the building creak in only one direction for more than eight seconds, you must evacuate." But this was like something else. It pushed the building to the right. I looked out the north windows and the debris was just raining down. I must have been in a state of shock because I can only remember staring out the window and just watching in amazement. The thing that brought me out of it was my supervisor shouting some sort of expletive. He was outside my cubicle saying we had to evacuate.

I was there in 1993 when the World Trade Center was bombed. Different job, same floor. In '93, we didn't know it was an explosion. We actually stayed on the floor for a while, a group of us. Then it was decided that we should evacuate. To evacuate me, a group of Port Authority employees plus two fellows from Cantor Fitzgerald, plus some other fellow from Deloitte Touche, were all there to help. I was in an electric wheelchair, which weighs 150 pounds, maybe. I'm a pretty big guy, six-foot-three, and I weigh between 250 and 275 pounds. So it was no easy task. They actually had to bounce the wheelchair down the stairs, one step at a time, from the sixty-ninth floor to the forty-third. We stopped often. On 58, there was some sort of command center, a meeting post where the firemen were determining what they had to do to get people. We eventually got to the forty-third floor where they transferred me to a stretcher. I got on the stretcher and we were ready to go back into the stairway when a fireman held us up and said no. We're told to stay out of the stairway because there must have been another bomb scare of some sort. Then we got the all-clear sign to proceed down. They carried me on the stretcher from 43 all the way down. The same people stayed with me the entire time. We would have to stop intermittently to let other people pass. It was an incredible effort by all of those people helping me, so labor inten-sive. It took us six hours to get out.

After the 1993 bombing, the World Trade Center purchased these evacuation chairs. I don't want to make this sound too easy, but these evacuation chairs are designed to more or less glide. It's a little larger than a child's stroller. Instead of rear wheels there's a sledlike device that glides on the stairs. It's a lot easier than bouncing.

So after the first plane hit on September 11, I proceeded to go out into the hall in my electric chair. Ten people were there, the ten people who wound up taking me down. The rest of the floor was already evacuated. Those remaining included the controller, the assistant controller, a few managers and supervisors who were making sure everyone had been cleared out.

We knew there were evacuation chairs. I had only seen them demonstrated once, when they were purchased after the '93 bombing. One of the accountants went back into the offices to get the chair. He found it and opened it up. There was no question of whether they were going to bring me. It wasn't even a matter of how. I don't even remember them deciding that they were going to bring me down. They just saw me there and they made it clear I was going with them, one way or the other.

We proceeded to go down and it was working out pretty good. Four fellows were on the chair at all times as we went down. We wanted to make time, but they were not absolutely sure how the chair worked or how it would handle. I know the company that makes the chairs, but I don't think they ever thought about the chair going down sixty-nine flights.

One of the fellows went down ahead of us to scout out the smoke conditions. It was because of him that when we got to the forty-fourth floor, we had to switch stairways. From here, they couldn't roll the chair any longer because of the debris. So they picked the chair up and carried me to the other stairway and we proceeded down again. We got to somewhere in the thirties and that's when we saw firemen coming up. And the firemen were carrying their equipment and their gear and some of them were exhausted on the side of the stairway just try-ing to catch their breath. But they cheered us on, encouraging us. "Keep on going," they said. "You're doing a good job. Keep going."

When we got to the twentieth, I remember hearing a rumble. One of the fel-lows looked at me and we knew it didn't sound good. It must have been tower 2 coming down, and we knew we had to get out of there and not stop for anything.

We made it out to the West Street entrance, but the doors were blocked. We saw a fireman outside the building and he was telling us, "No, go over toward the window." We went to the right side where the windows were broken out. There was glass all over the place. They had to lift the chair physically off the ground to carry me out into the street. We were maybe ten, fifteen feet away from the building and they put me down to rest. Our building was on fire. You could see flames. But we still didn't really know about the other building col-lapsing. Our view was blocked by the North Tower. We could see that a lot of windows were broken over at the World Financial Center and that the building was covered in white dust. But it didn't really click with me that the other building had come down. Then a firemen said, "You gotta get outta here. You just gotta keep going north."

We went to the intersection of West Street and Vesey, and they again put me down, near a fire truck. Now we could look up and see the debris raining down, and the bodies coming down. They weren't landing next to us, but you could see them maybe five hundred feet up and three hundred feet off in the distance. You knew exactly what it was. And again the firemen told us, "No, you gotta keep going north. Keep going north."

Eventually, we made it to the south side of Stuyvesant High School. We were still outside Stuyvesant when our building came down. I looked around and I could see the debris cloud chasing the firemen and the policemen, chasing them to our direction, toward the high school. A fireman in front of me grabbed the front of my chair and lifted me on the sidewalk, and they shoved me into Stuyvesant High School. The glass doors closed and everything just went black.

Just to give you a time frame, it took an hour and a half to get from the sixty-ninth floor down to the street level, and another ten to fifteen minutes to get to Stuyvesant High School. That was a far cry from the six hours it took in 1993. If it weren't for the evacuation chair and the ten people that brought me down, I would not have made it, that's for sure. That evacuation chair made the difference.

And the people who helped me weren't emergency evacuation personnel. They were accountants. I worked with a lot of them for twenty years. It's impossible to describe what they did for me. It was a tremendous thing. If this had been like it was for me in '93, I'm sure none of us would have made it, and possibly no one would have known what they attempted to do for me. I speak to three or four of them on a regular basis. Over time, I've contacted them all. I even spoke to their wives and some of their children. It's just incredible, what those people did for me.

PETER BITWINSKI
48, Assistant Manager in Accounts Payable, Port Authority

—◆—

"WE ENCOUNTERED MAYBE TWENTY TO TWENTY-FIVE FIREMEN, AND
YOU HAD TO KNOW THAT A LOT OF THEM DIDN'T MAKE IT DOWN.
IT'S ONE OF THE SADDER MEMORIES I HAVE OF THAT DAY."

I was sitting at my desk about eight-forty-five or so in the morning, just writing something, and all of a sudden something hit the building. Clearly it was something big because the building shook violently. I didn't even know whether I would survive because of the way the building was shaking. But a minute or two later the building stopped shaking and our director came running down the aisle saying, "Everybody off the floor. There's a problem."

So I was walking through the aisle, making my way toward the middle part of the floor (which is where you exit either by elevator or by staircase), and the first person I came upon was John Abruzzo.

I have known John for a long time, over twenty years. Our desks were side by side for many years in accounts payable, so needless to say, he was a close friend of mine.

I said, "John, where's your chair?" Meaning his Evacuchair.

I was with John in '93 when he was brought out of the building. It was very different then. They didn't have Evacuchairs. He had to be taken step by step down the staircase in his wheelchair, which is a very heavy chair. I think they only got about twenty floors and then the firemen eventually moved him to a stretcher and carried him the rest of the way down.

On September 11th, when I encountered John, he seemed to be in shock. He didn't even respond to me. He didn't say anything to me at the moment. So again I said, "John, do you know where your chair is?"

And he said, "I think it's over in revenue," which is the section where he worked.

I said, "John, don't go anywhere. Stay right here. I'm going to go get your chair." I knew what it looked like, so I began hunting, trying to find it. I looked first in revenue. I asked the guy who happened to still be there gathering some things whether he knew where it was. He thought it might have been in our other accounts payable section. So I moved back over to the north side of the floor, and I found it. It was sort of against a window behind some boxes. I figured it might be there because that was the office occupied by our fire warden. And the fire wardens were in charge of equipment and also in charge of the people who either had handicaps or were pregnant. So I looked there first and fortunately I found it.

So I grabbed the chair from behind the boxes and I started running over back to where John was. By then he was surrounded by a group of about eight or ten people, all of whom were in our group and were able to take him down.

We opened up the Evacuchair and we knew we had to shift John from his wheelchair to the Evacuchair. So we lifted him into the Evacuchair and strapped him in. We moved his wheelchair over to the side, and we gathered ourselves. By then everyone else who was on the floor had left. It was about ten or fifteen minutes after the impact.

We started to make our way down the staircase. We had to get a routine going, so we decided two people on the bottom would hold the Evacuchair, with two people at the top. We had eight people who were actively taking him down, four people at a time.

We started to move down and we developed a pace. There wasn't that much traffic in the staircase so we were moving fairly well. It was probably shortly after we started making our way down that the second plane hit. But I was oblivious to that. I didn't really notice the building shaking, or any kind of movement that would have tipped me off to the fact that the other building was hit. We just kept moving.

As we were getting down toward the forties, a lot more smoke started to come up the staircase. We knew that we had to do something, so when we got to the forty-fourth floor, which is the Sky Lobby, two of our guys searched out another staircase to see if it was better than the one we were in. They found that it was, so they came back to get us. We then moved out of the staircase we were in and we moved across the forty-fourth floor. There was a whole lot of smoke, even more so than in the staircase. But when we made it into the other staircase, it was better because the air was a little bit cleaner. I believed we moved from the A staircase to B. All we knew is that we needed a staircase with cleaner air. This turned out to be the right decision.

As we started moving down this other staircase, we started seeing people walking the opposite way up, like some operations people. I guess they were moving upward to see what they could do to rescue people up the higher floors. Eventually, firemen started moving upward. We encountered maybe twenty to twenty-five firemen, and you had to know that a lot of them didn't make it down. It's one of the sadder memories I have of that day. They were walking up with full equipment, these big metal picks, and you know they were sweating like crazy. It was just something you never forget.

When we got into the thirties, things started to slow a little. People behind us were gathering more, and we would have to move over when we reached a landing to allow them to pass by, because they were moving quicker than us. So although the air was cleaner, there was a lot more traffic.

Then we got to around the twentieth floor. A bunch of firemen told us that we had to move off the staircase and onto the floor because there was some heavier equipment moving up. Shortly after we moved onto that floor, there was a tremendous impact and the building rocked and shook just like it did at eight-forty-five. The lights went out. We knew something bad was happening. Much later on we realized that that was tower 2 collapsing, but we didn't know it then. But, needless to say, it heightened our determination to try to move down.

Eventually, there was no equipment moving up, and we convinced the firemen that we wanted to keep moving, and they allowed us to do that. So we started to move again. I think we got to around the ninth or tenth floor and everyone behind us started to gather and we were all stuck in the staircase. Some people got very nervous and antsy, and they started to shout out, "Come on. We've gotta move."

One or two of our guys from the front had heard from the firemen that we were just being delayed for a couple of moments. The firemen kept calling up, saying, "Please don't panic. We're going to be moving soon."

Soon we started moving again. As we got below the tenth floor, we encountered a lot more in terms of debris and water. So we had more obstacles to get John down. You have to remember, from 69 down we kept switching our team of people. The two guys holding the handles on top of the Evacuchair would move to the bottom of the Evacuchair after five flights. Then after you were on the bottom, you would move off of the chair, and two other guys would take your place. You'd be free of chair duty for about five or ten floors, and then you'd move to the top again. That was our routine. Our director, Peggy Zoch, made sure everyone was okay. Peggy and our revenue manager, Mike Ambrosio, were holding our briefcases and making sure we were okay.

Someone broke into a soda machine and we took out a whole bunch of drinks. With the exertion of moving John down it was heavy work. But everyone was holding their own, and we were making our way down.

When we reached the bottom area of the building, there was tons of that powdery soot and debris. They actually had to lift the Evacuchair to move John out through all of that debris and carry him through a broken window to make it out to the street.

When we walked out of that building, there was nobody around. It was like a ghost town. I still didn't realize that tower 2 had come down. We just started to move northward. There were some fire and emergency people moving us north. They kept telling us, "You have to keep moving." We'd go a block and then stop a little bit to catch our breath. Ultimately, we got about four blocks away and we were on the block where Stuyvesant High School is. It was then that we heard a tremendous roar and we saw the big cloud coming. It was tower 1 coming down.

We grabbed John and it seemed like we were literally running for our lives. We made it into the high school and the door closed behind us, and all you saw was blackness.

We were in Stuyvesant High School for about fifteen minutes when John started to get chills. It was cold because the air-conditioning was on in the high school. So we all gave him our coats. Then, fifteen minutes later, we moved out of the high school because he was getting too cold and we wanted to get him into the sunshine again.

Then he started to have a bit of a breathing problem, so we flagged down an EMT worker who took his blood pressure and checked his vitals. They got a flatbed truck to put the Evacuchair on, and then lifted him into an ambulance. I rode with him. We went to Beth Israel South Hospital. I stayed with him in the hospital. We couldn't make local calls, but he got word to an uncle in North Carolina that he survived and was in the hospital. I managed to contact my family and told them that I was okay and was with John.

John's breathing slowly got better. Obviously, he had no possessions at that point. He lost his wheelchair in the building, and the van he used to drive was parked four or five blocks away from the Trade Center. So he needed an ambulance to take him home. We made that clear to the nurses and the doctors that were looking in on us.

When we found out he couldn't get a ride home to Queens until the next day, I decided to stay the night with him. I was already with him and I didn't feel it was right to just drop him off and leave. I'm single, so it made it a lot easier. I had no major responsibilities. I had already contacted my family. So they got us a room and they got John into a bed. I slept in a convenience room. It was a long night, but they got John an ambulance at around 2 P.M. the next day, and they took him back to Queens.

I was happy that everything worked out the way it needed to, but our situation was very, very close. I mean, fifteen minutes later and we would have been buried in the rubble. There were so many instances where we were stuck in the staircase, stuck on one floor or another. What if we didn't have eight people and it took longer to get John down? Stuff like that crosses your mind. But as far as us doing anything extraordinary, John was our coworker and more than that, he was our friend. We all knew something bad had happened, and we wanted to get down. But he was one of us. He was with us. And we knew he couldn't get down on his own. So we were there to help him. As you're doing it, you don't really think of the extraordinary nature of the event. You just think of the fact that you're there and you're doing something and you want to be helpful.

STEVE GREENBERG

43, Senior Client Specialist, Aon

◆

"WE WERE RIGHT UNDER WHERE THE SECOND PLANE HIT. THE CEILING PRACTICALLY CAME DOWN ON US. YOU SAW THE WALLS STARTING TO CRACK AND SPLIT."

I started at Aon on September 4. On the eleventh, I got in around seven-thirty. I was in a training class with twelve people. Of the twelve, only four of us survived.

The class was held on the ninety-second floor of tower 2. All of a sudden we felt a low boom and the building shook a little bit. We didn't think anything of it because our entire floor was on a build-out. They were rebuilding the space for us. We thought maybe the construction workers popped something.

So we're sitting in the classroom, a couple of minutes after we felt that little boom, that shake. Someone stuck their head in the doorway and said that there was a small fire in the first building. Nothing to be alarmed about, they said, but we were going to evacuate just to play it safe. So they led us directly to a staircase and we started going down.

We asked what happened, and somebody said a small private plane hit the first building. We didn't know what to make of that because everyone knew you don't fly planes over Manhattan. So terrorism struck us as a possibility. And we talked about that possibility on the way down. I would say we got down to approximately the seventies when we heard an announcement saying the building was secure, that we could go back up. We said, "Oh, it's safe to go back up." And as we turned to go back up, everything came loose. The second plane must've hit, and the walls started cracking. We all fell to the floor and everyone was grabbing onto each other, holding onto each other.

We were right under where the second plane hit. The ceiling practically came down on us. You saw the walls starting to crack and split. And one of the women I was with, Gloria Novesl, was a grandmother in her fifties. She was part of my training. I met her the day I started. She had asthma.

She grabbed onto me and she said, "Please, don't leave me."

And I said, "Don't worry, I'll stay with you." And basically, I went down with her the whole way. But we had to stop at every flight because she couldn't breathe. The critically injured were passing us—people with things stuck in their heads, blood everywhere, bones sticking out through skin.

I couldn't carry her, but I stayed with her the whole time, and I kept motivating her, saying, "You know, we gotta keep moving, we gotta keep going."

She's like, "I gotta rest, I gotta rest."

"No, we gotta keep moving, we gotta keep going." At that point, we had no way of knowing the building was coming down. We were just looking to get down.

I got her all the way down. As we came into the mall area, the police and the FBI were there, and they're telling us, "You gotta get out of the building, you gotta get out of the building." Again, they didn't know the building was coming down either. But they were just trying to clear it.

They had ambulances all around there. I tried to get her some oxygen, but we couldn't find anyone. And then a fireman came over to us and told us to clear the area because of falling debris. We got to a little past Broadway when all of a sudden we heard this loud screaming. We turned around and saw the smoke coming at us, and we just started running for our lives. We only took a few steps before we realized we couldn't outrun it, so the two of us just stood there, holding each other, expecting it to crush us like pancakes. And then the cloud of smoke just hit us.

We stood there for a few minutes waiting for it to clear. You held your hand up to your face, and you couldn't even see your hand. And then once it cleared, we started moving farther and farther away. We got out of the building maybe anywhere from two to four minutes before it came down. We just started heading east with everyone else. We couldn't find a phone anywhere.

Gloria went the entire way with me. We just slowly walked until we got into Chinatown. I couldn't take it anymore. I had to let my wife know I was alive. So I went into a Chinese deli and I went behind the counter. I think the woman thought I was robbing her. But I just said I just want to use her phone. So she let me use the phone. I bought a bottle of water. I threw a five-dollar bill on the counter, and I walked out with Gloria.

We got to a construction site and we went into one of the trailers, where she was able to call her family. We continued to walk up to Penn Station, where there was mass of people standing out there. I think we went into Lindy's because Penn Station was closed at that point. We got a table after about five minutes. We were covered in soot. And we got ourselves a drink. There was a nice woman across the way who paid for our tab, and we just sat there for a few hours.

When they finally opened Penn Station, I asked Gloria if she wanted to come home with me. She had just relocated from Aon's Maryland office just five days before this happened. She started the same day I did. And here she was living in Jersey City. She had no pocketbook, no money, no nothing. She had left everything in the office too. So I offered to take her home with me, and she said, "No, I really would rather go home." So I took whatever money I had in my pocket, I gave it to her and I sent her home. I got on my own train and I went home to my family on Long Island. I have a wife and two kids. Gloria hasn't met them yet, but she's spoken to them on the phone. She bought them Hanukkah gifts. Her daughter sent us a beautiful card, thanking me for what I did. We're best of friends now. We sit next to each other at work, in an office Aon is using on Forty-fourth Street. When I went down to Florida for my niece's bat mitzvah a couple of weeks ago, Gloria handed me her rosaries and said, "Please, take these with you. It'll keep you safe."

Gloria Novesl, left, with Steve Greenberg.

GLORIA NOVESL
55, Insurance Broker, Aon

"AND AT ONE POINT, I SAID TO HIM, 'JUST GO,' BECAUSE HE
HAS TWO SMALL CHILDREN. . . . BUT HE WOULDN'T LEAVE ME.
HE SAID, 'NO, WE'RE GOING DOWN TOGETHER.'"

Steve and I only knew each other for a week. I came up from Baltimore and we had become friends. Of course, how friendly can you really get in a week?

When we were told that tower 1 was on fire, we proceeded to go down the stairwell. We stopped—I don't even remember what floor it was—and sat there for a few minutes to rest. When they said that everything was okay and that we could go back up, Steve and I looked at each other. We started to go up, but then we hesitated.

We kept going down and we got down to, I don't know, 74, 75, when there was another crash. Our building, tower 2, started to crack open. We just like looked at each other again and said we needed to get the hell out of there.

I have asthma. Basically, if I walk too much I just get out of breath and I have to use the inhaler. My asthma is nothing serious unless I overexert myself. Then I get shortness of breath. I've been suffering with this for the last five years.

So we just continued to go down the staircase, and as we're going down, people started to come down with glass in their arms, bleeding, with burns, and we just looked at each other and said, "What happened?"

They told us that another plane had hit, and we said, "Another plane?" So we just had to get out. Steve was in front of me, encouraging me, saying, "Come on, come on, come on. We have to go." And he just didn't leave my side, you know, all the way down. I could see that the staircase had cracked. There was smoke. And at one point, I said to him, "Just go," because he has two small children. I have four children. They live in Maryland. I have seven grandchildren. But he wouldn't leave me. He said, "No, we're going down together."

And then all I could see was my children and my grandchildren's faces, and I said, "We're not dying here. We're not dying here." And Steve was pushing me, pulling me from the front and staying next to me and taking me down the stairs.

I don't know if you believe in angels, but suddenly I just felt this pressure on my back. I lost my mom two and a half years ago, and I'm thinking to myself, "What is this pressure on my back?" And I'm thinking it's my mother, pushing me. So I had a guardian angel on my back and Steve was my knight in shining armor in front of me. There was no way I was going to let us die. And I'm thinking, He's not going to leave me. He's got two children, a wonderful wife, and he's not going to leave me. And the more I thought about that, the more energy I had to go down the staircases.

He saved my life. We got outside, everybody was going, "Hurry, get out. Get out. Get out." And we just kept running and running. And finally, we got outside and I was really having a hard time breathing. Steve took me over to an ambulance and the guy checked me out. We sat there for a few minutes, and I don't know, something just said, "Gloria, get up. Gloria, get up." And I just took a deep breath and I said, "Come on, Steve. Let's go."

And we walked across the street to where that church is, the one with the graveyard, St. Paul's, I think, and we were toward the back of it, and that is when the building collapsed.

A cloud engulfed us, and Steve just kept pulling my hand. "Come on, come on, come on," he said. "Let's go." We just kept running and running and finally got to a place where we could go into this little alcove, to get away from the dust and compose ourselves for a while. Then we walked with this crowd of people. We got to Chinatown and one of the proprietors at this store let us use the phone. Steve finally got through to his wife and she knew that we were okay.

We just kept walking and we got to Penn Station and waited and waited and waited for the trains to start up again. I had nothing with me, so Steve gave me money. He went to his home on Long Island and I used the money to get to Jersey City, where I live. As I was standing there waiting for the train, this young man let me use his phone, and I just kept dialing the numbers and finally I got a connection and got to my brother. They were screaming and crying that I was okay. And I know I was okay because of Steve. He absolutely saved my life, I will never, ever forget. He's got such a special place in my soul. I just love him to death. He's like my brother. We have a special, special bond.

LORI GUARNERA
39, Insurance Broker, Aon

"EVERYTHING IN MY NATURE TOLD ME NOT TO GET ON THAT ELEVATOR. I DON'T KNOW WHY I DID IT, BUT IT SAVED MY LIFE."

I work in Aon's alternative risk area doing captive feasibility studies for companies that are interested in setting up captive insurance companies. At the time of the incident I had only been with Aon for nine months.

I got to work that day around eight-fifteen, which is pretty much my normal time. My mother was a teacher, so when September rolled around it was always time to settle down and get back into a normal routine. So even though there was still a casual dress code for the summer, I decided to put on a dress and heels rather than wearing sandals and a skirt. I took the bus downtown, went into Starbucks to pick up coffee, thinking that it's been a great summer and that life is great, and I went upstairs to the 102nd floor of tower 2.

I work closely with four other people. Nobody in my group was in yet. My immediate boss was out for the day at meetings, and the other three people usually come in around nine. I was sitting there drinking my big Starbucks coffee and typing up some e-mails when I heard this enormous explosion.

I believe it was this girl, Tammy Lasiter, who worked across the hall from me a couple of doors down, who screamed, "Oh, my God, it's a bomb." I went back into my office, I grabbed my purse, I grabbed my bag, and I ran to the center of the floor. I mean, I'm just as guilty as probably most other people in this city: You go to these fire drills, you listen, "Oh, yeah, I know where the stairs are." But I was standing there with maybe five or six other people, and I said, "What do we do? What do we do?" We had no idea what happened. I could see papers flying around outside. I knew something was desperately wrong.

I never liked working in the towers to begin with. I'm not an elevator person. I'm a bit claustrophobic. I always felt the towers were a target.

So we get to the center of the floor, everybody's waiting, and they say, "Well, let's just wait for instructions."

And I said, "No. Where's the stairs?"

I start going down the stairs from the 102nd floor, and people are already coming down from the floors above me. It's one or two people, next to each other. It's not very crowded. One woman I know from the risk group, Judy Wein, is ahead of me, and another woman, Gigi Singer, is behind me. Gigi was very nervous going down the stairs. There was a man trying to comfort her, and people just kept going down.

Occasionally, we'd see somebody coming up, a maintenance worker, or another white-collar worker going back up the stairs. We were saying to them, "Come down, come down," but at that point nobody really understood what was happening.

We got to the seventy-eighth floor and Judy said, "Let's see if the elevators are working." I don't know what made me do it, because I'm thinking, I shouldn't be taking an elevator, but I guess the thought of walking down seventy-eight floors in my high heels was not exactly something I wanted to do. Judy was now a few people ahead of me. I followed her out onto 78, and at that point a lot of people were still coming up to work. A lot of people were starting to go back down, still trying to get into the elevators. People were milling around. Nobody knew what to do. The security people were saying, "Stay calm. The fire is in the other tower." In a way, thank God nobody knew what was happening at that point because there would've been a mass rush for the elevators.

I remember Judy saying, "Oh, I don't have my purse. All my stuff is upstairs."

And I thought, No, no, no. I'm getting out of here, I can't wait, I can't wait. I waited for one elevator to go down—they hold, I don't know, maybe forty people—and I almost didn't get on the next elevator. But I thought to myself, All right, you just put one foot in front of the other and get on the elevator.

The first thing I saw when I got outside is this letterhead and it's addressed to somebody at Cantor Fitzgerald. At this point, I hadn't even looked up. I'm trying to call my husband on the cell phone, and I finally turn around and look up. I'm thinking, Oh, my God, what is happening?

I'm on the back side of the block across from the Trade Center on Broadway when I hear another explosion. This is when the plane hits tower 2. The street just cleared. I ran into a GNC store and then ran right out and started running for the east side.

I later found out that Judy and Gigi were both badly injured on the seventy-eighth floor. They were with Judy's boss, Howard Kestenbaum, and a young man named Vijay Paramsothy. They all worked in the risk analysis group. Unfortunately, Howard and Vijay didn't make it. They were all waiting for elevators when the second plane hit. I think Howard was killed on impact.

Everything in my nature told me not to get on that elevator. I don't know why I did it, but it saved my life. If it hadn't been for the fact that Judy was two people ahead of me and said, "Let's see if the elevators are working," I would have still been in that stairwell. The only reason I left the stairwell was because I knew her.

I think it was Thursday morning when people at Aon were putting together lists of who was okay and who was missing. I remember talking to my boss and him saying, "Judy's in the hospital. Gigi's in the hospital. Howard and Vijay are okay."

And I said, "I didn't see Howard and Vijay, I don't know if they're okay." See, initially, they were on the survivors list. But I had a bad feeling about it.

Howard was a very bright man who had been with the company for thirty years. He put together the financial model for the captive studies that we do. Every day I have to open up that model and use it. And every day I think of him. He lived in New Jersey. He had a wife and a daughter. I don't know them that well, but Howard was a very sweet man. And some days I sit there working on the model he created, and I think, Oh, Howard, where are you when I need you?

It's been very hard for me. I wasn't in the building when it was hit. I wasn't on the seventy-eighth floor, and I feel guilty for having the feelings I have because there were people who went through so much more than I did. And, you know, there's guilt about still being here. Vijay was a young guy, twenty-three. I think his family is from Malaysia. He came to the United States five or six years ago. He used to work at my old company, Reliance Insurance. We were together there for a very short period of time. When he came here, he went to the College of Insurance. I used to joke with him about it because nobody comes here to go to the College of Insurance. A very bright kid. I just enjoyed talking to him.

Afterward, Aon set up a system where you could communicate with the families. There were some stories about Vijay that I wanted to share with his family. And I just—I couldn't do it. It took me a long time to sit down and write to his family and express my condolences, because I felt, How can I make this better for them?

MOSES LIPSON

89, Construction Inspector, World Trade Center

"WHEN QUESTIONED HOW I FELT . . . I SAID MY HEART
WAS PUMPING. PEOPLE LAUGHED. BUT I MEANT MY HEART
WAS PUMPING HARDER THAN USUAL."

At 8:46 A.M., I stood waiting to take the elevators down to the mechanical equipment room on the forty-first floor of tower 1. I was scheduled to open the door so that the electrician foreman working on the Lehman Bros. alteration could survey a proposed emergency power cable installation.

The plane crashed into the north face of the tower, causing the building to sway 1.5 feet south. My office was on the south side of the eighty-eighth floor. The plane hit the ninety-second to ninety-fourth floors. The strobe lights flashed, but there was no audio announcement.

After circling the interior corridor, the employees congregated in the director's office. A woman from an upper floor, who suffered some burns, joined us. We climbed over collapsed walls. Upon a signal we were directed by our manager to proceed to a side stairwell. My supervisor, who was directed to accompany me, offered on two occasions to carry me on his back. I refused him. A second colleague walked in front of me.

Despite flooding from activated sprinkler heads, we proceeded down to the seventy-eighth floor, where local elevators discharged passengers to express elevators. A female associate tried to open an elevator door for a man, but could not. She was told that a fireman would do it.

We were advised to change stairwells to a center stair. Of the three stairwells only the center stair exited at the street level. The other two exited at the second floor—the mezzanine. I learned at a meeting later that a door had been jammed shut by the crash, requiring people to return from the seventy-sixth floor up to the seventy-eighth floor for the clear stair.

Descending from the seventy-eighth floor, there were many occasions to rest on the stairs, and in the tenant spaces which were not as muggy—the floors were air-conditioned. On one occasion, when questioned how I felt—people were concerned—I said my heart was pumping. People laughed. But I meant my heart was pumping harder than usual. I am eighty-nine years old.

We were offered water and soda by people on several floors. I did not hear the collapse of 2 World Trade Center. The lights went out momentarily. We moved to the side railing to allow four men bringing an emergency carrying seat. We moved over for firefighters walking up.

At the tenth floor, my legs felt tired. Two colleagues held my arms until the street level. I didn't look at my watch until 12:15 P.M. I was told later that we exited the tower on West Street at 10:15 A.M., fifteen minutes before tower 1 collapsed.

At the doors exiting the tower, I saw three corpses under the canopy.

After climbing over debris from the canopy at the exit, I was taken to a policewoman who brought me to a Hatzalah ambulance. I was given oxygen for a short time. The oxygen was required for the people escaping the fireproofing spray which flooded the area.

I sat in the closed ambulance for a long time. I walked about a mile north on West Street, resting several times on the concrete divider between the West Side Highway and the service road. A mechanic recognized me and held my arm a short distance.

After hesitating, I climbed the passage walk over the Holland Tunnel exit ramp.

I looked for the driver of a parked taxi on the street north of Canal Street. I decided not to ask a group of women at a street telephone booth to allow me to call my home.

While walking north, I knocked on the window of a taxi making a left turn. The three men [inside the cab] okayed my sitting in the front seat. They dropped me at West End Avenue and Seventieth Street, where I found my cardiologist preparing for afternoon patients. His receptionist couldn't connect me with my home. The doctor would not tell me my blood pressure.

I caught a cab to Eighty-sixth Street. At 1 P.M., I rang the bell at my apartment. I worked at the World Trade Center from 1968 to 1982 as an electrical engineer. I had to retire in '82 at the mandatory retirement age of seventy. But I came back in 1989 and started working there again. As a construction inspector, I was part of the wrap-up team for [developer] Larry Silverstein to take over the World Trade Center. I was hoping to remain there until April 3, when I would turn ninety, so I could retire then.

I'm doing volunteer work now for Dorot, a community organization that shows younger people how best to help older people. But the biggest thing I take from my experience on September 11 was the dedication of those 343 firemen who kept going even though they knew the situation was impossible.

John Jester, far left, at the Pentagon.

If the tragic events on September 11 had been contained to just the area around the World Trade Center, what happened in New York that morning would still be considered the single most devastating attack ever unleashed on the United States of America.

But incredibly, it was proving even worse. Hijackers aboard two other planes had a second set of targets in mind, and while New York's Bravest and Finest were doing their best to save lives at the World Trade Center, a third commercial jetliner was diving for the Pentagon, where thirty thousand unsuspecting federal employees were just becoming aware of the unfolding horror in Manhattan.

And the heroism at work in New York and Washington would soon be matched by the heroism in the air, when forty men and women aboard United Airlines Flight 93 acted on information they received from wives, mothers, and GTE Airfone operators and overtook the hijackers and made sure that the fourth plane never reached its destination.

TED ANDERSON

42, Lieutenant Colonel, U.S. Army,
Legislative Liaison Officer to the U.S. Congress, Pentagon

———

"I AM COMPLETELY AND TOTALLY OUT OF MY MIND AT THIS POINT,
REVERTING TO FULL COMBAT MODE. . . . AND AS FAR AS I WAS
CONCERNED, THIS WAS A COMBAT SITUATION."

My portfolio deals with current operations for the army worldwide. So I go in extremely early, between 4 and 5 A.M., in order to read overnight cable traffic from Europe and destinations beyond. From there, I try to get in a little physical training and then begin the normal duty day with everybody else.

We had a morning meeting scheduled at 7:45, which I attended. I picked up a cup of coffee on the way back, chitchatted with a few folks, and made it back into the office. Then I noticed that all of my colleagues were huddled near an overhead television. Probably four or five lieutenant colonels and three civilian secretaries and everybody seemed extremely quiet. We're usually a pretty rambunctious group of folks. Some of the ladies were crying. I had no idea what had happened. And then I stared at the TV, and it showed the towers, both burning. Then the clip came on showing the replay of the second airplane striking tower 2. Two of the aviators in our office said, "Well, that's it. There's all the proof you need right there. That's no accident." And I knew he was right. And immediately I knew this was some kind of state-sponsored terrorism. Renegade terrorists cannot conduct a coordinated attack that successfully.

I walked back to my cubicle and sat down. I pulled up my e-mail and then all of a sudden I just got this real eerie feeling. I don't know, call it nineteen years in the army, combat experience, deployments worldwide, constant level of preparedness. So I immediately got up from my cubicle and walked out the mall entrance to the guard location, where the defense protective services folks are at. I knew the guys on duty. I asked them if they were aware of what had occurred in New York. They were just getting some of the details. And I stated, "Hey, look, guys, we need to upgrade security here. Has anybody given any thought of upgrading the threat level."

And he said, "Sir, I'm sure that they're talking about that now. Let me radio in." So he called in and found out that sergeants and the officers at the headquarters location were in a meeting talking about what upgraded security precautions they should take. So I felt a little bit better. I mean, we had talked about what a tremendous target the Pentagon was and how vulnerable we were, previously.

I walked back to my office, sat down, and pulled up some more of the e-mail and started corresponding with the daily activity across the Potomac on the Hill, and my phone rang. It was my wife, who lives in Fayetteville, North Carolina. My wife is a sixth-grade schoolteacher at Stedman Middle School, and she was in class with her students and they had the TV on and were watching the activity live and discussing what was going on. And my wife said, "Hey, I know somebody in Washington. Let's call him and we'll get an instant update as to what's going on and what they think in Washington."

So we talked briefly, and she was relaying information to her students as I was describing it to her. I told her that we could only assume at this point that it was some sort of coordinated attack. But I also told her to make sure that her students understood that we should not jump to conclusions and point fingers at anyone, because we had done that in the Oklahoma tragedy and we were extremely embarrassed that we had alienated the entire Arab community. I could hear her explaining that to her students, all about the Oklahoma bombing, when the plane hit the Pentagon. It was a loud roar, and I mean the building literally shook. And there was a sucking sound, which I believe was the oxygen escaping as the jet fuel poured into the corridors right down the hall from us and ignited, taking all of the oxygen out of the air.

Our ceiling caved in. The lights went out, but the phone was still working. I was still on with my wife. I was a little stunned, just for an initial second, and then I said, "Listen, we have been bombed. I have to go." And I hung up the phone. I didn't even wait for a response.

I didn't know at first that it was a plane. I initially assumed for about the first two minutes that a bomb had been left somewhere in the building, and the bomb went off.

I screamed for everybody in the office to get out. I got up and moved, and that was the last time I was ever in that cubicle. We lost everything: twenty years of medical records, everything on my hard drive, personal files, my Class A uniform, everything.

I moved out into the hallway out the back door and went into the main corridor between corridors 4 and 5. The plane actually hit between corridors 2 and 3. I positioned myself in the main corridor and was looking up and down the corridor to see if I could see smoke or fire or anything. And I noticed people just meandering out of their offices, looking around, having basic discussions, and I just started barking orders to get out of the building. Now here I am, dressed for legislative business with Congress. I've got on a nice suit with a striped shirt, tie, and suspenders. And I am screaming at full-bird colonels and general officers to move out of the building, just barking orders, screaming. And they listened to me. They all started moving and they tried to get out of the mall entrance but the guards had mistakenly thought that they were under attack from the outside of the building. So they secured that entrance. They had taken out most of their small arms, machine guns, etc., and brought them all out. It looked like they were preparing to defend the doors there. So I started moving people toward the center of the Pentagon. This all took place within two minutes.

The Pentagon is structured by a series of rings. The center of the Pentagon is the A-ring, and then it goes out in rings, B, C, D, and E. The E-ring is the last ring around the outside. It is basically the wall, the last corridor before you exit the building. So I'm at the E-ring and I kick open a fire exit door and scream for people to follow me out the door. I guess there were fifty, maybe one hundred people who followed me out that way. I motioned for them to move off to the northeast, toward north parking. We have two parking lots, north parking and south parking. I think you've got enough for about fifty thousand parking spaces on each side. I turned to my left and I saw a field of scattered debris. It was all gray and metallic. Everybody was moving to my right, and I turned to my left and ran toward the debris. There's nobody with me except Chris Braman, a noncommissioned officer, an NCO, and he is in civilian clothes. He's a cook for the chief of staff of the army, and he was wearing black pants and a polo shirt with his emblem on it.

As we get to the debris field, I know now that it's an airplane because of the chunks of charred steel. I'm running at full speed and I'm seeing the billowing smoke and the flames from around the helipad area of the Pentagon. I'm not paying attention to what I'm doing and I fall right into huge pieces of the aircraft and trip over it. I picked myself up and ran directly toward the fire, and at this point I notice that there are two fire trucks on that side which are maintained at the helipad area. It's basically the fire department at the Pentagon. One truck is parked outside and a truck is parked inside the garage. The outside truck was completely engulfed in flames from taking part of the impact of the airplane. The other truck was protected. It was inside the garage and there were three firefighters on duty, two of which I knew, and they pulled the truck out of the garage and were beginning to turn the water cannon on top of the truck. They were the only people out there. I didn't see anybody else.

I got as close to the building as I could, trying to find a door that we could get into. We found two women out on the ground next to the building. Initially, I thought that they had been blown out of their offices, or they had just jumped, but I found out later that they had been thrown out by people who were rescuing folks inside the building.

One woman was conscious. The other was unconscious. I picked up the conscious lady. She had a broken hip and was in horrible, horrible pain. She had flash burns as well. Both ladies had been terribly flash-burned. We were pretty close to the fire now. The fire was bearing down on us. The heat was horrendous. I made sure she understood that I was there, and that we were going to pull her out of there and move her away from the building. I told her it was going to hurt, and I picked her up and threw her on my back. She screamed in pain. I ran her about four hundred yards to the other side of the helipad and laid her down.

The NCO carried the other lady and followed me. We laid them there and other people came up to render aid to them.

Chris and I ran back to the building. We found a window that was pretty well blasted out and we tore the remaining shards of glass along the bottom out and gained entry. Inside we just screamed for people to come toward our voices. We couldn't see anything. The smoke was billowing and it was hard to breathe.

I got on the floor and I felt my way down the wall and I felt a body right in front of the door. It was a woman, extremely heavyset. She was conscious. She was bleeding from the ears and the mouth and she was definitely in shock. She was pinned against a wall by a huge safe. It was a six-drawer safe that had fallen and it was wedged up against her. We were either going to leave her there and let her burn, or we were going to waste some serious time getting her out of there. We had no choice. We had to go ahead and try to get her out. It seemed like forever, but we were finally able to pull her free. We weren't able to lift her. We had to drag her from the building.

Chris and I went back into the building and this time we were trying to figure out what we were going to do. We wanted to crawl from the outside door to the E-ring corridor. As we were trying to get our bearings, some type of fuel outside next to the fire department area blew up. A propane storage tank, I think. And when this thing blew up, it knocked us both down inside that office that we were in. When I pulled myself up, the whole time trying to shield my face with my elbow, I noticed this bright flash that went by me. I thought it was the ceiling caving in. And I heard Chris scream, "Help me." It was a person on fire, trying to get out of the building. Chris knocked him down and I jumped on top of him. We smothered the fire on this guy. He wasn't totally engulfed in flames, just the front part of this guy, from his head down to his lower torso including his legs. We rolled him on the ground and he was screaming, fully conscious, and we picked him up immediately and just carried him out. We got him as far away from the building as we could and gently laid him down. He was burned, horribly, horribly burned from the top of his head all the way to the bottom of his feet. He had no color in his eyes. It was all white.

There are three things that I remember from that day more than anything else. That is one of them. I could see it was a civilian because he had a suit on. You could see that he had a white shirt on, but the whole front of everything had been burnt away. The back of his collar was still affixed, the belt to his pants was still affixed and melted into the side of his body. Everything else was just charred black down the front.

Now this guy is screaming and we were finally able to figure out that he was saying something. He was yelling, "There are people behind me, in the corridor.

You have to get the people in the corridor out." He was just screaming this over and over again.

Chris and I looked around and we noticed that more firemen were showing up. Arlington County Fire Department was there, along with Fairfax County Fire Department and Washington, D.C., Fire Department. We ran back toward the same door and all we needed to do now was negotiate this twenty-five feet to that E-ring corridor, and we'll get to the people in that corridor. If we could just get to them, we can lead them back out.

We were getting ready to make entry again, and the firemen stopped us. We had a little confrontation there, I must tell you. I've been instructed by the army to not explain what really happened there, but it was a very lively conversation. I grabbed one of the firefighters and basically told him, "Look, I know you're doing your job, and I know you have our best interests at heart, but here's the bottom line. You have two choices: you can either stay out here, or you can go in with us, and that's basically all I want to talk about. We're wasting time."

Other firemen showed up and they physically restrained us and pulled us away from the building. I am completely and totally out of my mind at this point, reverting to full combat mode. So did Chris. He had been in the Ranger regiment. He fought in Mogadishu. And as far as I was concerned, this was a combat situation. You've got all the horrors of combat. You've got the smells, the sounds of agony and despair. You've got everything there, all of the elements of combat except for the actual lead that's flying through the air. Nobody's shooting at you.

Still, it's an unwritten code that we live by. If you saw *Black Hawk Down,* you know we don't leave anyone behind. I knew there were people inside the building, as did Chris, and it didn't matter that they were civilians. It didn't matter that they were contractors or vendors. We were all one team, one fight. I consider the civilians for the Department of Defense just as important, if not more important, than the military folks. The DOD civilians basically run the army and the Pentagon. I knew there were wounded in there and we needed to go in and get them. You can't leave your wounded behind, period. But I was restrained and pulled back.

A three-star general showed up, along with a couple other generals, and I explained to them what was going on. This three-star general basically felt the same way I did, and he went to the on-site fire commander and said, "Look, I will take full responsibility. We're going to mount a rescue effort. We've got two guys here that have already been inside. They will lead our rescue effort, but we need to make an attempt to go in and get our people out." He was overruled by the fire captain.

I have since come to know that the fire captain was correct. I am now certain that they saved my life and I'm certain they saved Chris's life, as well. My whole outlook on the American firefighter changed that day. I've become Mr. Fan of the Fire Department. Those guys were the real heroes of the day for me. I have talked to firemen who later went into that area and there was no way out. That last burned guy we brought out was the last person to come out of the building alive on the exterior side of the Pentagon. He is alive. The two ladies we brought out both lived. The heavyset woman, unfortunately, died.

Later that afternoon I was able to call and relay a message to my wife that I was okay. The firemen were fully involved in fighting the fire now. They were inside the structure and they were totally involved. I just sat and watched. I was in awe of them the whole afternoon. As darkness fell, the 3rd Infantry Regiment across the river, the old-guard soldiers, showed up in mass, about 250 soldiers, and they relieved us. Basically we were told to go home. "Thanks, you guys did a great job, but the infantry's here to take over."

I remember laying down outside along with a buddy of mine from the same office and we were trying to figure out how we were going to get home. Of course, we didn't bring anything out of the building with us. Everything was inside, including my car keys. Our cars were in the north parking lot and that part of the lot was now a crime scene because part of the aircraft had fallen there, so it was roped off. So we're trying to figure out where the closest metro is. The Pentagon metro site was closed down, so we needed to walk over to Crystal City, which was probably a ten-minute walk at most. So we started strolling off, two well-dressed guys who looked like they had fallen off the turnip truck and dragged through an onion field. We were caked in soot and blood, and it was just nasty looking. I mean, we looked like hell. So we walked over to Crystal City and walked down the metro station, which was running free. The gates were open. We got on a train headed toward Springfield, Virginia, and people looked at us in disbelief. But nobody said anything to us. We looked like bomb victims. And one of the other things that I remember—the first one was about that guy's eyes—the second thing is that nobody spoke on the train. It was total silence. Everybody was in shock. Even couples that were together, nobody was talking. They just stared out of the train, stared at each other in just total disbelief.

I got off at my stop and had to walk about four blocks to my house. I didn't have my keys with me, so I had to ask the manager of the building to let me in. He tried to let me in, but his key didn't work so he had to pull the lock off. I was exhausted. I went out and laid down in the grass and went to sleep. The maintenance guy had to come and find me. When I got in, I took a forty-minute shower, cried for thirty minutes, and then spent the rest of the night trying to answer about fifty voice mails. The phone just kept ringing all night. People called from Bulgaria, from Puerto Rico, from Colombia, all over the United States. Finally, you can only tell the story so many times. It physically wears you out. At about eleven o'clock, I had had it and I went to sleep. I slept for a couple of hours and then woke up, you know, and thought it was all a bad dream. I popped on the news and, of course, I couldn't get away from the story. This was about two in the morning and I just decided to get up and go to work. I put on my battle dress uniform, my fatigues and my boots. I grabbed gear figuring that I'm going to be at work for a while. I got in a car and drove up to the 395. And as soon as I turned onto 395, I could see the glow, the orange glow in the distance. As I got closer to it, the glow got brighter. Coming over the break in the horizon you could see that the building was on fire. The ceiling portion of the Pentagon was burning, and it was out of control. I remember very distinctively at about three-ten in the morning, parking my car and seeing this building on fire and people going into work. And that's the last of the three things I'll always remember about that day: Ten thousand people showed up to work at the Pentagon that morning and the building was still on fire. It just made me extremely proud of what I was doing and where I was working to know that a building can be burning out of control and still ten thousand people came to work because they knew number one, we were probably going to be at war, and number two, that there were still dead people in the building who needed to be brought out and identified.

CHRISTOPHER BRAMAN
33, Staff Sergeant, U.S. Army, Pentagon

"My wife met me at the door and wouldn't let me go.
She held me so tight, it was incredible.
She had never held me that way before."

I am an airborne Ranger cook, and on September 11 I got in at about five-thirty in the morning to open the kitchen. The crew came in, along with the executive chef and other preliminary chefs, to prepare for the day and set up for the morning. We had a prayer breakfast with some congressionals scheduled for that morning.

During the breakfast, I went through the shopping list for the afternoon lunch with the executive chef. Then I left to do the errands. I came back and grabbed some lunch for myself. I was inputting information on my computer when my wife called. She works out of the house, and she didn't know what had happened that morning until my dad called her from Texas. He said to her, "You need to call Chris. The Pentagon could be next."

My wife called me at about nine-thirty and explained what happened at the World Trade Center. I had had no idea either. Most military people are extremely busy all the time, and we often don't deal with outside items until we've finished the mission at hand. And that was typical of me.

I told my wife not to worry, and that I loved her. And as soon as I hung up the phone, I was thrown forward by what felt like an earthquake.

I exited the office, and there were people running down the hallway saying it was a bomb. I evacuated the kitchen area, turned off the stoves, and secured everything. My crew went one way and I went another. As I came down a stairwell, I saw people with clothes that appeared to be shredded off them, just walking aimlessly. As I stepped out the door, I saw a DPS officer running with a lady and a baby. There were over a hundred people standing around him, in awe. I grabbed the baby from the officer and we ran with the mother and her child about another seventy-five yards. I placed the baby down in the woman's arms, but the woman kept repeating, "Where's my baby? Where's my baby?"

I saw an ambulance pull up and I ran as fast as I could toward a medic kneeling down and pulling out aid bags and equipment. Medics were tending to a lady who was burned over 70 percent of her body—from the back of her head to the back of her thighs. She was bright pink and had no clothes on; it looked like they had either been burned or ripped off of her. As they lay her down, I knelt and accidentally put my hand on her shoulder. She didn't make any noise. As my hand pulled away, it was just gooey—a residue of skin—like mucus. I kept saying, "I need to get help. I have a lady and a baby." Everything seemed to be happening in slow motion.

I met Lieutenant Colonel Ted Anderson as he was coming out of the building. He was dressed in what appeared to be a suit, with a striped shirt and suspenders on, and he just kept repeating, "My general didn't die on my watch. I got him out."

Colonel Anderson and I went into the building at least four times. The heat inside was so hot it felt like the sun kissing you. My face was hurting, but I ignored it. We just kept going in and out, working our way around to the south parking area. We were looking for another way to get into the building. As we worked our way around, other men started joining us. They thought we knew what we were doing, but we were really just grabbing and going. It didn't matter what anyone's rank was.

A medical student named Eric Jones, who had initially pulled his car over to the side of the road and started giving medical aid, jumped on our litter team to give us a hand.

We would organize a group and all of a sudden there'd be another secondary explosion, and we were pushed back two hundred meters. I hadn't realized yet that a plane had hit. I was going on adrenaline.

During that time, Colonel Anderson separated from us. He grabbed a fireman's mask off the truck and went to get us some intelligence, so we could find out what to do. We were going to find another way in regardless of orders to the contrary.

Anderson was gone for quite some time. While we waited from him, a hundred of us shared one cell phone. I got to talk to my wife for thirty seconds, long enough to say, "I love you. I'm okay. I'm staying." I didn't talk to her again until Friday.

When Colonel Anderson got back, we tried to go inside again, but we were restrained by a man who said, "You can't go back in." We were so jacked up on adrenaline. Colonel Anderson kept getting into fights with different authority figures—firemen, military, it didn't matter who it was.

At around nine-thirty that night, Lieutenant Colonel Mauhei Edmundson walked up and said she was the officer in charge of the recovery team. I told her that I was a cook at the Pentagon, but that my background was combat search and rescue with a Ranger battalion. She said she could use my help.

From that moment, I became part of the solution instead of part of the problem. I found things to do. The FBI supply teams came and I told them I needed body bags, flashlights, and respirators. They asked, "Who are you?" I told them I was the noncommissioned officer in charge of the recovery team. By morning everything I'd ordered appeared, and Colonel Edmundson was amazed that I had acquired what was needed. Task forces from Tennessee, Maryland, and Virginia were showing up. Search and rescue teams were coming in from all over the country. The Salvation Army showed up. The Red Cross showed up with psychological support, food, and water, and were setting up tents all around us. The building was still burning all around us, but it was the most organized chaos I've ever seen.

The firemen said they had shored up an area on the far right side of the impact, which would serve as a safe haven for us to enter the building. I'll never forget that first hallway: ankle-deep water, full of debris, slime, jet fuel, and human matter. There was an arm, a hand, just floating in the water. As we went down the hallway, we began to feel increasingly claustrophobic. A marine got sick and started saying to himself, "I can do it. I can do it." We crawled around air-conditioning ducts, falling all over ourselves because of the debris constricting us. If your face mask came off, you'd take in a lungful of the still-smoldering fire, jet fuel, asbestos, and human remains. Then you'd reseal your mask and put it back on.

During that time, we came across our first victim, a heavy woman. She must have been answering the telephone when the plane hit, because she still had the telephone melted to her head. It took six of us to lift her, put her in a bag, and carry her out.

We passed four chaplains standing in the water—a Baptist, a Protestant, a Catholic, and a Jewish rabbi. They were there as one denomination. They didn't argue over the religion of each victim. They were unified. And they just gave the last rites as we carried each body out.

There were times when we got excited because we thought we'd found a whole body. But many times when we'd see the tops of shoulders, we'd reach down and see melted intestines and hardened lungs, deflated and black, through the rib cage. Other times, we'd reach down and there would be a pile of ash and rib bones.

I've been part of security teams that went in after the Navy SEALs and Delta Force. I've been to Iraq, Turkey, Yugoslavia, South America, and Central America. I've seen every armpit that's come down the pike. There was no question that this was another battle zone.

I saw Lieutenant Colonel Ted Anderson again on Thursday, when the president and some congressmen came down to survey the site. And Ted kept saying, "You're still here?" Even those who knew I hadn't left kept saying, "You're still here?" And every time I brought a body out there was a psychologist or a rescue worker trauma person asking me if I needed help.

I didn't want to talk about it. I just kept saying, "I'm fine. I appreciate it, thanks." I just kept going on about my business. I became numb, tuned my feelings out, compartmentalized everything, and just shut off my emotions. I was on such an adrenaline surge that my military training kicked in and I just reacted.

The last body Eric (the medical student) and I picked up was a woman. We looked down and her fingernails were painted red. There was a pink purse next to her that wasn't damaged and a wedding ring on her finger. As we picked her up, the back of her head opened up. We picked up as much as we could. That was the last person we brought out.

At about four-forty-five on Friday morning, Eric and I looked at each other, and I said, "You know what? Come to my house. We'll take a shower and we'll come back." He didn't say anything. He just followed me.

We got into my Jeep and went to my house. We undressed outside, leaving our clothes in a plastic bag. My wife met me at the door and wouldn't let me go. She held me so tight, it was incredible. She had never held me that way before. She was just in tears and shaking. I went upstairs and I took a shower, but she never left my side and didn't say a word. She just sat there while I took a shower. I came out and dried off. She said I looked very skinny. I had apparently lost twelve pounds in those three days. My wife kept staring at my face and saying that I looked like I had changed or aged. She didn't know what was different about me.

Eric lay on the couch and I lay in bed next to my wife upstairs. It was only for about ten minutes, but I just kept staring at the walls with images of the Pentagon going through my mind, and I knew had to go back. I kept saying, "I gotta go. I love you, but I gotta go."

Eric and I went outside, put on the same clothes we had worn since Tuesday, and left. Two exits away from the Pentagon, I had a mental dump and had to pull over to the side of the road because I suddenly couldn't move. I was so overwhelmed with feelings—with what I had seen and what I had done all week—that I just became paralyzed. I cried for forty-five minutes before I realized that Eric was still sitting next to me.

JOHN JESTER
59, Chief of Defense Protective Service, Pentagon

———

"IT WAS ORDINARY PEOPLE DOING EXTRAORDINARY THINGS."

Just prior to the incident at the Pentagon, I had received a call from our public-affairs office asking me what measures we were taking at the Pentagon based on what was happening in New York. I had just gotten into my office from a meeting and I was unaware of what had happened in New York, so I quickly hit the TV button, tuned into CNN, and saw the second plane hitting.

We have what we call "threat majors," and we increased our threat majors, which give a bigger appearance of security around the building. In fact, I was talking to some people about what we were doing, and I had just walked into my office when the building shuddered. My office is probably three hundred feet from where the plane hit. At first I thought it was a big load of furniture in the hallway. Then I thought, No. That was just too big.

And then someone said, "We've been hit." They saw the fireball and the smoke coming from the west side of the building. I ran downstairs to our communications center to get an assessment of what had happened, where it happened, and then what actions our communications center had initiated in terms of getting people to the scene and getting support from the fire department.

We had to deal with a building population of twenty thousand people. We had to get support from the Arlington County Fire Department, which actually had a fire truck on the roadway and saw the plane hit the building. Our officers and some Pentagon employees went in and rescued a number of people from the area, which was in flames. It was good to see how everyone just jumped to save their fellow employees.

It was difficult to manage an evacuation of the world's largest building. Using the public-address system, we advised people to leave the building. We had to get medical people to the scene. Ambulances were arriving from every location. Helicopters came in to evacuate people. And the fire departments and the local police departments have agreements in place so that Arlington County Fire Department is the one that supports us, but they are able through arrangements to call other adjoining counties and cities to support them. So fire trucks from all over the metropolitan Washington area came to support us. And police departments from all different areas supported us on the roadways to the Pentagon. Traffic control was a big issue all around the Pentagon. At the same time, we had to maintain a high security profile because we didn't know what was going to happen next.

Obviously, this was a very traumatic day. Three planes hit three symbolic structures, and for a while there was a report of a second plane inbound to Washington, which caused everybody a great deal of concern. So a lot was going on at one time. I would call it controlled chaos.

I always think about "what-ifs." What if certain things were to occur? How would you react to them? What kind of plan would you exercise? We had actually thought about planes hitting the Pentagon. We're so close to the National Airport. We're just a short distance from the runways. In fact, one runway for commuter aircraft comes real close to the Pentagon. So we're always concerned about a possible accident, as well as possibly terrorists using a small plane. But you're never thinking a 757. When you first see the enormity of it, you almost can't believe it occurred. And then you have to quickly snap out of that and get on with your mission. I think we were very successful. We were able to evacuate the building. We were able to get people out. People just got together—firemen, military officers, and civilian employees. Someone said it was ordinary people doing extraordinary things, working toward a common goal.

When the plane hit, it basically gutted three rings of the building. The plane went into the building at an angle. So when you looked at the destruction, it didn't appear to be as bad on the outside as it really was on the inside. The reconstruction effort, which is named Project Phoenix, has been fantastic. Five floors of the building have been rebuilt in a very short time. All the concrete work is completed, and our goal is to have some of those offices operational by this September 11. The entire Pentagon was originally built in sixteen months. There have been so many advancements in the technology of concrete and reinforcements in concrete that the part of the building that was destroyed will be a much more solid structure than it was before.

We've added more security measures since September 11, and our security around the Pentagon is much more visible now. It was visible before, but it's much more high profile now.

Still, there are some people in the building who are concerned about another incident. I mean, we are a target. We're a symbol of the United States. In my profession, we've always been concerned with terrorism, and not necessarily if it would happen, but when. I don't know anyone personally, but I've heard some people say they know others who would not want to work here now. When they hear loud noises, they look around more now. I do that myself. But this building is a military structure and most people grin and bear it and just keep on with the job. Morale now is probably higher than it's ever been. People feel, "You hit us, but you didn't stop us." The Pentagon kept working through the entire incident.

People around the country are just supporting the Pentagon like crazy. The hallways of the Pentagon are covered in banners and posters from school kids throughout the United States. It's a great story. I'll never forget one little girl, a toddler, who sent a card here, a get-well card to the Pentagon. It just said, "Get well. Hope you're okay."

JAMES SCHWARTZ

43, Assistant Chief of Operations, Arlington County Fire Department

"MOST AMERICANS HAVE AN UNDERSTANDING OF BUILDING
FIRES, MANY HAVE SEEN PLANE CRASHES BEFORE, AND SOME
EVEN KNOW ABOUT BUILDING COLLAPSES. . . . SEPTEMBER 11
WAS ALL THREE WRAPPED INTO ONE."

On the morning of September 11, I was, like many people, watching the events unfold in New York City. After the second airplane hit, we started looking at vulnerabilities in our own area.

At that time, the *USA Today* building and Gannett headquarters was operating in Arlington County. Their thirty-two-story office tower sits right on the

Potomac River in Arlington County and is along the flight path of aircraft on their final approach to National Airport. And we were beginning to get phone calls from people in those buildings concerned about their own safety after watching the Trade Tower events. Soon after that one of our units out on the road reported seeing a plane go down in the area of the Fourteenth Street Bridge. It took a few minutes, but then it was determined that the plane had hit the Pentagon. I immediately left my office and went to the Pentagon.

As the assistant chief for operations, my responsibilities include the management of the operations division, which is all of the fire stations, all of the emergency response units. And I have two battalion chiefs on each shift that report to me.

I arrived on the scene at the Pentagon in just a few minutes and met with the first battalion chief. Luckily, he was a man who has thirty-seven years of experience with Arlington County Fire Department and has a great deal of experience at the Pentagon itself. His name is Robert Cornwell, and he had established command and begun to implement our incident command system.

I assigned him to an interior group. I assigned him several companies of firefighters and assigned him to a particular portion of the building. He quickly went off with those assigned personnel and made his way to the building.

We had an awful lot of activity going on the outside of the building because a lot of people had self-evacuated, and there were a great deal of military and civilian personnel assigned to the Pentagon who were assisting others. We had a large number of injured people. And of course, we had a lot of fatalities.

I went on to assume command for the incident and was joined a few minutes later by Special Agent Christopher Combs, an FBI agent with the Washington field office Joint Terrorism Task Force. Chris and I have done a lot of work together in the past and we know each other very well. Chris came to me and said that another airplane had been hijacked and was headed for the Pentagon. Based on what we had witnessed at the World Trade Center, what he was saying was certainly a possibility. So I made the judgment to withdraw all of our troops, all of our responders from the area, to a place of refuge. We stayed in the protected area for about twenty minutes until the threat passed. Obviously, it didn't hit the Pentagon, but it's believed to be the aircraft that went on to crash in the field in Pennsylvania.

Most Americans have an understanding of building fires, many have seen plane crashes before, and some even know about building collapses. But from an operational standpoint, September 11 was all three wrapped into one. And the aircraft itself presented a significant problem because it brought with it six thousand gallons of jet fuel, which contributed to a tremendous fire that we were dealing with.

We called for plenty of additional resources and had responders from virtually every fire department in the area. We also called for some special response teams, including the National Medical Response team, which is a team of fire-fighters, paramedics, and law enforcement officers who are trained to respond to acts of terrorism. They bring special capabilities in that they are able to detect and monitor for chemical agents. They bring a mass casualty decontamination capability, and they also bring a large cache of pharmaceuticals that are available in case of chemical exposures. This was extremely important, because in the early stage of this incident we didn't know what we were dealing with.

At about two o'clock on the afternoon of the eleventh, I met with John Jester, who is the chief of the Defense Protective Services, which essentially serves as the police department for the Pentagon. John and I know each other from previous exercises and working together. Arlington County provides all of the fire and EMS protection to the Pentagon, and we go there almost every day for some kind of incident. In fact, we had a two-alarm fire at the Pentagon on August 2 of 2001, a month before the September 11 events. So we're very familiar with the building.

At six o'clock that night, John arranged to get the secretary of defense's press briefing room for me, and we gathered all the different organizations on the scene. I explained to them that while we had done a really good job in the first eight hours of this incident, we were going to be here another eight days, and in order to continue our success we were going to have to transition from the single command format into a unified command.

The command system is used by the American fire service every single day. We didn't make this up on September 11. We've been using it for the last twenty years. We simply expanded a system that we already use to a much larger degree for September 11.

At this meeting were military people, federal law enforcement, state representatives, local representatives, and civilian agencies. I explained to them that the unified command team was going to consist of the Arlington County Fire Department, the Arlington County Police Department, the FBI, DOD, FEMA, and an individual who was part of USAR, the urban search and rescue team. We explained to everybody that we would manage this incident under the unified concept and that the final decision-making authority would rest with the Arlington Country Fire Department. And we got everybody to sign on to that arrangement.

Also on the afternoon of the eleventh, Secretary of Defense Donald Rumsfeld announced that it would be "business as usual." I knew there was literally no way that there was going to be business as usual. And I certainly didn't want the twenty-five thousand people that normally work at the Pentagon to think that if they showed up on the morning of the twelfth, that they were going to be able to even find a parking space, let alone access their offices.

But the structure proved to be extremely productive. I cannot remember more than a handful of occasions in which issues that were raised at a particular meeting of the unified team came back at a subsequent meeting as being unresolved. It was an extremely cooperative, collegial, very professional, and productive relationship that really did contribute to the overall tone of cooperation throughout the incident. And it's important to note that this incident was extremely large. It certainly paled in comparison to the World Trade Center and all that they dealt with up there. But, you know, we built quite a little village down there at the Pentagon, both in terms of our operational needs to deal with the rescue and recovery efforts, as well as the logistical effort that was necessary to support the thousands of responders that were on the scene for the ten days that the Arlington County Fire Department was in charge.

It became apparent to everybody on September 11 that the risk has changed. There's no more graphic evidence of that than the 343 firefighters who died in the collapse of the World Trade Center. The stakes are now higher.

When people dial 911, they're not searching around for a service to come help them. They're calling for public safety to come help them, and it's largely fire and EMS that are on those front lines. You go back and look at the planning for these kinds of things. I couch it this way: planning is the result of experience coupled with assumptions. I go back to the firefighters. I can't necessarily speak for police officers, but I sense that it's the same thing. While we are extremely principled people as a group, we're very idealistic. We see what we do as having to meet certain ideals. If the average person were standing outside of your house at two o'clock in the morning while it was on fire, they would take a very realistic or pragmatic approach to what they were looking at. They'd say, "That's terrible, it's a lost cause."

But a firefighter is much more idealistic. He or she looks at that kind of circumstance and says, "I can make a difference here. I can do something that will make this better," which is what allows them to do the kinds of things that they do. And they do things today that the average person would not do. Not that the average person isn't capable of it. But the average person is not prepared to crawl down a smoky hallway with nine hundred degrees of heat above their head. Firefighters are able to do that because they have a high level of training and they have a sense of confidence that comes with that training, and comes with the knowledge that their equipment and the support systems that are in place are all going to contribute to a positive outcome that is going to make a difference. And I think that at the end of the day that's how they view their responsibilities with regard to response to terrorism.

I cannot tell you that if that airplane flew into the *USA Today* building today that we would act the same way that the firefighters in New York did at the World Trade Center. But I sense that an awful lot of what we would do would be very similar. And I'm not suggesting that we would put ourselves in harm's way to an extreme degree. We would certainly be mindful of the experience in New York City, but at the same time we're going to do a lot of the things that we would normally do in those circumstances. Our sense of duty and our sense of mission has us shoot for those ideals.

JOE FINLEY
46, Ladder 7, FDNY

"THERE IS NO CLOSURE WHEN YOU LOSE SOMEONE.
THERE'S AN EVOLUTION THAT TAKES PLACE, BUT YOU SPEND
THE REST OF YOUR LIFE GRIEVING."

I'm with Ladder 7, on East Twenty-ninth Street and Second Avenue. I just started my thirteenth year. I was off that day. I was planning to meet a friend of mine, a guy I had known since I was about six years old. We were going to go fishing at noon because that's when the tide is right. I live in Northport, Long Island. I have a workshop. I had a project I was going to work on that morning until about eleven. I build furniture, that type of thing, cabinets and woodworking. I was up in the shop and my wife called. She said, "You've got to put the television on. Something terrible has happened in the city."

I put the TV on and I couldn't believe what I was seeing. Even though the TV screen makes everything seem smaller than it is, I know how big those buildings are. Each floor is a square acre, over forty thousand square feet. And several acres of office building were burning after the plane hit. I thought that hundreds, maybe thousands of people were killed when that plane hit. I watched a little bit more and then talked to another fireman who called me when the other plane hit. We were talking about how we didn't think those buildings were going to stand, and then one of them fell. Then the other. I looked at my wife and said, "We just lost hundreds of firemen in that building. Hundreds of guys were just killed." You know firemen. People run out of a burning building and firemen run in. I knew that everybody down there was going to be inside the building. I told my wife I had to go into the city.

I knew my company would be down there. I didn't call them at all. I just got in the car and drove in. I didn't know what I was going to encounter. I didn't know if the Long Island Expressway was going to be bumper-to-bumper traffic or what. The police had every entrance and exit closed. The only way you could get on the expressway was with your badge and your ID. So it was actually a lot easier than I thought it was going to be. There were hundreds of cars filled with cops and firemen streaming into the city.

At a rally point in Cunningham Park, Queens, hundreds of firemen waited for city buses to come in and pick them up. We waited our turn. They had a sign-up list. We signed and then got on the bus. Fifty firemen were on it. They looked like guys who had been on the job for a while. And nobody was saying anything to each other. We all looked out the window at the skyline of New York City, and the huge plume of smoke going miles up into the air.

The city was closed below Twenty-ninth Street, but we went right down in the bus, which pulled up a few blocks before the Trade Center. Everything was covered with that gray ash. Millions of pieces of paper just rained down. Cars that had been on fire were damaged by debris that had fallen. Windows were broken all over the place.

There were several inches of dust. We couldn't even hear our own footsteps. Nobody was talking. There was no sound, no cars. Downtown Manhattan in the middle of the day, and it was absolutely silent. We got within sight of where the towers should have been when the church bells downtown started to ring. I took it as a reminder of hope. I couldn't tell you which church, or where it was coming from, or even if it was more than one church. I don't know how many bells they have in their steeple, but they were definitely church bells.

We went a little closer and I could see one of the buildings, I think it was number 4, and it was burning all across the top floor. Right in front of the building was a flagpole with the American flag still up. It was tattered and torn. Smoke was billowing out. Flames were shooting out the windows. And then one of the guys I was with said, "Hey, look, there's 7 truck. Your rig is here." And it was operating.

I ran down there hoping that it was going to be our guys on the rig, and it wasn't. Everybody was facing the building, and I didn't recognize anybody from behind, and then one by one I saw them turning around and there were guys from different companies operating the rig. I climbed up inside to look at the riding list. Every company's got a riding list of who's on the rig, in case of a disaster or something like that. I saw the names of the guys who were working that day. And you knew, just looking at the devastation and the enormity of this, that we would be lucky to find them.

Our firehouse lost nine guys that day, the six on the rig, two guys who had been promoted from our company, and a new guy who was on a rotation and was working on 15 truck down by the seaport.

A couple of guys from my firehouse went through an atrium and then climbed out onto that pile out on West Street. The guys from my firehouse were searching, and it was a very frustrating, overwhelming feeling. You wanted to search. You wanted to find somebody. But we were down there with our bare hands. We had nothing, no tools to work with. Those beams weigh forty-one tons each. So you couldn't move anything. And everything else was pulverized. I mean, you had 220 stories in all. Each story was a square acre of telephones, desks, chairs, rugs, everything that builds an office. And you couldn't identify anything. You couldn't find a single thing that you could identify as something like a handset on a telephone, or even a piece of wire. There was paper that blew across the river into Brooklyn, millions of pieces of paper everywhere. But nothing else.

We live out in Northport. It's about forty miles outside of Manhattan. My son was getting ready for school, and it was still warm that day. I was getting ready to head into the city. This was within a week or so, two weeks maybe. And he said, "Dad, I think there's something burning in the bathroom. It smells like an electrical fire or something." The bathroom window was open, and the smoke that day was blowing out over the island from the city. You could still smell the smoke forty miles away.

Following September 11, I had a chance to look back and think about it a bit. I was never prouder to be an American. The outpouring of compassion from everywhere was incredible. People from all across the country just filled up trucks with supplies and drove toward New York City without a final destination, without instructions or directions or anything. And when they showed up downtown, they asked, "Where can we give this stuff? Where it will do the most good?" It was just inspiring to see people like that, lines of people on the street waiting to give blood, volunteers from all over the country, firemen from all over the place coming down to help out in any way they could. People stopped by the firehouse, hundreds of people every day, with candles and flowers.

My family has almost a century-long history with the fire department: my great-uncle, my grandfather, my father, my wife's father, several cousins. My nephew is now in the same firehouse with me. Prior to September 11, the greatest loss of firefighters in any one time was in 1966, when twelve firemen died in a fire on Twenty-third Street and Broadway, right across the street from the Flatiron Building. My father was one of the guys killed in that fire. John Finley. He was a lieutenant. When I was a kid, my mother came into my room and gave me a little prayer that was framed. It was the Serenity Prayer. I had it on my headboard as a kid, the whole time I was growing up. It says, "Lord, grant me the serenity to accept the things I cannot change, the courage to change the things I can, and the wisdom to know the difference."

Down there on September 11 we lost fathers and sons. There were brothers looking for brothers down there, fathers for sons, sons for fathers. You hear the term "brotherhood" all the time, but the fire department really is a family. We spend as much time with each other as we do our own families at home. My great-uncle's name was John Finley also, and he died in quarters in 1915. His wife became the matron up there, at 8 Engine on Fifty-first Street. Back in those days there wasn't much of a pension system. They would reserve the job of matron for the widow of a fireman who died in the line of duty. So she was the matron there from 1915 until the late 1960s. And because there was no pension, all the firemen would chip in together, out of their pockets, and they would pay the matron to come by the firehouse and sew buttons on uniforms or fix a meal or make a bed.

My father worked in that firehouse when he was a fireman, and sometimes I went with him. We used to live in Queens. On payday, he would sit around and talk with the guys in the firehouse, while I played on the fire truck. I'd always want to ring the bell before I left. He would say to me, "Only ring it once," because they had a bell system back then, so all the firemen were always hearing bells. Five bells meant the engine, seven bells meant the truck, and they also gave the box number with bells.

I can relate to these families. They can't believe what happened. They're asking, "How can there be a God if this happened?" Why them? They probably all have some item of clothing that their loved one wore that they're not going to get rid of. They're not going to put it in the laundry and wash it because they can still put it up to their face and still smell it and smell the person that they lost. They won't talk about it, but they do it. I mean, they're in the very early stages. I've had thirty-six years to figure things out.

My wife and I have been married for eighteen years. When we first got married, my sister pulled her aside at a family gathering as we were telling stories about my father. She said to my wife, "Get used to this. You're going to hear these stories a million times." We often talk about good stories and bad stories and happy stories and sad stories, about people in my family who are gone. My father still lives in our memories. My parents had twenty-three grandchildren. My father only knew three of them, but all twenty-three of those kids could tell you stories about him.

You hear people talk about closure all the time. That's a big popular catchword. But there actually is no such thing as closure. There might be closure when you buy a house. There might be other kinds of closure, but there is no closure when you lose someone. There's an evolution that takes place, but you spend the rest of your life grieving.

When I first got to the firehouse, the other firemen didn't understand: "Why would you want to work here? Why did you want to become a fireman in the first place? Why did you want to work in this firehouse where your father was working when he was killed?" Well, I always wanted to be a fireman, but one of the reasons is because it makes me feel closer to my father. And I feel closer to him by working in the firehouse where he worked. It might make other people feel uncomfortable, but it makes me feel good. You can't run away from something like this. You have to face up to it. You have to deal with it.

KENNETH ESCOFFERY
43, Ladder 20, FDNY

"WORKING WITH GUYS THIRTEEN YEARS, TEN YEARS, EATING AND SLEEPING, WORKING AND LAUGHING AND SWEATING WITH THESE GUYS, THEN YOU COME IN THE FIREHOUSE AND THEY'RE NO LONGER THERE. IT'S LIKE THEY DISAPPEARED."

I got relieved from work about eight-thirty on the morning of September 11. I had worked the night before. We were standing outside the firehouse, on Lafayette Street between Spring and Prince, when a plane, flying low, showed up directly across from the firehouse. Before we realized what was happening, we heard the collision and saw the smoke.

We ran back inside the firehouse and alerted the others that the plane had crashed. Everyone that was working the day tour suited up in their bunker gear and jumped on rigs which proceeded toward the direction of the smoke. There were three of us left at the station—myself and two other gentlemen—and we turned on the TV. That's when we realized that the plane had hit the World Trade Center.

I was also involved in the '93 World Trade incident, so I knew they would need a lot of help. We decided to go see if we could help. As we pulled up in front of the North Tower, about ten minutes behind our company, we saw the devastation.

We went into the lobby, which was functioning as the command station. One gentleman took a radio and ran up the staircase, and that was the last time we saw him. We were told our company was working its way up from the twenty-seventh floor. The chief asked us to stay in the lobby and check the elevators to make sure everybody was out of them. Most of the elevator doors were blown off the track. There were a few elevators working in the lower bank.

The chief then asked us to go up to the mezzanine level, where you can actually walk around and look down onto the lobby. Someone had said there was a fire there. He wanted us to check it out. Sure enough, there was a fire in the corner. It looked like jet fuel was running down one side of the building. But it was pretty much contained. A Port Authority cop asked us if we could give him a hand with an overweight person on the staircase. I believe that's when the second plane hit. At that time we didn't know what it was. I thought maybe the elevators had fallen down the shaft and made that explosion. You could actually feel the wind from the blast when going up the staircase.

We didn't have a radio. We didn't have equipment. We didn't have a mask. We didn't have a flashlight. We had nothing. But we helped people evacuate down the staircase to the mezzanine level so they could cross over the catwalk and go north. Once you cross the catwalk, you can look down and see the street. We stayed on the staircase for about forty minutes trying to help evacuate people. There was not a lot of dust on the staircase, but there was enough that it was becoming difficult to breathe. So my partner George and I decided to work our way out. One of us stayed in the hallway and one worked forward, trying to get other firemen to come back with some flashlights so people could see well enough to evacuate safely.

We got into the courtyard and crossed over the North Tower to building 6. Somewhere in there, about thirty feet away from the West Side Highway, we heard what sounded like an incoming missile. We started to run. It seemed like we had a good five-second run when a blast knocked us down. We were lying on the sidewalk out on the West Side Highway. I happened to find a hose that somebody had stretched into the building. I crawled on it back to an engine pumper, so I was able to wash my face, wash out my mouth. I started shouting, "George," to my partner. I knew he was right behind me but I didn't hear him, so I started to crawl back on the hose to where I believed he should have been, and as I crawled, I yelled his name. Finally he yelled back that he was okay. Later on we found out that it wasn't the North Tower but the South Tower that had collapsed then.

We wet our hoods and put them over our mouths. It took until Chambers Street before we could breathe what is considered air. When we got close to Chambers, doctors came up and said we should wash all the debris off our skin. After that, we went back to look for our company, hoping they got out.

By the time the North Tower collapsed, we were far enough away that we were really out of danger. We basically walked up and down the West Side Highway just hoping to see companies coming out of that cloud of dust, especially members of our own. No one had seen Ladder 20. We waited the whole day hoping that we'd hear that the guys in our house were okay. Even late that night we went back to the firehouse, and I think that was the hardest part, when you had the loved ones calling and asking, "Did you see this person?" and you have to tell them, "No, I didn't." And the longer this went on, the worse it was. And you couldn't tell them that you didn't think they'd made it. People down there realized as the search went on that a lot of these guys weren't coming back.

For the first week or two, most of the company downtown was part of the recovery. For two weeks we didn't have a rig. We went back down to Ground Zero to dig and to search for survivors. But once you got down there, it seemed like such an impossible task. A lot of guys again didn't have any tools, and the guys who did have tools would cut and dig and the rest of the firemen would just get in the bucket line and move debris and dirt. That's basically what we did.

As for Ladder 20, we lost all six guys that responded on the rig and one guy that apparently came after. He had gotten off that morning and left the firehouse. Somehow he went back and drove down on his own. They found him with the engine company, Squad 18, that had also responded from our quarters. So between the squad and Ladder 20, we lost fourteen: six guys working from the engine, six guys from the truck, one guy that was off duty from the engine, and one guy that was off duty from the trucks. Out of the first sixteen that responded down there, we lost fourteen. Only George and I made it, because the chief asked us to check the elevators and then check the second floor, and we didn't go up the staircase.

September 10 was my eighteenth wedding anniversary. We do mutuals in the firehouse. If, say, I'm working Monday day, Tuesday day, and you're working Monday night, Tuesday night, I could say, "All right, since you're there Monday, you do my Monday night. I'll do your Tuesday." So I had a mutual partner, and we normally do our mutuals two weeks in advance. So when I realized that September 10 was my anniversary, and I was working, I didn't want to call him to switch it. I didn't want to inconvenience him. So I pretty much told the wife, "We can celebrate on the eleventh." Now if I had swapped it, and come in Tuesday morning, he would have been the one getting off, and I would have been the one on the rig.

I've been to a lot of funerals, too many. It was a wake one day, a funeral the next day. Every week. I mean, just for the fourteen guys that responded from my house, that was more than enough. I would say the average fireman probably went to twenty-five, thirty funerals, not even counting the wakes. It got to the point where a lot of guys just got burnt out. After a month or two of this, you just had to shut it down.

I still haven't quite adjusted yet. Working with guys thirteen years, ten years, eating and sleeping, working and laughing and sweating with these guys, then you come in the firehouse and they're no longer there. It's like they disappeared. Sleeping was really rough the first few weeks. I kept hearing the sounds of bodies hitting the pavement, hitting the buildings. I'm standing in the lobby and it sounded like every five or ten seconds somebody hit the pavement. You'd see a piece of body part fly by—a hand, ears. The most difficult part for me was getting that sound out of my head. I'd be sitting in the kitchen and if someone behind me dropped a chair, I would jump.

Most of the members of the firehouse were coughing for two months. The job gave us all a medical and they wound up taking blood. I guess they wanted to store the blood in case complications come up later on in our lives. And I believe they will. Ten years from now, who knows how many of these guys may die from cancer?

The fire department put a counselor in each firehouse that lost members. So we have someone that comes in. He spends anywhere from five to ten hours a week in the firehouse. But I don't know how much guys are using him. I've spoken to him, but it's not like we're in a private area. You can get away from one side of the firehouse, but you're still in the firehouse. People are still moving and walking around, so I don't think you'll get much out of me.

JOE GRAZIANO
47, Ladder 13, FDNY

"I REMEMBER AS I WAS LEAVING, I THOUGHT, MAN, THIS IS DÉJÀ VU.
I HAD THE WORST FEELING OF DÉJÀ VU I'VE EVER HAD. I SAID,
'I'VE DONE THIS BEFORE.' I JUST COULDN'T REMEMBER THE ENDING."

I was in the kitchen in the firehouse on Eighty-fifth Street between Third and Lex, watching CNN or one of those stations. As soon as the second plane hit, we got the call to go down to the Trade Center. We got on the truck and it seemed like the city just opened up for us. I mean, we got down there in no time. We didn't even have a chance to unbutton our coats before they told us that we were going into tower 1. There were six of us, and I was the only one that came back.

I don't really know the Trade Center that well because it's pretty far out of our district. But I remember we were on the west side, where the atrium was. We went into the lobby and got everything together and they told us that we were going to go up to the forty-fourth floor to start searching. We passed a spiral staircase, which I guess went up to the hotel. We got to the first set of elevators and there was nothing. We went to the second set of elevators and we found one elevator that went up to the twenty-fourth floor, and that's the one we got on. So we started to search from the twenty-fourth floor. We started to search offices which were as big as football fields. I'd never seen anything like it. We're in one office, in a little cubicle, and all of a sudden the glass blew in on us. I was with Dennis McHugh, and I looked out and saw a body on the setback, a smaller part of the building, which was the Marriott Hotel, I think. Dennis and I came back to the elevator banks and I turned to the captain, Walter Hynes, and said, "Cap, I think the building blew up above us. There's a jumper on the setback."

And Walter said, "I think you're right." And he radioed down. But in hindsight now, I know that that glass breaking was tower 2 coming down. But we didn't know that then. The windows we were near looked out in another direction, to the top of the hotel. We couldn't see the other tower. We just thought it was something happening above us. They always teach us, whenever there's any kind of terrorism, you have to be aware of secondary explosions. If they're going to blow up a building, they're going to put in more than just one bomb. So we figured it was some kind of secondary explosion within the building we were in.

A few minutes after Captain Hynes radioed down, they told us to evacuate the building. And that's what we started to do. We went down from 24 to 23, and there was a security lock, which we popped, and we went into those offices and started to search them for people. There was nobody there, so we dropped down to 22. We were on the B stairwell and we were grabbing people off the A stairwell and bringing them to the B. We continued down one more flight when we ran into a fireman, Billy Kasey, from Engine 21, who I know now but didn't know then. He was carrying a gentleman who was having heart problems, a big guy, and Billy was having trouble with him. So I turned to Captain Hynes, and I said, "Cap, I'm going to help this guy down."

And he said, "Good. Get that guy out of here." I gave my tools to Dennis and I proceeded to walk the guy down with Billy.

We coaxed him down. We didn't think anything of it. We told him we could stop and go into an office. We'd get him a chair. We'd do anything we could. We just said, "Look, we're not going to leave you. You don't have to worry. We'll get you out of here." We didn't think there was any urgency at all. The man's name was Ralph. That's all I remember about him. I remember saying to him, "Ralph, this is something you'll be able to tell your grandchildren about." I said, "Do you have any grandchildren?" and he said no. And I started laughing to myself, saying, "Come on, Ralph, you gotta work with me here." I found out that he did have some children, but he didn't have any grandchildren. I think he told me he had one child.

Eventually, we moved his legs a little. He was a trouper and we finally got him down after a long time. I remember passing other firemen in the stairwell. I passed all the guys from 2 Truck, and Captain Freddy Ill, who I knew from when he was a fireman up at 43. And the strap on my mask was falling down, and I said, "Freddy, do me a favor and fix my strap." And he pulled it up for me. I said, "Give it a tug so it doesn't move." So he tugged it, you know, and I just kept walking past him.

Billy and I finally got Ralph to the lobby. We started to go left, which would have been where all the stores were, in that walkway, and one of the guys from the building, I don't know who, told us, "No, don't go left. Go right. Everything is on West Street."

So we went right and we went out on West Street, and as we were walking on West Street, I asked somebody where the ambulances were and they told me, "Way down on West Street."

I said, "We can't make it that far."

They said, "Well, then turn left and go to Vesey," and as we did, tower 1 came down. I could see the building come right at me. And I still had no idea that the South Tower had already come down.

Billy got himself to the cyclone fence on West Street. Ralph fell, and I just lay on top of him. And waited. I was thinking to myself that something's going to hit me and my back is going to break. I thought about my four kids. I have three sons and a daughter. They're very athletic, and I wondered, What am I going to do?

We had water bottles that we had gotten from the forty-fourth floor, so I kept drinking the water and spitting it out. Finally, Ralph said, "Let me have some of that water," and I gave him some water. And I think I actually said, "Ralph, you gotta get up now. We gotta get the fuck out of here."

And I got him up. We started to walk a little farther and I got him to where there was a bagel shop and a Mexican restaurant, right across from the American Express building. And that's where all the ambulances were. So I sat him down and the guys from the ambulance took over and they made sure he was all right.

As soon as they cleaned me up, the first thing I did was get on the radio. And I kept calling and calling the others. And I got nothing. I was told to go to the river. They said everybody that came out of the building was sent to the river. So I went to the river and they weren't there. Then they said everybody was at Stuyvesant High School, so I walked. I just kept walking and calling and calling. Nothing. They were gone. And I remember thinking, I can't find them. They were nowhere to be found.

The guy that drove the truck that day, Tommy Sabella, who I worked with for nineteen years, was in the lobby. And he was the last guy I saw. I said, "Tommy, I'm going to take this guy to the ambulance and I'm coming back." I said, "Just tell Walter I'm at the ambulance."

So he said, "Yeah."

And I remember as I was leaving, I thought, Man, this is déjà vu. I had the worst feeling of déjà vu I've ever had. I said, "I've done this before." I just couldn't remember the ending.

I think about it every day. I think about Tommy in the lobby. Out of the nine guys who didn't make it from my firehouse, we've found seven, which is pretty good.

We thought Billy was lost, and he thought we were lost too, because we got separated when the building came down, but I saw him a couple of days later, so I knew he was okay. But people who had been standing next to me were now gone. Why didn't any part of that building hit me? I think about that all the time. I'm alive, but I don't feel guilty. Every day when I wake up, I wish I could go back. I just need five minutes. If I could go back and relive five minutes of my life, I would. I don't feel guilty because I know I didn't do wrong. I did what I was supposed to do. But I just wish I could have changed what happened. I wish I could have had another five or ten minutes to get them out.

MARCEL CLAES
47, Engine 24, FDNY

<small>"I SAW SOMEONE WEARING A HELMET WITH LADDER 5 ON IT.
I SAID, 'WHO'S HERE FROM LADDER 5?' THINKING, THIS IS GREAT.
THERE'S SOMEBODY LEFT FROM LADDER 5 HERE. BUT IT TURNED
OUT TO BE ANOTHER FIREMAN WHO SAID HE HAD COME FROM
HOME IN BROOKLYN OR QUEENS OR THE BRONX, AND HE HAD
GONE TO THE CLOSEST FIREHOUSE AND GRABBED SOME GEAR."</small>

We are with Ladder 5 at Battalion 2 in Greenwich Village, Houston and Sixth
Avenue, about a mile and a half from the World Trade Center. I was in Engine 24
the night before, and I was doing a mutual with someone in Ladder 5. The
engine was short so I stayed in the engine. Otherwise, I would have been with
Ladder 5 that morning. And they all perished.

So that morning I was sitting house watch. It was a really nice day. I remember some of the members coming in and things were normal. And just before the
change of tours, the call came in. I believe the ticket said, "An explosion at the

World Trade Center," which I didn't really hear at the time. I just heard the bells go off and I got on the rig and we headed toward the World Trade Center. On the way down, I looked out the window and I saw the damage, and I said to the probee sitting across from me that it was an explosion. When we got to the lobby of the North Tower, I found out a plane had hit the building.

I saw that the walls had buckled somewhat near the elevator banks, and the elevators were out. So my company started proceeding up the stairs along with other companies. It was single file of civilians going down and single file of firemen going up. It was orderly, and I was just thinking of the work that we had ahead of us, and I just kept climbing. I knew it was going to be a hard day, but I just kept thinking about putting water on the fire. That was my only concern at the time.

So we're climbing and after about a dozen floors we're exhausted carrying all our equipment, so we took a breather. We caught our breath and kept climbing. Civilians were thanking us, blessing us, and helping one another down. There was a woman on one landing and I thought she was having an asthma attack. She was really frantic and we were trying to calm her down. She mentioned something about her mother and her son. I asked her if they were in the building, and she said no. I said, "Don't worry, they'll be okay. Sit down." At that point, my company started climbing the stairs again. As far as I know, she made it out okay.

There were six of us and another probee, a new man on the job, a rookie, just out of school. I had one probee working with me that day, the nozzle man, and he was all excited. Another probee was off duty, and he went along for the ride.

We made it up to the thirtieth floor, which took some time, and we were catching our breath. At one point, we were catching our breath with Ladder 5. We made it up to the thirty-fifth floor, and one of our members was having a hard time. So I told the lieutenant, "Why don't we leave him behind because we have the extra man?" So he was sent down to the twenty-seventh floor, where there was a man in a wheelchair who needed help.

I was on my knees catching my breath, and all of a sudden we felt this rumble and we heard this noise, like a train was going through your living room. And I jumped up and ran. I wanted to run somewhere but there was nowhere to run. And then it stopped, so we figured we were in the clear. Someone said that maybe the upper floors had collapsed. We figured we were safe because the noise stopped. We heard members giving Maydays for chest pains. We just thought people were having a hard time hiking up all those stairs. I didn't know until later that the second plane hit the other tower.

Then the chief came by and told us to drop everything and get out. I was carrying a kit with tools for the standpipe. So I went back and got that. It was only a few feet away. Meanwhile, the other members from my company started down. So I'm the last one, and I forgot about the guy on the twenty-seventh floor.

They went into the hallway to get him, and I thought they were in front of me, so I passed them.

So I'm going down and I didn't see anyone until the tenth floor. I saw someone in the hallway telling me go to stairway B. I started up on A and I was coming down on A, but on the way down this man says to go to stairway B, for some reason. I didn't ask questions. I just went to B.

I saw our battalion aide and I asked him if he had seen anybody from 24 Engine because I was still thinking they're in front of me. And he said no. So I continued down, not realizing what was about to happen. So I was going down stairway B and I came across a woman walking very slowly. I was waiting because the hallways were narrow. There's only enough room for two people. I got impatient, so when we got to a landing I went around her and continued down. She was being assisted by a fireman.

That woman turned out to be Josephine Harris, and the fireman with her was Jay Jonas, from Ladder 6. But I didn't know that until much later.

I got to the lobby and I started getting confused because I saw a lot of dust and a lot more debris. There was some debris when I first started climbing, but nothing to this extent. I went out the same way I came in because I knew where my engine was parked and hooked up to the standpipe on the corner of West and Vesey Street. So I went out on the far northwest corner, out of a window. I saw a group of firemen standing there, and they weren't going out because a lot of stuff was falling. But I saw a man in the driveway waving me out. He's looking up waving me out. I went right out to the street, still carrying my tool bag and my cylinder on my shoulder. I turned around and was still confused because I didn't see the rest of my company. There was all this debris. I turned around and I saw one tower standing. Three people jumped from above the fire and my heart just melted for those people. Plus the fact that there was only one tower standing. I couldn't believe my eyes.

Not long after those three people jumped, the one remaining tower started to collapse from the top and it just pancaked down. I looked down West Street and I saw guys taking off. All I could think of was, How far do I have to run before I get crushed? I guess not really far because it came down fast. The cloud of dust started passing me so I ducked behind an engine.

When the dust finally cleared, I started walking away from the collapse area. Then I realized that I don't see anybody from my company. So I went back to the engine. It was still running. The supply line for water was cut, and there was a lot of rubble and cars and fire trucks on fire. I heard a lot of radio chatter and I tried to contact the other guys from my company, but I got no call back. I still didn't know what happened to them. At that point, I thought I was the only one that survived, and I was thinking, How could I be the only one that survived my company?

And then I heard that Ladder 5 was missing. I was hoping for the best. I mean, even for days after that: "Oh, they're probably caught in a void some-where."

By four o'clock that day I found some of the guys from the house. They didn't know I was working that day. But they knew Ladder 5 was missing because nobody had heard from them. At one point, I saw someone wearing a helmet with Ladder 5 on it. I said, "Who's here from Ladder 5?" thinking, This is great. There's somebody left from Ladder 5 here. But it turned out to be another fire-man who said he had come from home in Brooklyn or Queens or the Bronx, and he had gone to the closest firehouse and grabbed some gear.

After 7 World Trade collapsed, I started walking back to the firehouse. I knew family members would be there from Ladder 5. I saw some of the brothers that I knew. I told them that we had gone in there together, but now they were miss-ing. I tried to comfort them as best I could. People kept saying that they feared two hundred firemen were dead. I said, "I hope it's only two hundred."

I had a mission that day to put water on the fire. And that's that. I knew we were in for trouble, but I never thought the building would collapse. I was glad the chief said, "Drop everything and get out," because I didn't know what that roar and that earthquake feeling was. But once it stopped I figured I was safe.

I don't live too far from the water in Brooklyn. And whenever I go in that direction, I can see the lower Manhattan skyline. Something's missing. If you lose a leg, you'll always look for it—that's how I feel about the Trade Center. I've been looking at it for so many years, and now it's gone.

I'll always think about what happened on that day. It's not just the eleven guys from my firehouse that were lost. I've been on the job for twelve years. I've detailed to other houses on occasion. I know so many guys that have passed through, officers who have done spots at our house. I mean, we were like broth-ers. You could talk and sit at the table, joke around, mention your family. You're family with them.

The first three months or so were a blur. A lot of people come by the fire-house. They say, "I feel so bad. What can I do?" We set up a fund for the families with donations, so that feels good. People have been very generous with their cookies and cards, from all over the country, all over the world. A man from En-gland gave us a book with all letters from his students and a donation for the family fund. It never stops. But it does help. It does help a lot.

I feel like I aged twenty years in six months. My first few months, I was a bas-ket case. I couldn't remember anything. It's still pretty bad. I got glasses, early in August 2001, and they're no good anymore. I can't read with them. I've been meaning to go to the eye doctor to get a stronger prescription. And there are counselors and the help is there, but I haven't found it necessary to take any time and talk to any counselors yet. I'd like to, but I just haven't. The best people I can deal with are the guys at the firehouse. They know. They lived it with me, and that tends to be my salvation.

STANLEY TROJANOWSKI
45, Engine 238, FDNY

"LATER ON WE GOT A CREW TOGETHER FROM MY
COMPANY AND FROM LADDER 106, AND WE STARTED LOOKING
FOR LIEUTENANT WILKINSON. WE SAID, 'WE LOOK UNTIL
WE DROP, OR UNTIL WE FIND HIM.'"

I'm an engine chauffeur, Engine 238 in Brooklyn. I came into work that morning around eight. We received the original ticket around nine to respond to the first building that was hit by the airplane. We responded on a fifth alarm. There was an automatic second alarm—any high-rise fire or emergency is an automatic second alarm—and then it went right to an automatic fifth alarm.

We were instructed to take the Brooklyn Bridge, but it was closed to all traffic. We saw that the Manhattan Bridge was wide open so we took that and got over really quickly, made a left at the foot of the Manhattan Bridge, went underneath an underpass at 1 Police Plaza, and ended up on Barclay and West.

The area was already congested with emergency vehicles, fire trucks, ambulances, you name it. Port Authority personnel were running around with their walkie-talkies trying to direct traffic. They told us we couldn't get any closer. So our guys got prepared. They took the fold-ups, an extra cylinder. I actually hugged each one and said, "Come back safe." But I never got a chance to hug my lieutenant, Glenn Wilkinson. He had already jumped out and was helping the young kids get prepared, because he knew they'd be going into the building. So I just called out to him, you know, "Come back safe."

It's my responsibility to stay with the truck. After they left, I looked around for a hydrant and found one on Barclay, around the corner from West. I hooked up to it. There was a little water out of there, but not much pressure. Actually, it was showing zero on my hydrant gauge on the truck. But a little water was better than nothing in that situation. I looked around for a Siamese connection for any standpipes, or sprinkler systems that would be on the outside of the building, and while looking up, I saw debris falling, this and that, and then all of a sudden I realized it was people that were falling. Our guys actually had to cross West Street going downtown toward Liberty to avoid the jumpers. Otherwise they might've gotten killed too, just like my friend from 216, Danny Suhr, who was killed by a jumper.

I must have blessed myself between forty or fifty times, once for each jumper. Sometimes three or four of them jumped together. No screaming, no nothing. It was just crazy. I didn't realize at first that they were actually human beings. But you'd hear it every once in a while: a bump. Nobody really hit the ground close to me. I was on Vesey. But I could hear it in the distance: a bump, a dud sound.

You can't put out a fire without water or foam, and our guys were going up there with fold-ups. In any high-rise, you have pumping stations about every fifteen floors. I'm not familiar with the complex at all. I wasn't sure if they had any water tanks above the floors. The truck's responsibility is to rescue and evacuate. Finding the fire is the ladder's responsibility. The engine's responsibility is to put out the fire. Our orders were to go below the fire, to the command post, set up, and try to extinguish it. That's standard operating procedure in any high-rise.

So they went down to Liberty and got their orders to go to the north building, the first building hit. I heard from our guys. I'm pretty sure they were supposed to respond to the seventy-eighth floor, a couple of floors below the fire, and get together with other companies, and the chief up there would decide how to handle the situation. But they never made it up there. By the time they went through the lobby of the Marriott into the lobby of the North Tower, the south building came down.

I wasn't in contact with them at that time. I didn't realize it was a collapse. I thought it was just a couple of floors. You know, you hear Maydays, you hear all kinds of transmissions. I had seen an explosion, and everything just went black with the debris, and the dirt, and everything else falling. But I didn't realize the whole building came down.

I ran underneath the scaffolding of the building opposite the Verizon building. My rig was over there. Everybody was hightailing it, dropping their gear, and I was wondering, What the hell is happening? And I was cursing because I figure they planted some bombs there. I said, "Now they're killing us off. Now they have bombs throughout the buildings." I thought the initial impact of the airplane was just something to instigate us to go into the buildings, since they didn't collapse at first. So I was cursing and pissed off. And with the debris falling, I just managed to run underneath the scaffolding. A friend of mine from 229, a chauffeur, was running by, so I grabbed him and we managed to survive the first collapse together.

Then I went back to the truck to see if there was any water left, and I started washing off people running by and I made a little water curtain to try to clear up some of the air too. I started looking around to see if anybody was trapped, and I tried to contact my company on the radio. Between all the Maydays and all the transmissions I was trying to get 238. I knew I wasn't getting the whole transmission through, but I was just trying to make sure somebody from my company—the officer or the hookup man with the radio—could hear the call.

Somehow I heard 238 on the radio, so I figured they were alive. I started looking through the debris and lost track of time. You do what you can. You put out some fires, car fires, rigs. I managed to do what I could. And then all of a sudden, about a half hour later, I heard another rumble. I wasn't sure the first building came down because the north building was blocking my view. Now I heard more rumbling, and saw the big cloud and debris and fire and everything.

I got knocked down by the force and I managed to crawl over a three-foot divider. I didn't have any oxygen or gear. The guys from my rig who went had everything, even my mask. You're choking, trying to breathe, your eyes are full of debris, you can't see anything. But we pulled out one fireman. A couple of us got him into an ambulance. He was in cardiac arrest, bleeding. Four surgeons showed up out of the blue. I had a radio, but the command post was all in disarray.

We reorganized on Warren Street, just trying to do what we could. I grabbed one of the surgeons who was with the fireman, who was unconscious. I said to the surgeon, "Why don't you go with him? See what you can do in the back of the ambulance." I couldn't contact anyone. If there are important transmissions between the Maydays, you don't want to step on them. But I tried to call my company every once in a while, 238 again, and I thought I heard someone answer.

Meanwhile, I tried to put out some fires. A police car on the corner of Vesey and West was on fire, and a three-and-a-half-inch line that was supplying the ladder was severed. A couple of young kids, maybe in their teens or maybe their early twenties, tried to help me get the line from under all the debris to get some water on the fires. They were just civilians. There were a lot of cops sitting there dazed, all full of debris. I couldn't get their attention. "Come, give me a hand." They were just dazed.

I still hadn't seen anybody from my company. I thought I heard someone saying, "North of the overpass." I asked around, "Anybody see 238?" I saw one guy with 238 tags, so I knew somebody was alive. I tracked down two other guys from my company. It turned out later that everybody was accounted for except my lieutenant.

Later on we got a crew together from my company and from Ladder 106, and we started looking for Lieutenant Wilkinson. We said, "We look until we drop, or until we find him."

We actually found him in the debris, south of the north overpass, about 250 feet west of the Marriott Hotel. He was underneath beams and debris. It took us until six in the morning to cut him out. By the grace of God, somebody found him. I'm not going to get into too many particulars, but we recovered the lieutenant's body.

Our 238 just lost our lieutenant. The rest of us just got banged around. When the first tower came down, the guys in the lobby of the North Tower managed to get out with the lieutenant. But one of our guys didn't get out with them. He got out another way, but the lieutenant didn't know that. So he had gone back to look for him when the North Tower suddenly came down. We don't know if he got blown across the street, or almost managed to get away, but we had a body, so we're one of the lucky few, considering.

I've been a fireman for twenty-one years, and I'm retiring because they won't let me do full duty, and there's no way I'll sit in an office. I was given light duty because the CAT scans came back and everything was borderline. Nobody says I'm bad, nobody says I'm good. I had colon tests, I was coughing up blood, and I was out for a month the end of September and the beginning of October. I'm doing a lot better now. In January and February, things weren't so good. On Super Bowl Sunday they took me to the emergency room. The Sunday before that I was unconscious three times just from the coughing. They told me, "It'll all go away." I'm doing pretty well, considering. I still use an inhaler. I walk. I can't run. Actually in January, I tried to play a little basketball with my kids. My chest just tightened up after a couple of minutes. I couldn't catch a breath. That's when I went to my own doctor for some tests, you know, blood work and lung tests and everything.

But I ended up in the emergency room the Sunday before the Super Bowl. I actually started coughing and went unconscious in the emergency room for the third time that day. It also happened once behind the wheel. Luckily my wife was there. I went through a major intersection. Then once at my friend's house.

I cough, I wheeze, but I hope it'll go away. So I said, "If you're going to put me on light duty, I'm retiring." If they had put me on full duty, I would have gone back to work at the firehouse. I don't want to sit in some office delivering freakin' paperwork.

So I figure maybe my retirement was meant to be. I got pissed off after the World Trade Center. I figured, "Now we gotta kick some butt. We have to try to get even." And here I am, coughing myself unconscious.

JAMES FILOMENO
47, Marine 1, FDNY

"THEN THE SECOND BUILDING CAME DOWN
AND IT STARTED ALL OVER AGAIN."

On September 11, I was working at the Marine Division, Marine 1, off the West Side Highway. When I came into work, I was having breakfast with the guys when over the teleprinter it came that building 1 had had an explosion.

We looked to see. We went outside on the pier and we actually saw the big red fireball exploding into the building. And then it came over that it was an airplane that just hit. So right from there we went over on the boat. It only took us three minutes to get there. And as we were getting there, I watched the second jet coming, and I watched it going over our heads. We actually saw it crash into the building right over our heads. Shortly after the plane exploded, we watched people get thrown out of the building. They were cartwheeling on fire as they came out. We could hear the faint screams. Everybody was just about crying watching all this, all seven of us on the boat.

It wasn't too long after that the building started falling. We were already docked near the pier, right across from the building. I got off the boat and I was watching people running toward us. They looked like a herd of cattle. I watched debris coming down on them. I got back on the boat and people were jumping headfirst onto the deck, and screaming. People were trying to hand me their kids. "Take my baby. I don't want to stay here. Take the baby." People fell in the water. It was horrible, really bad. It's something I'd never want to see again, ever. And the debris was falling and it turned pitch black, like from daylight to nighttime.

At that point, I thought we were all dead. I thought, I'm going to meet the maker now. There was nothing I could see. Just screams in the background was all you heard, because there was no vision of anything. Then, after a while—it seemed like forever—it started clearing up, and I don't know how the pilot of the boat maneuvered out of there without seeing because he was literally blinded at that point. But he got under way and we took that boat to New Jersey.

I would say there were two hundred people or more on the boat. People were diving on the boat, just to get out of there. In Jersey, we dropped off a lot of people, including this old woman who dove headfirst onto the deck. I don't know if she lived or not, but she must have broken her neck hitting the deck. They carried her off the boat on a stretcher. There were people hurt all over the place.

So then we came back from Jersey after dropping off all those injured people, and we hooked up the boat and starting supplying water to all the engines that were headed toward the building. We had sixteen lines coming off the boat, because at that point the buildings had crushed all the pipe work for the hydrants in that area. So they weren't getting any water on land. They were depending on us. We were supplying all the water at this point. And it was really havoc. I mean, smoke and fire all over the place.

Then the second building came down and it started all over again, the same thing, people running, havoc, the worst. I don't ever want to experience anything like that again, ever.

And even now, you can't even begin to say what happened. The stuff that fell had asbestos in there, carcinogens, toxins, PCBs, you name it, it had to be in there. Psychologically, you don't even want to think about it. It keeps running through our minds like a tape that keeps rewinding and playing back.

I'm twenty years on the job and I don't know if my lungs can take any more of this stuff. I now have the end of asthma, the beginning of emphysema. I feel like my body's not working inside. I tire easily. I get winded right away, with minor exertion. They put me on light duty. I've gone for medical care. I'm on an inhaler. I do it twice a day, once in the morning, once at night. It feels like it's helping, but it feels also like it's bringing up the garbage that's in my lungs. My throat is raspy. It's hard breathing. My eyes are okay now, but they were real red in the beginning. Even the brown of my eyes was red. I was totally covered with debris when it came down.

At first it was hard to sleep. But now it's getting easier, I guess, because of the therapy I've been going through with the counselors. They help you get by this with other people. They talk about it. That's how we've been dealing with it. So I'm coming along better now, mentally anyway.

I've decided that I'm going to spend all my money, whatever's left. And I'm going to enjoy everything that I can enjoy, because nobody knows what tomorrow holds. Especially when you listen to the news. I think I'm going to get out of New York. Go someplace quieter, that's for sure.

Everybody was touched by this. Even on the block where I live in Staten Island, a couple of people around the neighborhood died that worked in the World Trade Center. It wasn't just firefighters. This affected everyone. And that's bad news. We're never as safe as we think we are. All these years, maybe we thought we were a superpower and that nobody would bother us. But after September 11, we now know different. I'm not going to be cocky anymore.

Lyzbeth Glick, right, with her late husband, Jeremy.

LYZBETH GLICK
32, Wife of Jeremy Glick, Passenger on United Airlines Flight 93

"I THINK HE SENSED PANIC IN MY VOICE,
AND WE JUST STARTED SAYING, 'I LOVE YOU.'"

I was actually on maternity leave from a teaching job at Berkley, a business college in New York City. On that Monday morning, September 10, Jeremy helped me pack up the car. He was going to California on business, and was booked on a flight that night. We live in Hewitt, New Jersey, right on Greenwood Lake, and I was going up to my parents' house in the Catskill Mountains while he was away. So he packed me up and then he headed down to Newark for a meeting. He called me at around five o'clock and said there had been a fire in Newark and he didn't feel like arriving in California at two in the morning. He was really frustrated, so he decided to go back home and get a good night's sleep and catch the first flight out Tuesday morning.

I was already at my parents' house with our baby, Emerson, who was just eleven weeks old at that time. Jeremy was a sales manager for Vividance, an Internet company. His plan was to take the red-eye back later Tuesday so he could be home Wednesday morning. He called Tuesday morning at around seven, before his flight took off. My dad answered and I was still asleep. He said, "Just tell her that I called and I'll call her when I get to California."

I must have gotten up just after the first plane hit, because the first thing I did was turn on the TV that morning and I saw that the World Trade Center, the first building, was on fire. I didn't even make a connection. I just thought it was a small commuter plane that had hit. So I didn't even really think twice about it. My parents were very nervous. They just felt something was wrong and were trying to turn off the TVs as I'm walking around the house turning them back on so I could watch the news. I saw the second plane hit, and I still didn't think that something could be wrong with Jeremy's flight. I just assumed those planes had come from JFK, and Jeremy was flying from Newark, so it didn't even register.

So I got the baby ready and I went downstairs. I was about to get some breakfast in the kitchen when I heard the phone ring and I heard my parents scream, "Oh, my God, Jeremy." I went into the room and all color had drained from their faces.

I think I started to panic, and I said, "Oh, my God, that wasn't Jeremy's flight, was it?"

And they said, "No. He's okay, for now." They added "for now" because Jeremy had told them that the plane had been hijacked.

They handed the phone to me. I was in the living room, you know, watching it, because we have a big-screen TV in there. So I was watching everything unfold as I'm talking to him. I think he sensed panic in my voice, and we just started saying, "I love you." We must have said it for ten minutes straight until it calmed us down. And then he explained to me what had happened, that there were three men who had hijacked the plane. One of them had claimed he had a bomb strapped to him. He said the other hijackers were wearing red headbands and he described them as Arabic-looking. He told me that they were going to blow up the plane. They told them to all stay seated. He said they had moved him to the back of the plane, and that he was free to talk. Nobody was stopping them from making phone calls.

Then he started asking me what was happening in New York and did they crash planes into the World Trade Center? I guess he had heard it from one of the other passengers. I hesitated for a minute, then I said, "Honey, you need to be strong, but yes, they are crashing planes into the World Trade Center."

And he said, "Do you think that is where this plane is going to go?"

I said, "I don't think it's going to go to the World Trade Center because there's really nothing, you know, to crash into."

He said he didn't think he was going to make it out. He told me he loved me and Emerson very much, and he needed us to be happy and that he would respect any decisions I made. And he sounded very sad. He kept saying, "I can't believe this is happening to me." I wasn't really agreeing with what he was saying. I mean, I knew what was happening, but I think my mind was saying, It can't be happening to his plane too.

So I told him to just be really strong and think good thoughts, and to put a picture of Emerson and me in his head, and be brave. And then we went into a kind of a planning mode. My dad had grabbed his cell phone and had called 911. They had tapped into my call, and they couldn't speak to me but they could hear what was going on. Jeremy didn't know who was flying the plane. There was no contact with the pilot, so he was unsure of what had happened to them.

Then Jeremy said there were three other guys as big as him, and they were going to jump on the hijacker with the bomb and try to take back the plane. He asked if I thought that was a good idea. We debated a little bit. He said that they were going to take a vote, and what did I think he should do.

I think I said, "You need to do it."

I also asked him if they had automatic weapons, or any type of guns, and he said he hadn't seen any. He had seen knives, but that wouldn't have been a problem. He's a very strong man, and large—six feet, 220. He was a national judo champion, so he was really well equipped with self-defense. I figured if it was hand against hand, or even with a knife, that nobody would be a match for him. So I told him to go ahead and do it.

And then he was joking. He said, "Okay, I have my butter knife from breakfast." So despite everything he was able to be a little bit humorous, which is very typical of Jeremy, always looking for the bright side of things. And then he said, "Okay, I'm going to put the phone down. I'll be right back. I love you."

I didn't want to listen to what had happened, so I gave the phone to my dad. And it wasn't until a couple of days later that I found out what had transpired. My father told me later that he had heard a series of screams. And then, you know, it seemed like an eternity, but it was probably only a few minutes, and there was a series of more screams, and then there was a sound that was inaudible, and it sounded like a roller coaster. And then there was nothing.

The 911 people then got on the line, and my dad stayed on the line for over two hours because it was the only connection, just really hoping beyond hope.

An hour or two later they told me that Jeremy's plane had gone down. The police were at my house and somebody said there had been some survivors on the plane. I thought, Okay, if there are survivors, he's going to be one of them because he's a survivor. My minister had come over and we just sat there and prayed. And I knew that since there was no call, it wasn't good news. United probably called three hours after the plane went down. And I said, "You don't even need to tell me. I know."

But six months later, it's still really hard for me to comprehend the magnitude of it all. Maybe it was when I got a call from Dick Cheney, which was three days later. He said that he considered Jeremy a hero and that he had saved Washington from further destruction. Maybe it was then that reality began to set in. It still comes in waves. I know that Jeremy just wanted to come home to me and Emerson. I think everything was moving so fast up there. They hit a rural landscape. Apparently, it was just a few miles from a high school in Shanksville, Pennsylvania. Had the plane been in the air for another minute it would have hit the school. So thank goodness it didn't. That gives me brief glimpses of hope, the thought that no other lives were lost. But at the same time I would do anything to have him back here with me.

Alice Ann Hoglan, left, with her late son, Mark Bingham.

ALICE ANN HOGLAN

52, United Airlines Flight Attendant and Mother
of Mark Bingham, a Passenger on United Airlines Flight 93

"AND THEN THE PHONE WENT DEAD."

When I first heard about the World Trade Center, I was standing in the living room of my brother Vaughn's home in Saratoga, California. Just a few moments before we had gotten a call from Mark, and he had told us he was on United Flight 93 and that it had been hijacked.

The call came in at 6:44 in the morning and a family friend answered it. We were all still in bed because we have young babies in the family and we were all trying to get some sleep.

Carol Phipps answered the phone, and I heard her pad down the hall past my room to rouse my sister-in-law, Cathy, out of bed. I heard Cathy run down the hall and I knew that something was wrong. I heard Cathy say on the phone, "Well, we love you too, Mark. Let me get you Mom."

Cathy saw me and she said, "Alice, talk to Mark. He's been hijacked." She also handed me a slip of paper that said "93 United." She had written this down while he was talking to her. I'm a flight attendant for United Airlines. My sister Candy is also a flight attendant and Mark was traveling on her companion ticket.

I took the phone from Cathy and he just said, "Mom, this is Mark Bingham." I knew that he was a little flustered because he was using his last name.

I said, "Hi, Mark," or something like that.

And he said, "I just want to let you know that I love you." Cathy told me later that he said, "I just want to let you guys know that I love you in case I don't see you again." But he didn't say that to me. He also said, "I'm on a flight from Newark to San Francisco." I spoke to Mark for about a total of three minutes. He said, "There are three guys on board who have taken over the plane and they say they have a bomb."

And I said, "I love you too, Mark. Who are these guys?" And then there was this long pause, as if he didn't hear me. It appeared as though someone was speaking to him and I tried to listen, but I couldn't tell what the situation was. I was so afraid that he was drawing attention to himself. But I didn't hear any signs of violence, no yelling or anything. And I was so relieved when he came back on and said, "I'm calling you from the air phone on the plane." I made a mental note that he was not using his cell phone. And then he said, "You believe me, don't you, Mom?" Or something like that.

And I said, "Yes, I believe you, Mark. But who are those guys?" There was another long pause, as if someone had set the phone down in an office. I could hear muffled voices and it sounded like there was probably a man's voice speaking English, sort of confidentially and low. And then the phone went dead. The three of us, Cathy and Vaughn and I, just sort of stood in the kitchen trying to figure out what to do. Vaughn turned on the TV, and we all stood there horrified watching the World Trade Center. One of the towers was on fire and there was a plane approaching the other tower, slowly and low, and it plowed into it. As I think back, it must have been a replay. We were still asleep in California when the first two planes hit the World Trade Center.

Vaughn said, "It's a suicide thing, and you need to call Mark back and tell him that he must do whatever he can to stop them." So I did. I called Mark's cell phone and left him a message that said, "Mark, this is your mom. Those terrorists on board probably intend to use your plane as a target." I meant to say "weapon," but I said "target." And I said, "Sweetie, you need to do whatever you can to try to stop it." I recited a couple of other things I can't remember, and I said, "Good luck. Good luck, sweetie." And then I hung up. Then I left another message. Almost a month later, when I was able to get access to Mark's voice mail messages, I replayed the forty-four unheard messages dating to September 11. Mine were on there and he had not heard them.

As it turned out, he didn't need to hear from me because, fortunately, he was seated right next to Tom Burnett. Tom Burnett was in 4C, Mark was in 4D, and Tom had the presence of mind and the good fortune to be able to speak to his wife, Deena, who told him everything about the World Trade Center. It was Tom who told Deena, "Well, some of us are going to do something." That's how Mark got involved. Both Tom and Mark were seated right behind two of the hijackers, two of the murderers who happened to be seated in 3C and 3D. The other two terrorists were seated in 6B and 1B, so that means that Tom and Mark were between everybody. I'm sure they saw the cockpit being breached. They probably saw one of the flight attendants being threatened. They may have seen the pilot being murdered, I don't know. But they saw quite a bit. It's interesting, Mark told me there were three men, so it's possible that one of them had not shown himself yet, I don't really know.

So I left those two messages and then I called United and asked them for information. The crew desk queried me. I had to establish my identity by giving them information about myself, my line of flying, and so forth. Then the crew desk told me, "Well, I'm sorry. We can't tell you anything. We don't know anything, basically." Then I made another call to United and I heard the automated voice say, "United Flight 93 left Newark International Airport at 8:01 A.M., and will arrive at 11:39 A.M., in San Francisco, Gate 83," Or maybe it was Gate 89. But I knew that I had more current information than that, so I called the FBI and I recited to them that we'd heard from my son. The agent there asked me, "Did he say that they had any weapons? Did he give you a description of these people?"

And I had to say no. He didn't mention any weapons, except the bomb, although we know now that they had box cutters and knives. They did tell passengers they had a bomb, and my conclusion and what other people have concluded is that there really wasn't a bomb but they were using the bomb threat to keep people in line. After I got off the phone with FBI—and they promised they would send agents out, and as a matter of fact they did—Cathy, my brother, Vaughn, and Carol Phipps, and I watched TV, and we were just thrashing around trying to think of things to do. We had called Mark, called the FBI, called United to get some kind of confirmation, and then we heard the news that Flight 93 had crashed in Pennsylvania. They had the footage so fast on television, and it showed rescue workers already on the site with a just a big, gaping, smoldering hole. That's the way I found out that Mark had been killed along with the other passengers. It's still hard to believe. I could accept it intellectually, immediately right then, but even now when I wake up in the morning, it hits me like shocking bad news.

The uniqueness of Flight 93 is that it was in the air longer than the other flights, and for that reason the people on board were able to find out about the fate of the other three flights and were able to mount an effort to thwart the hijackers and were successful, even if they weren't able to save their own lives. My family has received congratulations and thanks and condolences from many people, including a lady who runs a nursery near the White House. She said she knows that because of the efforts of Mark and the others that her life was spared.

We received a letter of thank you from the spouses of the members of Congress. A whole bunch of people signed the letter thanking me for the life of my son and his heroic effort. That makes me feel much better. Other family members who lost loved ones on Flight 93 have expressed the same feelings that, yes, it is a great comfort to know that our loved ones, in dying the way they did, saved the lives of hundreds of people on the ground.

Deena Burnett, left, with her late husband, Tom.

DEENA BURNETT
37, Wife of Tom Burnett, Passenger on United Airlines Flight 93

" 'YES, HE IS, BUT DON'T WORRY, MOM, THAT'S NOT
HIS PLANE. HE WOULDN'T BE ON AMERICAN.
HE'D BE FLYING UNITED OR DELTA.' "

Tom was in New York for a business meeting. I did not talk to him on the tenth. Normally, he called at least once a day unless he was terribly busy, and he did call on the tenth, but I was out. He left a message on the answering machine and for whatever reason he did not call my cell phone. I took it to mean that he was very busy. It was very unusual not to talk to him.

On the morning of September 11, I was awakened by the three children running into my room, as normal for most mornings. They came in a little before six [Pacific time] and I immediately got up and out of bed. It was Anna Clare's first day of preschool, so we were very excited about getting downstairs and getting breakfast over and being on time. Anna Clare and our two five-year-old twins, Halley and Madison, told me what they wanted for breakfast. I turned on the television. Our kitchen and family room are connected and you can easily see the television. I normally turn it on to check the weather so I can see how to dress the children.

I noticed that on every station there was a news report about the World Trade Center, and as I turned it back to channel 7, ABC News, they showed an airplane flying through one of the towers. I thought, My goodness, air traffic control must be terribly messed up. They're sending airplanes into the towers by accident.

The phone rang, and it was my mom, who said, "Deena, have you seen the television? They're saying this is an American Airlines flight that's gone into the towers. Tom's in New York, isn't he?"

I said, "Yes, he is, but don't worry, Mom, that's not his plane. He wouldn't be on American. He'd be flying United or Delta."

She said, "Well, do you know what time he was leaving?"

And I said, "No, but it should have been fairly early in the morning. He said he'd be home by noon." I could tell by her voice that she was concerned, and I reassured her: "Mom, don't worry. Planes crash all the time and Tom's never on them. Of all the thousands of planes in the sky, the likelihood of that being Tom's is just very slim. It can't possibly be his." She said, "Okay, I'll stop worrying," and she hung up.

I turned the news up again. The more I watched and listened, the more concerned I became. I kept trying to do the math in my mind: if he's coming in at noon and there's a three-hour time difference and it's a five-hour flight, what time would he have taken off and which airport would he have taken off from?

And then I thought, Okay, I can call his cell phone. I tried to remember if he had an itinerary. Normally he would have left one with me, but it was such a short trip that he did not leave one. I thought about calling his secretary, Kim, and realized it was too early to call, that she wouldn't be in at the office. I couldn't find her home phone number and didn't want to wake her anyway. And then I thought about calling his mom. Maybe she would know what time he was leaving and what flight he was on. And while I was trying to decide whether or not I should worry her, the phone rang again and it was Tom's mother. I made breakfast for the children while I was on the phone with her. And her first question was "Do you know where Tom is?"

I said, "No, I don't. I was hoping you would know." And while we were trying to provide each other with information and figure out the situation, the phone rang in on call-waiting, and I said, "Oh, let me go. That may be him."

And so I clicked over, and I looked at the phone and I saw on the caller ID that it was Tom's cell phone. I was relieved, thinking that if he was on his cell phone, he was in the airport somewhere and was fine. I brought the phone back to my mouth and ear and said, "Tom, are you okay?"

And he said, "No, I'm not. I'm on an airplane that's been hijacked. It's United Flight 93." And he told me what was going on. "They've already knifed a guy. I think one of them has a gun." I started asking questions, and he said, "Deena, just listen." He went over the information again and said, "Please call the authorities," and he hung up.

I just felt a jolt of terror run through my whole body. It was as if I'd been struck by lightning. I couldn't believe how I felt. I started reaching for the phone book, and for papers, going back and forth in the kitchen, pacing up and down the counter, trying to figure out who to call. I didn't even know what I was looking for. Then I thought, 911. I have to call 911. Maybe they can tell me who I need to call for a hijacking. I dialed their number, and while the phone was ringing I thought, They're going to think I am nuts. What can I say to them to make them believe me?

A woman answered 911. She asked, "Is this an emergency?"

And I said, "Well, yes. I don't know. Yes. My husband is on a plane that's been hijacked. He called me from the airplane and told me that they have guns on board the plane."

And she started repeating me. "Your husband's on a plane that's been hijacked?" I said yes, and she said, "Okay, let me transfer you." She transferred me to another lady, I believe a supervisor, who eventually transferred me to a man at the FBI. And he transferred me to a special agent. As I was explaining the situation and Tom's phone call, the phone rang in again on call-waiting, and I said, "I have to go."

He said, "Call me back if it's him," and I wrote his number down quickly.

And I clicked over and it was Tom again, and the first thing he said was, "They're in the cockpit." And I told him about the World Trade Center. He hadn't known about it yet. As soon as I told him, he relayed that information to the people sitting around him.

And he said, "Oh, my God, it's a suicide mission." And he started asking questions: "Who's involved? Was it a commercial airplane? What airline was it? Do you know how many airplanes are involved?" He was really pumping me for information about what was going on, anything that I knew. And he was relaying my answers to people sitting around him. Then he told me he had to go and he hung up.

I started calling United to find out what kind of plane he was on and they told me it was a 757. And of course, they didn't know anything about the hijacking.

I was sitting in a chair. I had fed the girls their breakfast. They were sitting on the sofa watching an airplane fly into the World Trade Center and saying, "Mom, is that Dad's plane?" And I said no. Because when he first called, they had gathered around me and they wanted to talk to him, and I said that he would talk to them later. They seemed to be fine with that. I just reassured them that Dad was fine and they shouldn't worry about him.

And then a news reporter came on saying that the Pentagon had been hit, and I started wailing. I mean, really wailing, making a noise that I did not know I could make, thinking that it was Tom's plane that had hit the Pentagon. I began to tremble. The girls were watching me and they started laughing. I had made a strange noise, not a crying noise but a sound of sorrow and grief and pain.

And when they saw the tears fall down my face and that I wasn't laughing, that I wasn't playing with them, they began to get concerned, and they ran over to me, and they started crying. I realized at that point that I needed to get control of myself, that I was alarming the children. And so I tried to contain myself.

The phone rang again and it was Tom and he said, "Deena."

I said, "Tom, you're okay," thinking that he had survived the plane crash. He said no. And I said, "They just hit the Pentagon." And I knew that he was assessing the situation and trying to figure out how to solve the problem that they were in.

He repeated the same questions: "Who's involved? How many planes are involved? Which airlines?" And he told the people around him that a plane had just hit the Pentagon, and I could hear people talking and spreading the news in the background and I could hear their concern and I could hear people gasping as if they were surprised and shocked. Tom came back on the phone and said, "I'm putting a plan together. We're going to take back the airplane."

I asked, "Who's helping you?"

He said, "Different people, several people. There's a group of us. Don't worry. We're going to do something." Then he said, "I'm going to call you back," and he hung up. And then he called back about five minutes till seven. I didn't even say hello. I just said, "Tom."

He asked, "Is there anything new?" I said no. He was very quiet this time, very calm. He had been very calm and collected through the other conversations, but he was very solemn in this conversation, and I couldn't hear anything in the background. I could hear the roar of the engines and I could tell that he was sitting in a seat and very still and not walking around like he had been. He asked, "Where are the kids?"

I said, "They're fine. They're sitting at the table. They're asking to talk to you."

He said, "Tell them I'll talk to them later."

"I called your parents. They know about your plane being hijacked," I told him.

He scolded me: "You shouldn't have worried them. How are they doing?"

"They're okay. They're with Mary and Martha."

"Good." It was just silent, and I could feel my heart racing. Tom said, "We're waiting until we're over a rural area. We're going to take back the airplane."

I became very frightened and I begged, "No, no, Tom. Just sit down, be still, be quiet, and don't draw attention to yourself."

He said, "No, Deena. If they're going to crash this plane into the ground, we're going to have to do something."

I asked, "What about the authorities?"

He said, "We can't wait for the authorities. I don't know what they can do anyway. It's up to us." He said, "I think we can do it." And neither of us said anything for a few seconds.

Then I said, "What do you want me to do? What can I do?"

"Pray, Deena, just pray."

"I am praying. I love you."

Tom said, "Don't worry. We're going to do something," then he hung up. And he never called back.

I kept waiting. I held onto the telephone for almost three hours waiting for him to call back to tell me that he had landed the plane and that everything was fine and that he would be home later. I started thinking about what I could cook for dinner. I was thinking about sending the kids to school, and who could come pick them up, because I didn't want to miss his phone call when he called. I thought about calling his parents to tell them that everything was fine, that Tom was in control, but I was afraid I would miss his call if I called anyone. So I just sat there.

A policeman showed up around the third or fourth phone call to sit with me. A neighbor who had seen the police car came over to see if the children were okay. Tom's sister, Mary, called from her cell phone, and I told her about the hijacking. Their other sister Martha and she went over to their parents' house, and called me to let me know that they were there. So there were actually many telephone calls coming in that morning, between his phone calls. Police officers and FBI agents called on the phone to ask if I had talked to Tom again. I updated them briefly, so I wouldn't tie up my telephone.

By the time his fourth phone call came, firemen had shown up on the front lawn. The children went in and out of the house, looking at all the police cars and fire trucks. I dressed them for school while still holding onto the telephone.

At about ten o'clock I realized that I had been running around the house all morning in my pajamas. I had Tom's old blue robe on. I had not showered or anything. I had not heard from Tom for about three hours, and I just thought I really needed to get dressed. So I went upstairs. I had the telephone with me. And it was really the first time I had released it. I put it on the ledge by the shower so that in the event I didn't hear it, I could see it ring. I never took my eyes off the telephone while I was showering. It was a very fast shower. I got dressed, and I went downstairs. The policeman was standing at the bottom, and I could tell by the look on his face that something was wrong. I asked him what was wrong, and he said, "I think I have bad news for you."

I remember turning toward the television and seeing that there had been another plane crash. And I ran over to the TV and I asked, "Is that Tom's plane?"

And he said, "Yes, it's Flight 93." I just felt my knees buckle and he pretty much carried me over to the sofa. I was so weak I couldn't even feel the ground beneath me. And I just started crying. It felt as though the tears were coming from the depths of my heart. I was just incredibly, incredibly sad. And I felt so alone. I've never felt such an emptiness as I experienced in those few moments.

I handed the policeman the telephone. But I kept thinking, People can survive a plane crash. And if he survived, he's going to call. But I looked down and I noticed that the phone battery was dead. The policeman hung it back up on the charger.

It was very difficult. All I wanted to do was go to church. I knew that my children were fine. They had gone off to school, and the principal had called to let me know that the kids were okay and that they did not know about the airplane yet. Several parents were picking up their children from school that day, but I decided to let mine stay in school. I thought that being there was better than being at home and seeing me fall apart. I felt like I needed some time to decide how to handle the emotions. And so I went to church. The policeman took me to church, and by the time I left, I knew that the media was looking for me. I went out the back door. The media was already there, questioning the priest who had been brought in earlier that day. I went home. The policeman who had been staying with me all day told me that I needed to brace myself because they were going to find out who I was and where I lived, and I needed to be ready for the onslaught of the media.

I remember being incredibly frightened about speaking to the press. I didn't know what to say. I didn't know what to do. But by six that evening, they had found our house and began knocking on the door and asking to come in or have me come out. And I spent the evening just crying and being with friends and having neighbors come in and out and having family call me on my cell phone to offer their condolences.

And so the next day, I decided that I would face the media, hoping that if I did interviews for one day, they'd leave us alone and we could go on with our lives. They came in droves, packs and packs of news reporters, as many as could fit in my living room. And I remember them saying that my husband was being touted as a hero. It made me laugh to think about Tom's reaction to being called a hero.

They asked me why I was laughing, and I said, "If you knew my husband, you would know that he would laugh at being called a hero. He would tell you that all he was trying to do was get home to his family." He realized the danger of the situation he was in, and he assessed the situation and tried to solve the problem based on the fact that he was a good man and knew right from wrong. He knew it was the right thing to do, not because he was trying to be a hero.

I found that having people call him a hero was a very difficult balance, maybe even an impossible balance. There was incredible pride on my part for his actions on Flight 93. And yet, there was the incredible pain of this loss that we suffered and the fact that my children no longer had a father, and that their father had been cut so short of being able to accomplish what he had planned to in life. I think we still struggle with the balance of the loss versus the pride.

LISA JEFFERSON
43, Customer Service Supervisor, Verizon Airfone

"THEY TOLD ME TO RELEASE THE LINE, AND I KEPT CALLING HIS NAME. THEY SAID, 'THAT WAS HIS PLANE, LISA. JUST RELEASE THE LINE.' AND I FINALLY RELEASED IT."

I work in a small office right outside our customer service center in Oak Brook, Illinois. On September 11, the name of our division was still GTE Airfone. It was recently changed to Verizon.

I had just heard about two planes crashing into the World Trade Center. It didn't sound to me like an accident, so I wanted to hear the news. The radio was on in the call center. As I proceeded out of my office to hear the news on the radio, I was stopped by a representative who told me she had a call from a gentleman who said that his plane was being hijacked. I immediately went to her station and I asked her for the appropriate information. I needed to report it to our surveillance center. In turn, they called the FBI and the airlines and all the appropriate authorities.

When I came back to her station she appeared to be traumatized. I told her that I would take over the call. I sat at her desk to take the call from a calm-speaking gentleman, and he told me that his plane had been hijacked by three people. He said that two of them had locked themselves into the cockpit, and one had a bomb strapped around his waist with a red belt. The flight attendants were standing and they asked everyone to sit down.

He was seated near the back of the plane. I asked him if there were any children on that flight, and he told me none that he could see. He asked me if I knew what they wanted. He said, "Is it money, or a ransom or what?" I told him I really didn't know.

I asked him if anyone was hurt. He said he could see two people lying on the floor in first class, and they appeared to be hurt. One of the flight attendants was sitting next to him and she told him it was the pilot and the copilot. He said he didn't know if they were dead or alive. At that point, the plane started to fly erratic, and he said, "We're going down, we're going down. Jesus, help us." I could hear the commotion in the background, and the screams and hollering. But then he said, "Wait, we're turning north. We're turning around. We're going back north. I don't know where we're going."

Then he called out, "Lisa."

Let me back up a little. When I originally took the call, I said, "My name is Mrs. Jefferson, and I understand that your plane is being hijacked. Could you please explain to me in detail exactly what is happening."

So when the plane started to fly erratically, and he said, "Lisa," I was surprised and said, "Yes?"

And he said, "Oh, that's my wife's name."

And I said, "And that's my name too."

And he said, "Oh, my God." Then he started telling me about his family. He told me he had two sons, David and Andrew. He gave me their ages. He told me that his wife was expecting their third child in January. And then we had a small family conversation.

I asked him his name, and he told me, "Todd Beamer, from Cranberry, New Jersey." He gave me his phone number. And he told me if he didn't make it, would I please call his family and let his wife know how much he loved them. And I told him that I would.

Then the plane took another dive, and he hollered, "Lisa. Lisa."

I said, "I'm still here, Todd. I'm not going anywhere. I'll be on this line as long as you." And he asked me to recite the Lord's Prayer with him. I told him I would, and we recited the Lord's Prayer. Then he asked me again to make him a promise and make sure that if he didn't make it, I would contact his family. I told him not to worry, I would. But we still had hope that they would be able to land that plane safely.

He told me that a few of them had gotten together and they decided to jump the guy with the bomb and gain control of the plane. I asked him if he was sure that's what he wanted to do. He told me that he didn't have much of a choice at that point. He said he was going on faith, and yes, that's what he was going to do. I told him I would stand behind him and support his decision.

Then he turned away from the phone, and he said, "Are you ready?" Someone answered him, but I could not hear them. And then he said, "Okay, let's roll."

I kept the line open for about fifteen minutes after the plane went down. Our surveillance center had traced the call to Pittsburgh, and that's where it stopped. They told me to release the line, and I kept calling his name. They said, "That was his plane, Lisa. Just release the line." And I finally released it.

I was very upset and started crying when I heard that the plane had crashed.

I never gave up hope that they would land safely, although I knew in my heart there was a possibility they would not. When I originally took the call, I felt like I was just doing my job. I still feel that way today. Lisa Beamer called me a pillar of strength and a rock for Todd. But I would have done that for anybody, and I would do it again.

When I got home and I watched all this taking place on TV, I realized that I was put in that situation by a power larger than myself, and that it chose me to be the messenger for the Beamer family that day. My name is Lisa, Todd's wife's name is Lisa, and when we called 911 to reach the FBI that day, the dispatcher's name was Lisa. I just feel that God definitely works in mysterious ways. I don't normally take calls out on the floor, and I probably hadn't taken a call directly on the floor in years. But that particular day, I stepped out of my office and went straight to the call. I just didn't think twice.

I met Lisa Beamer and I've talked to her several times since then. I haven't spoken directly to Todd's parents, but they wrote me, his parents and his grandparents and his aunt, to thank me for being there for Todd. I don't know, I feel like Todd and I formed a bond in that little time that we had together. I just wish there was more that I could have done for him. It's like I had him right here in the palm of my hand, but there was nothing I could do for him.

JOE BLOZIS
47, Detective Sergeant, Crime Scene Investigator, NYPD

"AFTER THE BUILDING CAME DOWN, THERE WAS A CALMNESS I'LL NEVER FORGET."

I was inside my office on Jamaica Avenue, preparing for a three-day training course that was to have started on September 12, when we were first notified that a plane had hit the World Trade Center.

I'm sure, like most people, civilians and law enforcement, my initial reaction was that it must have been a small prop plane that had difficulties of some sort and inadvertently struck the tower. At this point, I'm looking at it as a highly unusual occurrence and figuring that Crime Scene should be responding. I'm a senior sergeant in the office. I've been in the forensic field for over fifteen years, in Crime Scene for over ten years. I made the decision that we should start gearing up and head down to the World Trade Center.

While en route, I heard a transmission over the radio that I will never forget in my life. An officer was saying that another plane had just struck the other tower. As soon as I heard that, we knew it was a terrorist act, and we knew that this was an act of war.

I was in an unmarked car with three other detectives. We had two other vehicles directly behind us—our crime scene van, and I believe one other vehicle, our crime scene auto. As soon as we started hitting lower Manhattan, I remember distinctly that there were thousands of people running. The fright was etched on their faces. I could tell this was going to be a bad one. Something else that I won't forget is that the civilians, the pedestrians on the streets and sidewalks, were actually directing traffic to help us get through. Not only us, but all emergency vehicles. Streams of people, lines of people, were stopping other pedestrians and clearing traffic ways to get the emergency vehicles in. If it weren't for the pedestrians doing this, it would have been a nightmare getting emergency vehicles down to that site.

Neither tower had collapsed at this point. Both were on fire. Thousands and thousands of people were running. We parked the cars a few blocks away, in the vicinity of Church and Vesey. It was seven of us, including myself, and it was quite evident that this no longer was a crime scene investigation. Right now we were there to search and rescue and help the people getting out.

I will never forget when I heard the screams: "Run, the building's about to go down." Then I heard a large roar. The best analogy I can think of would be that it sounded like an elevated subway train coming in, but a thousand times the decibel level of a train. And that was the building coming down.

We had to look for shelter. People were running into alcoves, into buildings. We tried to get into one building and couldn't. I went under an emergency service truck, one of our emergency response vehicles. I couldn't get my whole body under the truck, but I tried to just protect my head region. After the building collapsed, there was a calmness that I'll never forget. That and the dust cloud, which came simultaneously. And when the dust cloud came, you heard nothing, and you saw nothing.

I made it back to where one of my partners, Detective Curtis Harris, was. He is a detective at Crime Scene. Once I got a hold of Curt, we went back into the dust storm. We were holding hands because we didn't want to lose one another. We didn't want to become totally disoriented. We put face masks on that we had brought down with us. Before we left Jamaica, I had the terrible thought that some type of biological warfare may have been used. I told the guys to grab the masks. I'm certainly glad I made that decision because at least we could breathe.

We tried to scoop up as many people as we could hear calling for help. We went out, we grabbed them, literally, brought them into our chest area, and tried to get them into an enclosed area. We knew those buildings were relatively safe. But more important, if you put a person in an enclosed structure, at least they could breathe. They're not outside in that dust. And that's what we were doing. We were just grabbing anyone that we saw coming out from anywhere, coming up from under trucks, coming up from their own little alcoves, coming up from subways, wherever it may have been. We were taking people and putting them inside buildings just so that they could breathe. All you could see of these people was the blinking of their eyes. That's all. You didn't know what color they were, you didn't know anything about them. They were in states of shock, I could tell. They couldn't really talk to me. I'd ask, "Are you hurt?" And I'd get no response. This was such a disaster that you either made it out alive or you were dead. The triage centers and the trauma units had a small number of victims going in. And that was the reason: you either made it or you didn't.

Maybe I'm exaggerating, but it looked like maybe eighteen inches of paper were covering the streets. Just tons and tons and tons of paper from all those office buildings. And the paper was catching on fire, which caused our emergency vehicles to go on fire. We needed oxygen for the people, and I remember breaking into emergency service trucks that were on fire, to clear them, to get at the oxygen tanks. We needed equipment before it was burnt up, so we were emptying out the trucks, taking the oxygen out, tools, ropes, and everything.

When that first building went, my first thoughts were for the guys in the building from the PD, from Fire, and from Emergency Services. We tried to do what we were supposed to do, but it's nothing compared to the people who lost their lives. The emergency workers and their families, those are the true heroes of what happened. Our mayor and our governor have often said, and our new mayor has said it too, that it takes a certain breed of people to run into a building as thousands of people are running out.

Then came that roar again, that same sound, and then the second dust cloud. That's how I knew the second tower had fallen. The second time I think I went into one of the buildings that was close by. Then you start to look around. "Where's the rest of my guys? We came down with seven. Are we all together? Yes, we're together." Now at that point I'm walking up Vesey, down by 7 World Trade and 5 World Trade. Our sister unit is the bomb squad, and I was stopped by Detective Danny McNally, and he says, "We just lost Danny inside the Federal Plaza area, between 5 and 7 World Trade." He was talking about Claude Richards, but we always called him "Danny" Claude Richards. A bomb squad guy. So Danny McNally says to me, "Joe, Danny is trapped on the other side. Can you help us?"

I say, "Okay. Let's go see if we can get him out." So we start to make our way. I remember we were met by firefighters who got on the radio and within a matter of seconds we probably had thirty firefighters from one of the rescue units. I relayed to their chief that we were looking for one of our detectives. At this point, no one knows the extent of the devastation. There were mountains of debris, stories high, that you had to climb over. The debris was smoldering. A lot of it was on fire because of the paper. I remember leaning up against a wall and I could feel that the back of the wall was oven hot. And this building wasn't even damaged. But it retained so much heat. Bottom line, the fire department wanted to send in an advance team to make sure the building was structurally sound, which they did. They came back out and said it was not structurally safe for anyone to enter. This was right between 5 and 7, right off Vesey. But these guys said their brother detective was in there.

"We gotta go back in there," they said. "He can't be too far into the World Trade." But thankfully, the fire department said no. That building did collapse. We would have had another thirty-eight, maybe forty more casualties, including the rest of the bomb squad, if we had gone in.

Unfortunately, Danny Claude Richards never made it out of there. I subsequently found out he was with Sergeant Mike Curtin, who I know from numerous jobs, and police officer John D'Allara, from Emergency Services. Gone. I feel terrible because John wanted to come into the crime scene unit from years ago. He put in an application, and every time I'd see him at different crime scenes, because we work hand-in-hand with Emergency Services, John would always be saying, "Joe, how's my application?" I always tried my best to get him into the unit, and it ended up he was in there with Danny and Mike Curtin.

MARK DeMARCO
49, Emergency Services Unit, NYPD

"A LOT OF THE PEOPLE WHO WERE LOST WERE A
LOT MORE TALENTED THAN ME, A LOT MORE KNOWLEDGEABLE
THAN ME. THEY'RE PROBABLY BETTER PEOPLE THAN I AM. . . .
WHAT AM I DOING HERE? HOW DID I GET OUT AND
THE OTHERS DIDN'T?"

I was assigned to Emergency Service Truck 1. On the morning of September 11, I responded to the corner of Church Street and Vesey Street. That's where we were told the responding units were mobilizing. When I pulled up, there was a male who was injured by falling debris, which looked like plane parts from the first plane hitting the first tower. We were starting to treat him, myself and Officer Brian McDonald, who is also from Truck 1, whose body was never found.

We were able to get the man on a stretcher and get him out of the area immediately. I was getting some tools out of our truck when I heard a massive explosion behind me. I turned around to see what it was, and it was the second plane hitting the South Tower. More debris was beginning to fall down. I dove into the truck to avoid some of the debris. Luckily, nothing in my immediate area was hit heavy. When everything settled, more emergency units responded. We all began to get together at Vesey and Church, getting our tools and equipment together. Some of us were donning ballistic helmets, vests, and heavy weapons because after the second plane had hit we figured it was a terrorist attack.

I was now assigned to a group, four police officers and one sergeant, five of us altogether. It was a team, headed by Sergeant Mike Curtin. The four officers were John D'Allara, Steve Blihar, Bill Beaury, and myself. At this time, Mike Curtin and John D'Allara are still among the missing. They've never been recovered from the site.

We were assigned to go to tower 1, to stairwell C, and help evacuate people out of the building. We had gotten to somewhere between the ninth and the eleventh floors when we saw a few people who were overcome, or unable to walk out on their own. We tried to calm them down. We got them some water. We did a search of that floor and then we proceeded back to the stairwell to go down with other people still coming down the stairs, when there was a massive sound. It felt like an earthquake, a rumbling. It turned out to be tower 2, and it was collapsing. People out on the ground—one person in particular, Ken Winkler, who was assigned to our truck—came on the radio and said that tower 2 had just collapsed. He told us to evacuate tower 1. In the confusion of coming down the stairs and evacuating people, Steve Blihar was separated from us.

It took us about a half hour to evacuate down the stairwell. Mike Curtin, D'Allara, Beaury, myself, and about eight to ten firemen and a civilian who was brought down the stairwell on a chair were all in the lobby together. There were no other civilians in the area, so we figured we had done our job in that location. So we started to exit tower 1 on the north side, out of the second-floor lobby. We were crossing over to building 6, approximately thirty feet away. As we crossed over, we were looking up because there were still bodies coming out of the building. Debris was still coming down and to avoid getting hit we had to constantly look up. When we got over to the lobby area on the outside of building 6, Mike Curtin directed myself and Bill Beaury to check the lobby quickly to make sure nobody was in the lobby, and then we would proceed through the plaza area west, over to Church Street to evacuate the location.

Two members of the bomb squad showed up, and the four of us entered the lobby. We got about three-quarters of the way through the lobby when we heard a massive rumbling again. And that was when tower 1 began to collapse. Everything went black in less than a second. It sounded like a freight train coming. I dove on the floor and you heard this crashing and banging going on, this deafening sound going on around you, with everything shaking. I said to myself, "I guess this is it," and I said good-bye in my head to my wife, Phyllis, and my three boys and I just laid there waiting to get hit by something because everything was turning to shit.

When everything settled, I said, "Is this death? Am I alive, or am I dead?" And then I realized that my leg was moving. I started moving my hands and I realized that whatever had happened, I was still here.

Everything was pitch black. It was like being in a closet at nighttime with the lights off. Three of us hooked onto each other—myself, Danny McNally from the bomb squad, and Bill Beaury. And in total blackness we felt our way along the wall. We yelled out to other people and managed to locate three more who were nearby. Little by little you could start to see. Little fires were breaking out. They looked almost like campfires.

The people who had been with us by the lobby door, Sergeant Mike Curtin, D'Allara, and the firemen, were in the whole part of the building that had caved in. It was like a massive crater. I felt that they were more than likely gone. We just happened to be in a small pocket of the lobby, and we survived. Three-fourths of the lobby was devastated. When I went back the next day, I brought my supervisor back to show him exactly where I was when it happened, and where I thought our missing people were. And when the dust had settled and the sun was coming in, I just couldn't believe how much of building 6 was gone. At the time I felt there was no hope for them. It was just going to be a recovery.

A lot of the people who were lost were a lot more talented than me, a lot more knowledgeable than me. They're probably better people than I am. And to think they didn't make it out. Why did we get out? Was it just luck, or was it something else? In the beginning, I had this guilty feeling. What makes it even harder is we've gone off to all the funerals and the memorial masses, and I look at the wives and the kids of the guys who are lost, and I ask, Why am I able to go home to my family and still go on with my life? All the other lives have been so drastically changed. I don't think I did anything wrong that day, and I don't know if I did anything right that day. Our purpose was to go in and help get people out. If I had made a right instead of a left. If I had been five minutes or two minutes slower. If I had gone with a different team. There were so many variables. Everybody who was there says the same thing: It was just luck, nothing more than luck. Or, if you believe in God, it was God's plan. I don't know. What am I doing here? How did I get out and the others didn't?

STEPHEN BLIHAR
42, Emergency Services Unit, NYPD

"I KEEP LOOKING FOR TOWER 2. . . . I KNOW IT SHOULD BE RIGHT
THERE BUT I DON'T SEE IT. . . . I LOOK UP AND BUILDING 1 IS JUST
CURLING OVER MY HEAD LIKE A WAVE."

I normally work out of Queens, on Emergency Services Truck 10, and my regular partner before September 11 was Paul Talty. But that day they flew me off to Brooklyn to be paired with Santos Valentin in Adam 7. When I got to work, Ronnie Kloepfer asked me whether I would mind switching with him because he had some errands to run, and I said, "No problem." Then we all went upstairs and we had drunk two sips of coffee when the call came over.

I rode into Manhattan from Brooklyn with Bill Beaury in the large truck, which is Truck 7. Santos and Ronnie rode in Adam 7, and we followed them. Tommy Langone and Paul Talty came in from Queens. We came in from Brooklyn. We all pretty much pulled up to the scene together. Both towers had already been hit. Santos and Ronnie pulled out their gear and went to tower 2. I ended up on the team with Sergeant Mike Curtin, John D'Allara, Detective Joe Vigiano, Vincent Danz, and Bill Beaury. Mark DeMarco ended up on the team too but I didn't know it until afterward because we started moving right away.

The streets were littered with debris from the planes. The first things I noticed were luggage, shoes, clothes, and papers. I took my gun belt off, threw it in the truck, and threw on my rappelling gear. We grabbed tools, rope, sledge-hammers, a medical bag, anything we thought could help us, and made our way down Liberty Street to the escalator behind the Customs Building.

The whole courtyard was full of body parts and burning debris. The scene was almost worse than what came later. Sergeant Curtin stopped us for a moment because debris was falling. He said, "Let's take this easy." So we started moving one at a time. He sent me first and I ran to what was a day-care center, across from the Customs Building. John D'Allara followed me. I moved around the bend, just opposite tower 1. John D'Allara caught up with me and I moved into building 1. It took a few minutes to run across because I had to keep looking up. Debris and bodies were coming down. I made it to the door, opened it up, and wedged a fire extinguisher under it, for the next person to come in, which was John, and then somebody else. They were filing in behind him and everybody was moving into the building. I radioed back to Sergeant Curtin. I said, "The only way to get to building 2 is to go through building 1. We'll never make it across the courtyard, between all the debris and other things falling. It's just not going to happen."

I found Stairwell D. A crush of people were coming down. Water was running down the staircase. We just started making our way up, floor by floor, searching, making sure nobody was trapped, making sure nobody was hurt. A lot of people were very grateful to see us and they gave us pats on the back and said, "Thank you."

We made it to the ninth floor and I remember filling a coffee pot with water and grabbing some plastic cups for everybody, because by that time we were hot and sweaty and I knew we were going to be going up at least another seventy floors. So we all had a drink of water and gathered by the stairwell. All of a sudden we heard screaming, "Get out, get out, get out," over and over again, and you felt the rumbling. Everybody hit the floor. I remember rolling against the wall, and the rumbling lasted for about ten seconds. Things were falling over. Lights were flickering and went out. Then the rumbling stopped. Then it was just confusion over the radio. Sergeant Curtin said, "Let's get back downstairs and find out what's going on."

We started down, and then at about the third floor we hit a group of people who were coming back up. The smoke and the dust were coming up the staircase, and these people were choking in the stairwell. There was definitely some confusion on the third floor. Sergeant Curtin looked at me and said, "Let's get these people back upstairs." So I started leading. I had a flashlight. I threw my mask on and started leading them back upstairs to the last place I knew, which was an open office on the ninth floor. I think it was a Bank of America office. I directed them to a sink and water because people were coughing and choking. I said, "Take a drink, wash your eyes out." I turned around and walked back to the top of the stairwell to look for my team. And they weren't coming. So I radioed to Sergeant Curtin and asked, "Where are you?"

And he said, "We're on the third floor. We see light, and we're working our way out." From what I remember, we were on the third floor and there was a civilian directing the men into a darkened doorway. I think they were worried about people being trapped in there. So they went forward in there to look. And that's the last I ever heard from them.

I checked the center stairwells and found one that was light and smoky, but not too bad. We went down nine floors to the bottom mezzanine area. We sent people out in the direction others in line were heading.

I looked down to the lower concourse and saw a team of ESU officers. I thought they were mine, and I went down there, but it was Lieutenant Holyfield with another team. I said, "Sergeant Curtin and a team went out another way. I got separated from them. I'm going to stick with you, all right?"

He said, "Sure, yeah, of course." So I stayed there. I still didn't know that the screaming we heard on the stairway of tower 1 meant that tower 2 had fallen. I had no idea that it fell completely. I figured it was just a facade collapsing, maybe the upper floors.

Then Lieutenant Holyfield made the decision. He said, "We gotta get out of here." So we took a chance. Even with the debris falling, we hugged the wall and we made our way out to West Street, next to building 1.

We were out there for about a minute. We're all just catching our breath and I keep looking for tower 2. I know I'm on West Street. I know it should be right there but I don't see it. I figure, Maybe I'm in the wrong spot. Maybe it's behind 1. I walk down West Street in order to look behind myself and then I heard this sick cracking noise. I look up and building 1 is just curling over my head like a wave. So I take off running down West Street. I remember running and then feeling this warm wind coming up behind me, and then I was just bowled over onto the street. And it was just an eerie silence because I was buried—by dust, concrete. I could still hear debris piling up behind me. I knew I had to get to my feet, so I threw things off me. I was totally blind. I took my first breath and it was like breathing in pure dust. So I threw my helmet off and pulled my mask on. I started breathing air, but I was still blind.

I had a general sense of direction and started feeling my way along parked cars heading away from the building. I walked for a few minutes when my alarm suddenly went off. I was running out of air, and I still couldn't see an inch in front of my face. So I started pulling on car door handles. I finally pulled open the door on a tow truck and saw the back of a firefighter in there. I pushed him in and I climbed in with him. He was throwing up on the floor from breathing in the dust. I took off my mask and I just purged the rest of my air into the cab for him and I to breathe, because the inside of the cab was also full of dust and smoke. I remained there for about ten, fifteen minutes until the dust settled enough where I could see about twenty feet. Then I left the cab and started heading away from the buildings to look for my group and the rest of the ESU officers.

Later on that night at Stuyvesant High School, when we were taking a head count, Tommy and Paul and Ronnie and Santos came up as missing. Same with Sergeant Curtin and some of the men in his group. It was a day of lefts and rights. All these little changes somehow worked out to my benefit and kept me alive.

Terri Langone, left, with her late husband, Peter.

TERRI LANGONE
39, Wife of Firefighter Peter Langone

"I'M EXPECTING WHEN THEY FIND HIM, IT WILL BE JUST LIKE THE FIRST DAY, YOU KNOW, WITH MY FEELINGS. I THINK EVENTUALLY THEY'LL FIND SOMETHING. THE MEN IN HIS COMPANY ARE VERY HOPEFUL. THEY'RE ALWAYS SEARCHING, AND THEY THINK THEY HAVE A GOOD SHOT."

My husband had worked overnight at the firehouse, Squad 252 in Bushwick, Brooklyn. I put the girls on the bus, and when I came in, the phone was ringing. He called me to let me know, "Turn on the TV, Ter. We think a plane crashed into the towers." He said he thought it was a bomb.

And then he proceeded to talk to me like it was any other day. He has a landscaping business, and he wanted to know, "Are the guys getting out on time?"

Then he said, "Keep the TV on and watch. I'm not going to be home anytime soon." And that was that. He was gone. That was the last time I spoke to him. And I was fortunate. I'm one of the fortunate ones to have spoken to him that day.

I stopped everything. I was hooked to the TV. And then, when I saw the second plane crash into the towers, I went to get my girls at school because I was really afraid. I knew he was already there. The first thing I did when the second plane hit was call his firehouse. And he had already been gone fifteen minutes. So he must have hung up with me and just went to the call.

So I went to get the girls, and I definitely knew he was there. I came home, and as I tell everybody, when I saw the building come down I knew in my heart he was gone. I knew that instant. I knew without a doubt, because I know my husband would have taken a cell phone and tried to call, or gotten in touch with me some way just to say, "I'm okay."

Did I check hospitals? No, because I knew the fire department. He would have been in his gear. They would have notified me. And he was definitely in his gear. There's footage of him in his gear. I just found out that CNN has footage of him and the other five men getting off the truck in their gear, loading up, ready to help people out.

He was in the second tower to fall, tower 1. The lieutenant must have split them up into two groups. The lieutenant took the two junior men and went up to answer a Mayday call. The last I heard, my husband and the other two senior men were downstairs in the lobby trying to take five people out of the building when the North Tower came down. They tried to exit the door closest to the fire truck. I guess the general way to operate is that you go out the door you came in. But, apparently, that door was blocked by the first tower that came down.

I found out about Peter's brother, Thomas Langone, later on that afternoon. He was a police officer with ESU Truck 10. He was in the other tower. We were calling my sister-in-law Joanne, who was working that day, to get her to come home. We knew Thomas was working, but we didn't know his whereabouts. She didn't get any information until later on that afternoon or evening.

Peter was with the fire department for sixteen years. We were married for eleven years. This was his career and he lived through a lot of close calls. I remember this one call when they lost three men. Three companies responded to that call. One went to the left, one went to the right, and one went to the center. And the one that went to the center lost three men. It was devastating. He came home in tears, hugging the children. It all depended on which way you chose to go. This was similar.

We had a memorial service. I still don't have Pete. They didn't find him yet. When they do, obviously, we'll finalize it. But we had a very nice memorial for both Peter and Tommy. I live this every day, and I'm expecting when they find him, it will be just like the first day, you know, with my feelings. I think eventually they'll find something. The men in his company are very hopeful. They're always searching, and they think they have a good shot.

MICHAEL McAVOY
43, Associate Director, Bear Stearns

—•—

"I CALLED HIS FIREHOUSE. NO ANSWER.
I KNEW MY BROTHER HAD TO BE DOWN THERE."

I was in my office, in downtown Brooklyn, with a clear view of the World Trade Center towers. Myself and two coworkers were walking back from the elevator bank after getting breakfast when someone announced that a plane had hit the World Trade Center. We walked over to the windows and there was light grayish-looking smoke. We presumed it was a small aircraft, maybe a Cessna. People from all over the floor were walking toward the windows saying it was a commercial airliner. We went back to the window. Now the smoke was thick and black.

I walked back to call my buddy Jimmy, my best friend for over thirty years. He worked for Cantor Fitzgerald in tower 1 on the 104th floor. No answer. Maybe, just maybe, he took the day off and went golfing. Man, I hope so. I tried his cell phone. No answer. I called Jimmy's wife, Sheri. She was frantic, and who wouldn't be? Jimmy was at work. She wanted to know what floor Jimmy worked on. I blurted out 104, the one with the antenna on it. I had hoped he had gotten out. At this point, no one knew what type of damage was done.

All of a sudden people here started to scream. The second plane had hit with half the office watching. I started toward the windows thinking, no way is this an accident. It's terrorism. We are being attacked. I saw flames coming from the middle of tower 2. I was thinking, how are any of those people above it going to get out? Then I saw a horrible sight: flames, smoke, and huge holes in both buildings. I ran back to my desk and called my mom. She told me that my brother John, a New York City fireman in Ladder 3 on Thirteenth Street, had worked the night tour, so he was still in the firehouse when the planes hit.

I called his firehouse. No answer. I knew my brother had to be down there somewhere, but I couldn't get in touch with Paula, my brother's wife. She was at work. My mom was in shock. At work, we looked on the Internet to see what info we could get. Everything was going fast and in slow motion all at the same time. I tried Jimmy's cell phone again. It just rang and rang.

We were staring right at the World Trade Center when tower 2 collapsed. In seconds it was gone. People screamed again. I looked at my coworker, Brian, and said, "Holy shit, twenty thousand people just died." Then I cried knowing my brother was there somewhere. I just knew. I still had hope my friend had gotten out. I called my buddy's house and his wife, Sheri, told me he was on the phone with a client when the plane hit, and the phone line went dead.

Again, I tried calling Jimmy's cell phone. Nothing. We went outside to see what was happening. Pandemonium, dust, smoke, sirens. It was like a war was going on. I guess it was. The city was like a war zone, people everywhere, police everywhere, and lots of dust.

We heard there were more planes, some going toward D.C. Jesus, what is happening? This is a war. God help us. I called my wife again and I told her about John and Jimmy and that she should go to Sheri's house in New Jersey to support her and maybe watch the kids.

Then tower 1 collapses. Now there is nothing there except smoke and dust. I'm thinking, another ten thousand to twenty thousand people dead. Then we heard the Pentagon was hit. I said no way, impossible. Christ, what's going on? This is not happening. It's a bad dream or a movie. There are still reports that more planes are heading toward Washington. Where the hell is the military? Scramble some F-14s!

I thought about going home, but it made no sense. What was I gonna do at home in New Jersey? Plus, Penn Station is going to be a zoo. I decided to go to my brother's firehouse. From a few blocks away I saw a ton of firemen plus a ton of fire trucks outside John's firehouse. I started to run. I had a little hope. I got there and I didn't recognize any of them. Most of the firemen there were from firehouses from all over the city. It was total pandemonium. I was nervous and scared. I just knew John was gone. I had a feeling.

Then I see a fireman I know. He is covered in soot. I look him in the eye. I say, "Was my brother down there?" He says yes. I say, "Any chance for survivors? You can tell me." He says, "Mike, I wish I had better news, but no. The place is the worst any of us has ever seen."

I spent the rest of the day at hospitals, or at the firehouse, or at my friend's apartment in Greenwich Village. I looked over lists of people who were taken to various hospitals. No John McAvoy. No James Ladley. You look at the list and try to will a name on it. I went to a special makeshift information center on West Eleventh Street and found a table for Cantor Fitzgerald missing persons. I started checking lists and filling out forms. I put Jimmy's name on the list, anything I could do. I was walking back to the firehouse when I hear a plane. Everyone in the street stops and looks up. It was like *The Twilight Zone*. At the firehouse, the fireman had no better news. I walked back to St. Vincent's Hospital on Seventh Avenue. Maybe I should give blood. At the hospital, there were stretchers and gurneys and tons of nurses and doctors, but no new arriving patients.

My brother was in terrific physical condition. He prided himself in being in shape. If he could have, he would have spent days helping people out of those buildings. He would have stayed there until the last person was removed. Period. He lived helping people. That is him in a nutshell. I think he got up as high as the fiftieth floor.

I have cried so many times some nights until I fall asleep. To put in perspective what I lost that day: I got married in 1981. My brother John was my best man. I had a child in 1985, Michael John. Of course, the middle name John was after my brother. John was his godfather. I got remarried in 1998. Jimmy was my best man. He was to be the godfather to my daughter, Marlena Joy, born October 12. The *J* in her middle name is for Jimmy and John. The terrorists took two of the nicest guys on the planet. Each had two kids. My friend's kids are two and four. They will never know Jimmy like I did. John's kids are eleven and fifteen. They are now fatherless. My best friend and my brother are gone. My heart is missing a big piece.

According to the teachings in the Talmud, "Whoever rescues a single life earns as much merit as though he had rescued the entire world."

On September 11, much merit was earned as rescuers in New York and at the Pentagon pulled person after person out to safety. Sadly, though, there came a time when it started to become painfully clear to authorities at both sites that there was probably no one left alive to rescue.

Some miracles did occur, as evidenced by the amazing story of Josephine Harris and the firefighters of Ladder 6 in Chinatown. However, despite the prayers of others who continued to hold out hope that their loved ones might also be found, a sense of futility and of the incomprehensible reality soon descended over operations that were now forced to change in scope from "rescue" to "recovery."

JAY JONAS
44, Ladder 6, FDNY

"WE WERE BEING BOUNCED AROUND THE STAIRWAY
LIKE PING-PONG BALLS. AND WE'RE ALL LYING THERE
WAITING FOR THAT BIG BEAM, OR THAT BIG CHUNK OF
CONCRETE, TO COME AND HIT US."

Today I'm a battalion chief with a covering assignment in the first division in lower Manhattan. On September 11, I was the captain of Ladder Company 6 in Chinatown. I had worked the night before, and I had come downstairs at about eight o'clock in the morning. Everybody was checking tools and equipment, making sure everything was up to snuff. And I was having a cup of coffee in the kitchen when I heard a noise. We didn't know what it was, but it was the jet trail of the jet plane going into the World Trade Center. And then we heard a loud boom. It was so loud I thought it was a truck driving off the Manhattan Bridge, which is very close to my firehouse.

My house watchman was standing in front of the quarters, and he saw the plane go across, and he was banging on the intercom. He said, "A plane just crashed. A plane just crashed into the World Trade Center."

So I went running out in front of the firehouse and I started questioning him, "What kind of plane?"

He said, "It was a big plane."

"Was it a commercial jet?"

"Yeah, it was a commercial jet."

"All right, turn out both companies," I ordered.

I couldn't believe what I was seeing—a large gaping hole in the upper floors of the North Tower of the World Trade Center with a tremendous amount of fire and smoke pouring out. Up to that point, it was the most amazing sight I'd ever seen.

We came up over by City Hall, cutting across Broadway on Vesey Street. A tremendous amount of people were running away from the World Trade Center on foot. We had to weave our fire truck through the pedestrians. We parked the fire truck on West and Vesey, just south of the pedestrian overpass that goes across West Street.

We started gathering the tools that we'd normally gather for a high-rise fire. Pieces of the building were coming down and hitting the fire truck, so we sought shelter underneath the walk bridge, and we kept shuttling back and forth to gather all our tools whenever we saw there wasn't anything falling down. Once we gathered all our tools, I made sure everybody was ready. We looked up and we said, "Okay, ready, run." And we all ran to the front of the building—six of us, including me.

Once we got into the building, the first thing we saw were two badly burned people right near the lobby entrance. And that was just a sign of things to come.

We reported to the lobby command post, which was in the northwest corner of the building. Chief Joe Pfeifer literally had two phones in his hands trying to talk to two different people. Deputy Chief Peter Hayden was now in charge of the fire. Lots of other company officers were just reporting in, so I had to wait my turn to report in and get my name recorded. We would then get our orders from there. While I was waiting in line, I saw this big black shadow on the ground outside. All of a sudden we heard another loud explosion. And that was the second plane hitting the second tower. We didn't know what it was at first. We thought it was something happening in our building. And a guy came running in and told us that a second plane had just hit the second tower, which dramatically changed the demeanor inside our building. Now it was painfully obvious to everyone that this was not an accident. They were trying to kill us. And we all verbalized to each other, kind of winking to each other, that we were going to be lucky if we survived this.

I looked at Chief Hayden. It was my turn to get my orders. I said, "You know, a second plane just hit the second tower."

He said, "Yeah, I know. Just go upstairs and do the best you can."

And we did. When I saw the badly burned people when we first entered the building, it was significant because it told me they were in the elevators. Which meant taking the elevators to the upper floors was not an option. So I told my guys, "This is going to be hard, but this is what we gotta do. We gotta proceed on foot."

We had all our gear on and we started up the B stairway, from the ground floor. I told my guys we would take it ten floors at a time. We'd go to the tenth floor, catch our breath for a second, go up to 20, catch our breath again. This way, we would have some energy to fight the fires, make rescues, and then do whatever we were going to do when we got to the upper floors. So we just kept going upward.

We made it to the twenty-seventh floor when I realized I was missing two guys. They were lagging behind us. So I told the other guys to wait on 27, and I would go look for them. I found them. They were just a floor behind. We all gathered together again on 27. With me was Captain Billy Burke from Engine 21 and fireman Andy Fredericks from Squad 18. I knew both of them very well. We were taking a quick drink of water and then we were going to press on, when all of a sudden we felt an earthquakelike rumble. Our building swayed. The lights went out for about twenty seconds and then they came back on. I looked at Billy Burke, and I said, "You go check the south windows. I'll go check the north windows."

And we did, and we met back at the stairway. I looked at him, and I said, "Is that what I thought it was?"

He said, "Yes. The other building just collapsed."

I said, "All right, it's time for us to get out of here."

We started gathering all of our equipment, and we start heading down the stairway. I hadn't picked up a radio notification to evacuate the building yet, so I was a little nervous that I was jumping the gun. I saw from the *9/11* tape that they were giving out the orders to evacuate even before the South Tower had collapsed. But I didn't get that on my radio. I finally picked up the radio transmission to evacuate the building when we were around the twentieth floor. And then somewhere in there, probably between 18 and 20, we came upon a woman named Josephine Harris. She was an employee with the Port Authority. She was fifty-nine years old, and she had walked down from the seventy-third floor on her own, and now she was having trouble walking. She doesn't walk well on a good day, and she was standing in a doorway crying.

One of my guys looked at me. He says, "Cap, what do you want to do with her?"

I said, "Bring her with us. We'll make do as best we can."

So now we had Mrs. Harris, and our progress was greatly slowed. She was able to take one step at a time. One of my guys, Billy Butler, has her arm around his shoulders. Billy Burke and Andy Fredericks started evacuating with us, but they had both peeled off. So now it was just my five guys, me, and Mrs. Harris. We were proceeding down the stairs as a unit.

We got to the fourth floor and Josephine fell to the floor and she said she couldn't stand up anymore. And in the back of my head I knew that the clock was ticking. "Come on, we gotta keep moving," we said to her. "Let's go, come on, come on." Once we had her we couldn't let her go. If we had let her go and we made it out and she didn't, I'd be a basket case right now. So she collapsed at the fourth floor, and I started running around the floor looking for a chair that maybe we could throw her in and run with her. But I couldn't find anything, and I came to the realization that we were just going to have to drag her. So I went running back to the stairway, and I was about four or five feet away when the collapse of the North Tower started. I felt a wavelike action in the floor and a tremendous vibration in the building. My first attempt at opening the stairway door failed. I couldn't open it. On the second attempt I was able to get it. And I opened the door and I just dove for the stairway. My first thought when the collapse started was, Ahh, we didn't make it. I felt like I had almost let them down a little bit. We were so close and we didn't make it.

When the collapse was happening, every floor that hit fell in a pancake fashion. One floor would hit the other floor and every time that happened, there was just tremendous boom and vibration. And we were being bounced around the stairway like Ping-Pong balls. We were getting hit by debris. And we're all lying there waiting for that big beam, or that big chunk of concrete, to come and hit us. And it never came.

Once it stopped, I said, "Oh, man, I can't believe we just survived that."

Now we're all gasping for air. We're coughing, we're vomiting, there's that gigantic dust storm. I know where Ground Zero is. I was in the middle of it.

We're taking chunks of this stuff out of our mouths, using our fingernails to try to get this stuff out of our eyes, and we're trying to get acclimated to what had just happened. We had very little visibility. And then we started getting Mayday radio messages from other firemen, most notably from Ladder 5 who we had passed in the stairway on the way down. They were working on a man who was having chest pains, a civilian. I knew the officer. He and I are friends. I said to him, "Mike, come on, let's go. It's time to get out of here."

And he says, "Yeah, I know. You have your civilian and I have mine. We'll be right behind you." He gave out a Mayday message after the collapse saying he was on the twelfth floor of Stairway B. I tried to go up to help him out. I got to the fifth floor, but I couldn't move the debris, couldn't move anything over my head. It just wasn't working. That was difficult for me because I knew him and I knew there was nothing I could do to help him. The whole time I was in the stairway I was thinking about that—that if we got out, we had to make sure somebody got up to him.

It wasn't until after we got out that we realized that the twelfth floor no longer existed. His Mayday was coming from the rubble someplace.

We couldn't go down any farther, and so we started evaluating ways for our own survival. We knew we needed to save our flashlights, if possible, and our air, because we could hear fires breaking out around us. Immediately adjacent to us was 6 World Trade Center and on the other side of that was 7 World Trade

Center, and both of those buildings were fully involved in fire. We could hear firemen calling for lines over the radio to fight those fires. And we wanted to save our air in case we had a fire to deal with in the future.

Josephine was very quiet. We heard a secondary explosion that was very close to our location and she just started crying. She said she was scared. I said, "You know, we're all a little scared, darling. Just hang in there." She was very brave. She held her own. My guys kept taking turns talking to her and comforting her and trying to keep her mind off of what was happening around us.

The first person I got hold of was Deputy Chief Tom Haring. He recorded my location and he said they would start assembling rescue teams to come and get us. Then I spoke with Deputy Chief Nick Visconti. He's a very close friend of mine, and he assumed command of the rescue operation to find us. It was comforting talking to the guys that I knew. Other rescuers, my neighbor Cliff Stabner from Rescue 3, Battalion Chief John Salka from Battalion 18 in the Bronx, Battalion Chief Bill Blaich, who had assembled a rescue team from Ladder 11 and Ladder 6, were all out there coming to help us.

I could see out of a hole in a stairway. There was a wall of twisted steel around us. We knew it was bad but we weren't sure how bad it was. We thought that maybe the top half of the building fell off. Then I heard one guy on the radio ask, "Where's the North Tower?"

I said, "Oh, boy, they don't even know where the North Tower is. Doesn't sound good."

We kept waiting and evaluating things, and after about the three-hours-and-fifteen-minutes point of entrapment, the smoke and dust had cleared enough for us to look out and see a beam of light through the stairway. And I just looked down to the guys, and I said, "Guys, there used to be 106 floors above us, and now I see sunshine." And then about ten minutes later, we saw in the distance a fireman from Ladder 43 walking across the rubble.

Josephine Harris wasn't walking before the collapse and certainly after the collapse, she wasn't walking very well. But she was an incredibly brave woman, I'll tell you that. She really held her own.

Once we got out, I finally found the command post and Chief Hayden was standing on the roof of a pumper so he could see across the whole area. He was running the show like he was General Patton. I yelled up to him and finally got his attention and he looked down. It was a pretty emotional time. I worked for him for a long time. He's a terrific fire chief. And I could feel myself starting to cry as I'm looking up at him and he's looking down at me.

He says, "Jay, it's good to see you."

I gave him a salute, and I said, "It's good to be here, Chief."

BILLY BUTLER

38, Ladder 6, FDNY

"PEOPLE WERE ACTUALLY BREAKING INTO SODA MACHINES
AND GIVING US BOTTLES OF WATER ON THE WAY UP.
BUT WHEN THE BUILDING EVENTUALLY COLLAPSED,
WE HAD NO WATER WITH US BECAUSE WE HAD GIVEN
IT ALL BACK TO PEOPLE ON THEIR WAY DOWN."

On September 11, I was in the midst of studying to become a lieutenant. The test was supposed to be October 13, and I left my house at about four-thirty in the morning on September 11 to make the trip to the city to get a couple of hours of study time in prior to starting my tour. I got to the firehouse between six and six-thirty and immediately went into the basement study rooms and began to work. At about seven-thirty, I came up to take a break, and two guys were in the kitchen from the night tour from Ladder 15. Tommy Falco and I relieved them. Those two guys ultimately went back to Ladder 15, and I believe they were killed later that day.

I went back downstairs to continue my studies. At about eight-forty-five, somebody came over the intercom in the firehouse and said, "Let's go. Everybody out. We've got a plane crash." We had a couple of probees in the house, and I believe this was the first day for one of them. When they first made the announcement, I just thought they were playing with the probee. But what a vicious way to play.

I immediately ran up the stairs. And by that time they were saying that a plane had hit the World Trade Center. I started putting my gear on, and looked out the door to see that it was real. From our firehouse you can't see the Trade Center because of Confucius Plaza, the big high-rise building at the corner of Bowery. But you could see the smoke coming around both sides of it. So it was obvious that something had hit the Trade Center, and hit it high.

We were dressed and out the door very quickly. When we got to the corner of the Bowery and the Manhattan Bridge, you could see that there were probably fifteen or twenty floors of fire. We proceeded down the Bowery past City Hall. We got to the corner of Park Place and Broadway and all of a sudden there were thousands and thousands of people. And it seemed like everybody had a camera.

We went down Vesey the wrong way and people were lined up from the curb to the buildings, all the way down, thousands of people. When we went by the Trade Center, underneath where the plane had gone in, there were pieces of the plane lying there and people were standing right next to them. It was almost as if they were going to hike their leg up and take a picture, you know, stabilize themselves on a piece of the plane. It was unbelievable.

Sal D'Agnostino had the roof of the rig, so he was on the side of the building where the plane had hit. He looked over at me and says, "Billy, this is bad."

I said, "Yeah, I know." We didn't have to say anything else. We both knew.

When we got to West Street, we got off the rig and there was stuff smashing in the street. We actually had guys looking up and making sure that things didn't hit the guys that were getting their stuff off the rig. We got all our stuff and took refuge underneath the north walkway, which eventually collapsed. We waited there for maybe thirty seconds for stuff to stop falling. There was a momentary lull, and the captain said, "Let's go," and we sprinted for the building.

We went in the front doors and there was debris all over the first floor, and people were lying there. Some were burned up pretty badly. Typically, when you come upon an injured person, you take care of them. We get paid to take care of injured people. But there were security guards and police officers caring for people, so we had to go by them because we knew how many people were in that building and we knew how many people we had to get out that day.

Captain Patty Brown from Ladder 3 is originally from Rescue 1, and our captain, Jay Jonas, is originally from Rescue 3. Patty said to Jay, "Let's go. They want us to go up."

But my captain is a stickler for doing the right thing. We call him a straight shooter because he does the same thing every day. He is the model firefighter for the fire department. And he said, "Patty, the rules say that you're supposed to go check in at the command post, and I have to go check in at the command post." During that CBS *9/11* show, you can actually see him standing at the command post waiting for an assignment. It was utter chaos, and it took them a few seconds to give him an assignment. And they basically told him, "Go up and see what you can do." The time it took him to check in wasn't much. But it was eventually relevant as to our position in the stairwell.

When he came back, he said, "Let's go, boys. Let's go up." He was always calling us boys. We're like brothers and sons to him.

We were in a line to get into the stairwell. Ladder 3 was three companies ahead of us. And eventually, what that did was separate the two companies on the stairwell. It seemed like every little thing that happened that day put us in the position to be saved, or for that miracle to happen.

The firefighters had a problem getting through the doors to go upstairs. The stairwells themselves were wide enough. But they still only put a thirty-six-inch door on them. So you can have as many people as you want going up and down, but when you get to the door you can't get through. You have to go through one at a time. So we'd let a few people out, and then a few firemen would go in, and then a few more people, then a few firemen. Obviously, the important thing was to get the people out of the building.

Once we did get into the stairwell, we began our trek up. It was very orderly. The people coming down stayed to their right. We stayed to our right. People were coming by us, saying, "God bless you guys. You guys are the best. You're our heroes."

And at the same time, we told them, "Okay, you've got five floors to go. Go down and out of the stairwell, make a right and get out of the building." Or, "You've got ten floors." But we kept talking to these people, coaching them, and telling them where they had to go. Everybody was doing that. The firemen were coaching people on how to get out, because we couldn't physically spare someone to lead them. We didn't have enough resources to do that. So the best we could do was coach them verbally.

People were actually breaking into soda machines and giving us bottles of water on the way up. But when the building eventually collapsed, we had no water with us because we had given it all back to people on their way down.

When we came upon Josephine, somebody said to me, "Help with this woman," and then went to take care of somebody else. Guys were trying to take care of ten different people at one time. And it wasn't working.

I said, "I got her."

Jay said, "Billy, take her and go."

So I started down with Josephine. Sometimes in a fire we'll put civilians in a straight-backed chair and try to carry them. As we went down, we looked on each floor for a chair for Josephine, but the only thing we could find was a swivel-type chair, which is typically very bulky. So that wasn't really a choice because we were afraid that we'd put her in it and she'd flip right over. And we might have had to deal with some totally different consequences if we had knocked her out. These things do run through your mind when you're doing such a thing. We opted not to do it and we kept walking down.

Everybody was trying to push us along and it was a very slow process. We would push Josephine into the corner of the stairwell and let other guys slide by. Josephine is not small and neither am I. We had to let people pass. I remember guys going into the fourth floor to look for another chair. And then the whole building started to rock. Josephine was coming straight at me, and then everything went black.

Immediately, you look at yourself to make sure all the fingers are there, the toes are there, and you wiggle them to make sure that nothing is broken. I felt like I was beat up, but I was okay. I was trying to extricate myself and pick these large pieces of drywall off myself when Josephine suddenly came up out of the dust, like the Blob coming out of the swamp. She scared the shit out of me. I jumped. Then Jay checked on us, and I let him know both Josephine and I were all right.

Guys have tried to call Josephine every few weeks since September 11. One person or another calls her and tries to keep in contact. We all exchanged Christmas cards. She sent us an Easter card. And we actually took up a collection and gave her money for a vacation.

We've been treated pretty well by the fire department. People have been sent on trips to represent the fire department and receive awards. But we felt that Josephine was a victim in this whole thing. She's not getting anything from the funds. It's been pretty much the fire department, police department, and Port Authority police getting the money, along with the families of people killed. She's a survivor and she didn't get anything. So we took it upon ourselves to do the right thing and give her some money for a vacation.

Jillian Volk, right, with her late fiancé, Kevin Williams.

JILLIAN VOLK

24, Preschool Teacher

—

"I THOUGHT HE WAS ADMITTED TO A HOSPITAL WITH A
HURT LEG, A HURT ARM, SOMETHING. I THOUGHT
HE WAS SOMEWHERE."

I was on corner of Church and Thomas, at work at the preschool. It's about a
five-minute walk from the Trade Center. My fiancé, Kevin Williams, worked in
tower 2 for a small investment banking firm on the 104th floor.

I didn't see the first plane hit tower 1, but I felt something because my classroom has floor-to-ceiling glass windows in it, and it shook. One of my students
looked at me and said, "It's thundering." I knew it wasn't thundering. There was
no way it was thundering. It was a beautiful day. A woman came running into
the hallway and said a bomb had gone off in the Trade Center. I panicked. I
called Kevin, hoping I would get an answer from him. He picked up his line and

told me that a plane had gone into tower 1, and he had to go because they were being evacuated. He wasn't panicked, or anything like that. He just said he had to go because they were leaving. And that was it. Very short.

Once the second plane hit, panic broke out. I did not actually know there was a second plane. We were not aware of what was happening. But there was panic outside our door. Panic. You would see the people walking north up Church. Then all of a sudden we felt something and they started to run like they were being chased by who knows what. People screamed and banged on our doors trying to get in. We took a lot of the kids and tried walking up Church too, but the owner of the school got a hold of us and said the safest thing would be to go back into the school and stay in a classroom that doesn't have any windows, and just sit in there. So that's what we did. We still didn't really know what was happening. I must have been in shock because nothing was sinking in.

I thought Kevin was out. I truly thought he was going to walk into the school and get me. I waited at the school, I guess, until maybe ten-thirty or so. Most of the kids had gone by then, so I just started walking north. I didn't know where to go. Kevin and I had an apartment on the East Side, and my sister had an apartment on the West Side. Kevin and I were planning to get married on December 1, and had just gotten our place two weeks prior to September 11. We didn't set up the phones yet, so I didn't know where he would try to reach me since cell phones weren't working. I figured I may as well go to my sister's and wait there.

When I got there, I still hadn't heard anything about Kevin. I tried calling his parents. His father started driving in from Long Island as soon as the first plane hit. The plan was for him to pick me up so we could both try to find Kevin and figure out where he went. Everyone was calling—hysterical, crying, everyone, just kind of waiting. He was missing. He should have gotten out by that point. I thought he was admitted to a hospital with a hurt leg, a hurt arm, something. I thought he was somewhere. I didn't believe that he wasn't going to come back.

We spent the whole night going from hospital to hospital, checking the admittance lists. Then, at seven o'clock that night we got phone call from Bellevue Hospital saying that Kevin was admitted there. His dad got there before we did and he found out it wasn't the right Kevin Williams. It was somebody else. We had been on this whole high, screaming, like I was thinking, I'm going to get married tomorrow. I was so excited. I was flipping out. Then to find out it wasn't Kevin.

I searched the city for three days. We went to hospitals, we went everywhere. I called places in Jersey, just kept calling. I carried pictures of Kevin everywhere. I went on *Good Morning America.* Lara Spencer from ABC brought me back to her office and let me screen through tapes because one of our family friends thought they had seen Kevin on a stretcher in one of the brief news clippings. I went through the footage trying to find this person that they swore was Kevin, and I didn't find anything. Random people called and sent e-mails, people I never knew from across the country saying, "Oh, you know a man was interviewed and they mentioned a Kevin, and it sounds like the Kevin we saw you talking about on TV." I went with any little piece I could.

I didn't give up hope for weeks. The hardest thing to do was go home, because I felt like I was giving up on him. We waited a month until we had a memorial service for him. There was no recovery of him, no nothing. I have this image of him just being truly taken out of there. I feel like if they find something, it kills that image for me in a little way. I just want him to not have felt or known anything. I believe from the information I've received that he was right in the area where the second plane hit. Of all the people he was friendly with, the people in his firm that all left together, nothing has been recovered.

I don't know if I'll ever get married. I can only see myself with Kevin. We had been together since we were sixteen. I grew up in Wading River. He grew up in Shoreham. But it's pretty much the same town out there on the north fork of Long Island. We went to high school together. I'm twenty-four. He's twenty-four. He's a part of me as much as I'm a part of him. There are things of my personality that I know I've gotten from him, and I know there are things I taught him that are part of his personality. What I had with him was true love, and I can't imagine ever experiencing something like that again. I wouldn't want to. Kevin was my everything, perfect to me in every way. I feel like I'm eighty and I've lived my life and now it's over. I'm scared. I'm so lonely and confused. But I have an amazing support system. My family and friends have been amazing. Every day is a trial for me to wake up and get going, but I know I have to because that's how Kevin was. He'd be looking down on me saying, "Pull it together. You're still alive." I don't feel like it, but I know I am, and there's a reason I am, I guess.

THOMAS VON ESSEN

56, Former Fire Commissioner, FDNY

"THE MAYOR'S ASKED ME TO SIT IN ON SOME OF THOSE MEETINGS OF CIVILIANS MIXED IN WITH THE FAMILIES OF FIREFIGHTERS AND POLICE OFFICERS, REALLY NICE PEOPLE. . . . THEY JUST WANT TO BE TALKED TO AND TREATED WITH RESPECT. THEY'RE JUST REALLY NICE PEOPLE WHO HAVE SUFFERED SO MUCH."

I got picked up a little later than usual. I guess it was about eight-thirty. We were going along East River Drive when I saw some smoke. I asked my driver if he thought it was a cloud. He said, "No way. It's a fire."

We got a little farther down and the buildings opened up and I could see a big hole in the side of the North Tower. At first I thought it was probably a private plane. Maybe some rich guy had a heart attack, something like that. We raised the volume on the department radio and heard that there was an explosion of some sort at the Trade Center.

So we drove over there, went around to the lobby entrance on West Street, and went inside. Many of the chiefs were there already, including Chief Pfeifer and Chief Hayden. They were just doing what they would be doing in a normal job: trying to get a handle on communications with the people that were still up there, trying to set up our people who would be going up, trying to assist people on the way out.

It wasn't that unusual in the lobby at the time, except as you went in, you could see that jumpers had already started jumping. It made you realize that there was a tremendous fire up there. People would never jump from that kind of height unless they were absolutely desperate. Inside the lobby, I think we knew less of what was going on than people outside or in the street, or the people watching television.

When the South Tower got hit, there was more confusion. Obviously we knew it was terrorism then. I remember seeing Ray Downey in the lobby at that point, and he said to me, "You know, these buildings can collapse." He just said it in passing, not that these buildings will collapse in forty minutes and we have to get everybody out of here, or not that they'll collapse by tomorrow, or not that they necessarily will collapse at all. Just that they *can* collapse. That was the first sense I had of the enormity of this: when the second plane hit, and what he said.

I was in the lobby quite a while, I guess. Somebody told me the mayor was looking for me. They said he was over at the other command post. I said I'd be right over. I went out through one of the big windows without even looking up.

Later I thought about how dumb that was, because a body came down probably fifteen, twenty feet away from me and just splattered on the ground. And I thought, Holy mackerel, if that had hit me I'd be dead. It was a rookie move, and I was lucky.

I ran across the street. The mayor had already left. There was a lot of confusion over there. They weren't really set up yet. A few more minutes went by, I don't really know how long, but again somebody told me the mayor was looking for me. So I left and walked over to the Office of Emergency Management, at 7 World Trade Center. I thought that was where we should all be because that's what the command center was built for. But they were evacuating that building. I was really upset. I said, "How can we be evacuating OEM? We really need it now." But somebody had made a really smart move evacuating that building. Making that decision was probably a tough one to make at the time, but it was a wise decision.

So the mayor had already left there as well. They told me he was up near Barclay. I started walking up there, and maybe I was a block away when there was this unbelievable sound of the South Tower collapsing. I still didn't focus on how bad it was. I just assumed it was part of the building, not the whole thing. I ducked into a building to get away from the large volume of dust. It reminded me of videos I had seen of Mount Saint Helens, and that volcanic dust and dirt coming across all those people out there.

I was with two of my guys. They ducked to the right and I ducked to the left. We all ran in buildings. A few minutes later we came back out and started walking again, trying to talk on radios, trying to get a sense of what was going on. I didn't focus on how many guys would have been lost. I was thinking that maybe twenty floors toppled and maybe none of our guys had gotten up that high yet. So I still didn't have a sense.

We ran into the mayor's group, which had been in a basement down on Barclay Street. People were running in the streets, and he just kept telling people, "Keep calm. Walk north, walk north." We tried to figure out a place to go to get some information and some working telephones. We talked about going to the firehouse on Duane Street. We decided that was too close. Then they said City Hall, but that might be a target. We went into a hotel, but it had a glass ceiling. Not a good idea. We kept walking and got up to 5 Truck, which was near Houston Street on Sixth Avenue. We watched television, since it had better information than we did.

The mayor was talking to the White House and the governor, trying to get help and air cover. They weren't sure if there were going to be more attacks. They found out about the Pentagon. We realized we needed a command center. Bernie Kerik suggested the police academy on Twenty-first Street. The mayor asked me how many of my guys I thought were up there. And I had no idea. It was numbing, and it gets me upset just to talk about it. I'm sitting here crying now just talking about it.

We treated it like a rescue operation for weeks, even after we knew we weren't going to rescue anybody. We wanted to let our guys and the families keep some hope. We spoke to experts from FEMA, earthquake experts, and landslide experts from all around the world in the first couple days, and they told us there was no way anyone could have survived. And I just kept asking the mayor not to say that. Just try to be positive, at least for a while, and we'll see what happens.

We were winging it from day one. I remember going to the first meetings with the families. Maybe it was ten days after the tragedy. The mayor and I had talked about it and said, "We've got to prepare them for the inevitable. We've got to tell them tonight. We're not going to find any of their loved ones. It's time to do that. It's going to be painful. It's going to be horrible, but we have to do it."

And you know Rudy's a tough guy. But we went to the meeting, and by the time we got to the stage, he grabbed me and he says, "They're not ready. They're not ready yet. Don't say anything."

So I walked up to the stage and I had to have a whole new plan. Instead of giving them tough love, we just bought more time. And sometimes I look back on that and I don't know whether it was the right decision. But it was a decision that we made from our hearts. It was a decision that we made, thinking, If we say this, it will hurt less than if we said this. Everything we did was with that intention. Everything. There was never a decision that was made because the rescue effort or something cost too much money.

I remember people accused us of cutting back the manpower because we had found the gold. And I thought, Holy shit, how pathetic. The mayor said to me, "What gold?" He didn't even know there was gold. Neither did I. One of the banks had some gold there, and got some rescue guys to find this gold. And that was coincidentally the same time that we lowered the manpower at Ground Zero. We thought we had too many people. But they said we lowered the manpower because we wanted to save overtime. They said, "They found gold. How could you do that to these people? How could you be such a lowlife?"

There was one man who yelled and screamed at me at one of the meetings, about his son and about the construction, about how we didn't do this and how we didn't do that. It was one of those really horrible meetings with some of the families. We just couldn't tell them anything that they wanted to hear, so we just stood there and let them beat us up for a couple of hours.

Well, I ran into that same man the other night, and he was so nice to me. I couldn't believe it. He was like a different person because they eventually found his son. I think he understands now how much we did and how much we tried to do. And I knew that even at the first meeting. I knew this guy was a nice man, a good man, but he was heartbroken and he needed someone to scream at. It was just a horrible time. The department will be reeling from it for years.

And people still come to Mayor Giuliani for advice. He's asked me to sit in on some of those meetings of civilians mixed in with the families of firefighters and police officers, really nice people. They want a memorial the right way. They have issues to deal with every day. And they just want to be talked to and treated with respect. They're just really nice people who have suffered so much.

I had to get away from it because I really felt it was just too much for me. I'm not away from it even now, but I couldn't live it every day. I was just so close to it. I would have loved to have stayed in that job forever, but September 11 really changed it so much. Made it so painful.

I said to my wife, "Well, it's three months since I left. Maybe in another nine months it will be easier." But the fact is, it will never be. I'm never going to forget all those people. I was in a department for thirty-two years, was president of the union and a commissioner who lived, slept, and ate it. And it's devastating to lose people like that. So many great people got killed that day, God. But what are you supposed to do? What choice do you have? Just to keep going. You got a job to do so you do it. And even when you don't have a job to do, you still have a responsibility. I'll always love those guys. And now I'll just try to help from the outside rather than from the inside.

Daniel Donadio, left, with Veronica Hammer and Smitty.

DANIEL DONADIO

45, Lieutenant, Canine Commander, NYPD

"FROM DAY ONE HERE THE DOGS WERE VERY DEPRESSED,
AND THEY WOULD WHINE LIKE THEY WANTED TO DO SOMETHING.
THEY KNEW SOMETHING VERY BAD HAD HAPPENED, BUT
IN THEIR MINDS THEY COULDN'T COMPREHEND IT."

My job is the overall operation of the NYPD Canine Unit, which consists of thirty-one patrol dogs, all cross-trained with SAR, search and recovery, and three bloodhounds.

On September 11 I was at the canine base when the planes hit. When the first tower collapsed, Bobby Schnelle was with canine Atlas on the West Side Highway. If Bobby hadn't stopped to help an emergency service unit, he would have been too close to the building to escape in time when it came down.

Within fifteen minutes of the collapse, we had Peter Davis with canine

Apollo, an American Kennel Club Ace Award winner, trying to get to the North Tower because people were calling for a dog. Peter had to go through what would have been considered a river of water to get up on the pile. The ground under Apollo gave way, and he fell into a pit and was engulfed by flames. Peter had to pull him out and brush the embers off him so he could get back to work.

It was at about that time that I reached the site with maybe ten more canine teams. I couldn't really go further than City Hall because you couldn't see twenty feet in front of you. From there we had to make it on foot. I was scared to let any of my people go anywhere, because I wanted to keep them all next to me. We didn't know if any more terrorist attacks were coming. And my biggest concern for maybe the first hour and a half, in between being stunned, was trying to account for my people who were already there.

Our memory for a lot of us on September 11 is very vague. Forty-eight hours seemed like one hour, or an eternity. It's hard for me to explain, but when people ask what else happened that day, we have problems remembering. I remember walking across to the World Trade Center on the Church and Liberty side and looking up at the part of the facade that was sticking out of the ground and up into the air maybe four stories. It reminded me of the scene in *Planet of the Apes* where Charlton Heston finds the Statue of Liberty buried in the sand.

For about the first two weeks we were trying to locate survivors. Anything. Anybody. We didn't care if they were cops, firemen, people. These were New Yorkers, and these were our neighbors, and we wanted to find them.

By the second week we were into recovery. Officially, they waited a little longer to declare it a recovery, as opposed to a rescue and recovery, because nobody really wanted to acknowledge it. But once it was declared simply a recovery, the other canine teams all started pulling out. The FEMA team left. A lot of local teams that had come down from Jersey and other places started pulling out too, leaving it up to just us. God bless them and God bless their dogs, but they still had to get back to their homes and their jobs. I would say by the fourth week it was all ours, with some help from the state police. And at that point we were using the dogs for cadaver recovery.

No dog was instrumental in recovering anybody from the World Trade Center alive. We're always prepared for a building collapse in New York, because quite often old buildings collapse and we bring the dogs in right away. And these are dogs that we relied on every day for their noses. I mean in life-and-death situations. Their noses didn't fail us, and their spirit didn't fail us, and their loyalty didn't fail us. From day one here the dogs were very depressed, and they would whine like they wanted to do something. They knew something very bad had happened, but in their minds they couldn't comprehend it. They sensed the depression and the severity in their handlers. They just wanted to work and get up there and help out.

And to this day we're still doing it. We still have teams there on a twenty-four-hour basis, helping to recover people and letting us know where to dig.

The dogs are fine. The one dog who died was the Port Authority police dog that was left in the Port Authority Station in the tower. His handler went to go help people from the plane crash, so he left his dog behind. No search dogs that I know of died. My dogs suffered the same minor injuries we suffered, the same fatigue. There were always veterinarians right outside the perimeter, so when the dogs were done working they would go right to them. There was never a shortage of veterinarians volunteering their time to take care of the dogs. As soon as the dogs would come out of the site, they would get washed down, they would get treated for dehydration, they would get an examination from a veterinarian. The dogs were very well cared for.

But the men are feeling it, some more than others. Help is available to all of us, but we haven't made ourselves available yet. When we're done with the operation, it's going to be mandatory for all of us to go to counseling.

As for the dogs, most of them want to work. They don't want to stay home. Apollo is about ten years old now, and you can see that he's old by looking at him. But he still has a lot of heart and energy. And as long as he wants to do it, we'll let him do it. When he doesn't want to do it anymore, we'll let him stay home.

You know, when they speak of the towers, there were smaller towers in there, and they were man's best friend—the dogs. At least three hundred of them pulled service at the World Trade Center, and the twenty-five from my unit were there from day one. I like to consider them the little towers in the middle.

MARK DAWSON
43, Canine Handler, FEMA

—

"WE WENT INTO A HALLMARK STORE, AND IT WAS
PRETTY WEIRD. . . . THERE'S ALL THIS DESTRUCTION AROUND YOU,
AND THEN THERE'S THIS CARD SHOP WHERE ALL THE CARDS ARE
PERFECTLY PLACED IN A ROW."

I'm a paid firefighter and a canine handler for Massachusetts Task Force 1, which is part of the Federal Emergency Management Agency program, FEMA. We are one of twenty-eight teams in the country.

We arrived in New York City at 10 P.M. on 9/11. We went down to the site on Church Street for a review of the area we were going to search. We gathered

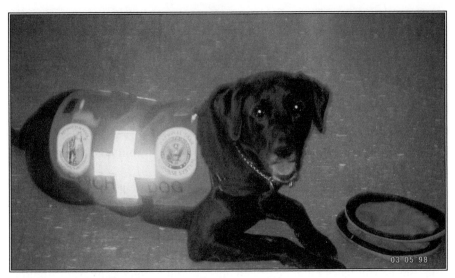
Mark Dawson's dog, Elvis.

information and split up into two groups, a day shift and a night shift. I worked the night shift for the next eight days.

There were still some large fires burning in the crater area on the night of the attacks. First I went to the edge of the rubble at building 2 with my dog, Elvis, who is a six-year-old black Lab, an advanced, certified dog in the FEMA program. I was taken aback by the devastation and I wondered whether we could work effectively in the pile. Elvis worked extremely well through a lot of hazardous areas. There were large void spaces under the surface of the rubble. We were able to climb down into them on ladders. We also lowered the dogs with rope harnesses down into void spaces that we weren't able to climb to, or that ladders couldn't reach. We got to one elevator shaft area the first night. We heard a pass alarm, which is the device firefighters use in an emergency situation, so they can be located. But in this case, there was no one in the area. It was just the device.

After that, we went to another area, about five stories down. There were streams of water and an out-of-control fire. Sometimes we were pulled out of areas because of the possible collapse of several buildings. We did a search of the first and basement floors of 4 World Trade Center and came up with no victims and no alerts in the area. Then we were asked to go down to an area where they thought they heard some pinging. We went a full story down into a large void area, a store area. We did a search and came across a number of mannequins. Apparently, it was a Halloween shop and they were used to display things. Elvis was searching through that area and he showed some unusual behavior when he approached the mannequins. They looked like deceased bodies.

We then worked the rest of the mall area into the subway. We went into a

Hallmark store, and it was pretty weird because the cards and everything were still on the shelves. There's all this destruction around you, and then there's this card shop where all the cards are perfectly placed in a row. It was pretty eerie. There were no indications of any survivors. In a lot of the shops it appeared like people had dropped everything and run out. Things were still in place. Back in the clerk's room, the money trays were still sitting on the desks.

We did a number of void searches on the second night, and again we came up with no live victims. Elvis is not a cadaver dog. Elvis is an air-scent dog. He has been exposed to cadaver work, but when he does hit a cadaver, his tail will go between his legs. He's usually very cautious, as if he's nervous of the area. We did have two indications of cadavers the third night, on the back side of building 6. One was confirmed. We work with two dogs in an area. If a dog has an indication or an alert, we bring a second dog in to verify it. Then we bring the technical search people in with cameras and listening devices to pick up sight or sound of any trapped victims. Then the rescue guys follow to extricate the subject.

On the fourth night, or maybe the tail end of the third night, thunderstorms rolled through, and they did not allow us to go back on the pile because the metal was slippery. They were concerned with risk and safety issues. So we ended up doing building searches of the surrounding buildings. Elvis and I went to the Federal Building with a team out of Sacramento and searched the eighteen stories. We found some plane parts on the roof and systematically worked each floor after that. Again, the scene was eerie. Usually when you do building searches, things aren't in place. But here we were finding offices with briefcases on the desks, Dunkin' Donuts coffee cups with only one or two sips gone, jackets and sport coats on the backs of doors and chairs.

We learned in Oklahoma that a dog's drive decreases over a period of several days when there is a lack of live finds. The cleanliness of the dogs is also important. Some of the dogs were depressed, and a bath would start to spark them up and drive them back to work again. Knowing these things, we positively rewarded our dogs for every act that they did. Whenever we came out of an area without finding anyone, we hid a rescuer, which would serve as a live victim for Elvis. That kept his drive and his spirits up.

What we did down there proved to be beneficial to the animals. As a FEMA team we're made up of a little bit of everybody: doctors, regular citizens, engineers, firefighters, police officers. And although we don't see the magnitude of what the firefighters see, we do deal with death on a daily basis.

Elvis's drive has not changed one bit. He still loves his job. If I tell him he's going to go search somewhere, he runs to the front door. There are so many things that we do with our animals to get them ready for days like September 11, and since then I think we're even a little more alert too. As we go by buildings today, we think of possible search scenarios. It's part of the world right now. But you know, we can do the job if called upon again.

MICHAEL MICHELSEN

48, Lieutenant, Wilton Fire Department, Wilton, Connecticut

"AS THEY WERE PULLING THE TRUCKS OUT OF THE WRECKAGE
THAT FIRST DAY, STARTING TO MOVE THINGS, YOU'RE LOOKING
AT A FIRE TRUCK, WHICH MOST PEOPLE VIEW AS INCREDIBLY
STRONG AND INCREDIBLY INDESTRUCTIBLE. AND THESE THINGS
WERE BROKEN LIKE LITTLE KIDS' TOYS."

I am a former firefighter from the New York City Fire Department, who was assigned to Ladder Company 3 in lower Manhattan. So I was very familiar with the area, and I had responded to the World Trade Center before.

I was at the Wilton firehouse when the tragedy began. We could hear the radio traffic that was going on in New York through a monitor that we had at the station. When the building came down, we could hear the initial silence. Then we could hear the dispatch desperately trying to contact someone, anyone. And we could hear the men calling that they were trapped within the building. We could hear what we call "pass alarms," which are the devices that will initiate when you're trapped and you can't move. It sets off a sounder so other firefighters could come, and hopefully extricate you from the wreckage.

But we weren't prepared to watch the buildings come down. I think that notion was well beyond our imagination. Of course, when the buildings did collapse, it created a sense of urgency for us to go. Luckily, we had the support of the Wilton Fire Department. We were able to commandeer a vehicle. We took air packs because we knew the basic supplies that would be unavailable down there. We brought bottled water and other equipment that we could use when we got on site.

When we got to lower Manhattan, we reported directly to the staging area. Five of us went down. You talk about things that tug at you emotionally. One of the things that I had everyone do before we left was write down current notification of next-of-kin information. Because we were heading into a set of circumstances that were completely unknown. We didn't know whether we would be coming back and you wanted to make sure that if something went wrong, at least the people that needed to be notified would be notified. That kind of set the tone for the seriousness of what we were walking into.

When we got down there, it was chaos. The fire service usually does things in a very orderly fashion. You have a complete command structure and you have the ability to use all your resources in a very organized fashion. But on September 11, the senior command staff was lost, the communication systems were lost, and getting simple information was a colossal challenge. We had a completely primitive staging area. We had runners, like it was a hundred years ago, running from point to point to relay information because the handheld radios weren't working. The hard-line radios that they were trying to wire up were constantly collapsing.

The fire service is a family. You're coming into somebody else's area. You're not there to take over for them. You're there to give them whatever they need. If it's a matter of you being an extra man to help them with their crew, that's what you'll do. You're just trying desperately to work with the circumstances. As they were pulling the trucks out of the wreckage that first day, starting to move things, you're looking at a fire truck, which most people view as incredibly strong and incredibly indestructible. And these things were broken like little kids' toys. It was like they were made out of papier mâché and then stepped on. The following morning one of the sites that particularly changed my thinking was my old Company 3 truck. Their truck had been dragged out of the wreckage. It was crushed and I knew that my old company had lost eleven men, almost half of the entire firehouse. That tragedy was repeated in so many of the houses. One of the reasons the loss of life was so significant was because the tragedy occurred at the change of shift. The way we work, it's not a matter of "Hey, I don't want to go." It's a matter of "Hey, you guys are going there without us? Come on." And then you have firemen fighting over the limited resources. The truck is set up for six people, there are only radios for six people, and yet twelve guys go in to help, so at the very least half of the people don't have the ability to communicate.

America lost its virginity that morning and we're forever changed as a society. Where we're going now is the big question. Not what's going to happen next, but when is it going to happen? You appreciate things differently. If you had made long-term plans before and your life was a very structured, orderly thing, I'd say there's a pretty good chance that you've spoken to your children, hugged your wife more, and talked to your parents, or renewed some sort of contacts that you were putting off. Because everything now has become tentative. It's no longer a circumstance where everything is simple, guaranteed, and I'm going to do this and I'm going to do that. You have to take each sunrise and look at it like you never did and appreciate it like you never did because it's no longer promised to anyone.

On day one, there was an ominous quiet down there because we were desperately trying to hear any cries for help or tapping or anything else. And a particularly astounding moment occurred when everybody was working and all of a sudden we heard this horrific roar. Everybody just hit the ground and covered their heads. You didn't know what was happening. And it was two F-16s doing a flyby, and after you saw them, you realized, Okay, at least they're our guys. But F-16s flying patrol around New York City? That's something I never expected to see. Driving out of the city seeing armed troops on the steps of City Hall and personnel carriers, seeing armed troops at every bridge and tunnel coming in and out of the city, you know, these were things I never expected to see in my lifetime.

A week after September 11, all the major resources had come to bear. FEMA was in place, tents were there, the perimeter was controlled. There's a whole series of images, none of which can be undone, none of which photographs do justice to. When you're seeing it, hearing it, smelling it, and tasting it, it's anchored in you, it's not going away.

EDWARD "BUD" McGIVERN JR.

65, Forensic Dentist

➤

"WE WEPT ON EACH OTHER'S SHOULDERS, HOLDING EACH OTHER.
WE HAD NEVER MET EACH OTHER, AND THERE WE WERE
JUST WEEPING AND HANGING ONTO EACH OTHER
IN THE MIDDLE OF THE NIGHT."

I have been an oral and maxillofacial surgeon since 1962. I have been chairman of several different hospital programs at both St. Vincent's and at Bellevue. I have been on the faculty at NYU as associate clinical professor of oral and maxillofacial surgery since 1965, and have maintained my own private practice in Staten Island. I essentially retired as an oral surgeon in January 2001, but I maintained my contacts with the medical examiner's offices in New York as a forensic dentist.

My assignment as a forensic dentist has always been to go the medical examiner's office and not to the scene of any disasters. For example, with airplane disasters we would just go to directly to the ME's office to identify or assist in identifying bodies.

On September 11, I was in Orlando, Florida, as a delegate to the American Association of Oral and Maxillofacial Surgeons' annual meeting. I was sitting in a bootblack's chair having my shoe shined when another delegate approached me with a cell phone in his ear and said, "My God, I just talked to my wife in Tampa, who tells me that the World Trade Center has been attacked, as well as the Pentagon, and that bombs have been set off."

The next few days were a washout for all of us. The meeting actually went on. We decided that since we couldn't get out of town, the hundred or so of us in the association may as well just continue the meeting in the spirit in which it had begun, but also in the spirit of great sorrow at what had happened.

By Thursday night, some of the delegates had rented cars and others banded together to rent. We talked about renting a Trailways bus. There were twenty-five of us, mostly faculty members from the University of Virginia, NYU, Columbia, Harvard, and the University of Connecticut, who banded together and rented a Trailways bus for six thousand dollars. We left on Friday and were able to get home late Saturday afternoon. The next day I put on a scrub suit and drove into town using emergency lanes and my identification from the medical examiner's office and the New York City Police Department.

The associate medical examiner, Jeff Burkes, who is an oral surgeon, got me into the main part of the medical examiner's office on Thirtieth Street and First Avenue, and we went to the basement where a lot of the dissecting of the bodies was being done. I need to explain the routine of this: Bodies were brought in vans or trucks or ambulances from the scene at the World Trade Center. A large tent had been quickly erected, and it was being occupied by chaplains, the Port Authority Police Department, the fire department, police department, and members of the medical examiner's office.

Bodies were assigned to a detective who took them all the way through fingerprinting, if there were any hands left. Where possible there were full-body X rays and then it was into the dental session, where we just cut out the jaws and x-rayed them. Not every person I saw had an intact face, or even a face that you could recognize as a human. Heads were coming in, heads and body parts. If it was a member of the force, meaning a member of the fire department or the Port Authority Police Department or the New York City Police Department, everybody would be called to attention to salute on the street. The ambulance would then be opened up and the body was brought out and placed on a gurney. If it was a fireman, the person's fire helmet would be placed on the chest of the body bag or on an area where the chest should be. Or in the case of a police officer, the officer's cap would be placed on the bag and they would be wheeled into the triage area where members of the FBI, CIA medical anthropologists, forensic pathologists, and members of the uniformed forces who were involved in remains recovery were waiting in scrubs and gowns and gloves and respirators.

It was just like standing around at an operating table. The clothing, if it could, would be taken off, either cut off or helped off gently. Sometimes people's flesh and pieces of their body would come off with the clothing, so this had to be done very, very gently. The boots, which have a bar code in them if they belonged to firemen, were identified. Keys and wallets would be found with pictures of loved ones. They were all put into evidence bags and put with the body. Then the body would be taken to the fingerprinting area. When I first got there, I saw a fingerprint technician using his cigarette lighter to burn the char off the ends of a finger. It is a well known fact that charcoal or dirt or any organic matter can be burned off and the print can be made much clearer. Fingerprints, thumbprints, footprints, toe prints, everything was taken that could potentially be used to identify someone.

Occasionally, the body was sent down to the dental forensic team, which is generally comprised of about eight to twelve volunteer forensic dentists who are trained in forensic identification. There were times when we'd open a body bag and we didn't really know whether these particular dental components—a piece of the jaw, upper or lower, or a section of three or four teeth—belonged to the person that we were trying to identify.

There were times when we found one tooth. And here we are, eight or ten people, most of us professors in dental school, standing around identifying a tooth, one tooth, x-raying it and looking at it from all angles and photographing it. You have to remember, many of the people who were killed in the 9/11 tragedy were from other parts of the country. And if they were missing, their families called their dentists to send in X rays. We received X rays in all kinds of states: mounted, in perfect order, and sometimes just in an envelope full of films, which we had to sort out. All kinds of order and disorder. X rays would be viewed with magnifying glasses and then photographed and entered into the computer program which hopefully would then be matched with the post-mortem computer program we were dealing with.

I remember this one man, a homicide detective from the Bronx. He probably stood five feet eight, or five-nine, and he was solid muscle. He looked like a pro football player, perhaps a guard. He had almost no neck. His shoulders just went up to the top of his head. If you didn't know he was a police officer, you certainly wouldn't want to encounter him in a dark alley.

He had been in Florida, hunting down some murder suspects from New York, at the time of 9/11, and he came home. I think he and his partner drove home from Florida. Anyway, his ex-partner had two brothers who were members of the fire department, both of whom died. We had the remains of one of the brothers of the ex-partner. The detectives were asked to sit off to the side and not get involved in this. And this guy had just been sitting there and watching the whole thing. He was a personal friend of the deceased's brother and he started crying in the middle of this, and we all started crying. We wept on each other's shoulders, holding each other. We had never met each other, and there we were just weeping and hanging onto each other in the middle of the night. And like I said, this was a guy you wouldn't want to meet in a dark alley. But he got so emotional, as did we. It defies description. This fellow was a hardened homicide cop from the Bronx, and soon to retire himself. But we had something for just half a second, something that made life at that moment a little easier.

After you got through with this kind of work for the night, we'd hang around the canteen that the Salvation Army set up on First Avenue, and you'd have to have some levity. There were times when we had two or three hours of nothing to do, waiting for bodies to come out of fingerprinting and full-body X ray. We'd sit around and talk and listen to the World Series.

I could never get accustomed to waiting for bodies to come in, hearing the sirens come up First Avenue and knowing that there were some more coming in, or that a fire officer or a police officer who was of high rank was coming in. And knowing that this was still a crime scene and that the FBI wanted everything positively identified.

I don't take anything for granted anymore. Every day is a new day. I used to read one or two books a week, now I find it really hard to concentrate. In fact, in the middle of January I started to read a biography of Joe DiMaggio, and I'm still reading it. I would normally knock that off in a week. But I still have a quarter of the book to go. I just can't concentrate.

JAMES LUONGO
43, Deputy Inspector, NYPD

"As the DNA comes back, we'll identify more."

My permanent assignment is with the fugitive enforcement division, but now I'm the interim commander at the Staten Island crime-scene site, Fresh Kills.

The fugitive enforcement division is on Gold Street in downtown Brooklyn, and that's where I was when I became aware of the planes hitting the Trade Center. I changed into my uniform. We jumped in the car, Sergeant Bootles,

Detective Lannigan, Detective Michael O'Brien, and myself, and shot over the Brooklyn Bridge. Both towers were burning. A female sergeant sent us down Vesey Street, between Church and Broadway. One of the first things that I saw that amazed me were the shoes, pairs and pairs of shoes, mostly women's shoes, lots of heels. People were so scared they just ran out of their shoes.

We were looking for temporary headquarters and watching the debris come down. I stopped looking after ten or fifteen. I just didn't want to see it anymore. There was nothing I could do to help. You'd say a prayer and look away. At one point, we had to hide underneath that overpass so we wouldn't get hit with a body once it hit the ground and exploded. I remember running down Vesey Street and seeing the huge hole in the north side of the North Tower. I said to myself, "How the hell are they ever going to fix that?" I never thought the towers were coming down.

The four of us rendered assistance to anybody that was injured. We kept God knows how many people from going back into the buildings. We had a surge of people that wanted to go back into the area to look for their loved ones. It was difficult trying to reason with these people because they did not want to hear direction. But for the most part everybody cooperated with us. However, I remember one woman in particular, by the Winter Garden. I was arguing with her. I said, "Lady, you have to leave." And she wouldn't leave, and I said to her, "I hope this person is worth your life."

And she says, "He is." And she stayed there. We tried to pull her away. I hope to God she's still alive.

When the South Tower came down, I'll be honest with you, I thought it was another plane coming in. We looked up and the cloud was coming at us and people were running. We directed them as we ran ourselves. And as you were running, you could feel the shrapnel flying by your head. I remember trying to look over my shoulder to see whether or not I should duck.

Same with the North Tower. Once again, I'm running like a bastard. I hear the tower crumbling. I feel it crumbling. And as I'm running, I'm about to pass a fire chaplain. So I start running with him, and as I'm running with him, I ask him if he's a priest. He said yes. I ask him if he's a Catholic priest, and he said yes. I said, "How about some absolution?" So, as he's running, he blesses me, he gives me my absolution.

Over by Battery Park City, we're still running. Another cop falls down and people are tripping over him. As he goes down, I reach and grab him by the gun belt and by his shirt to pick him up to get him out of there. He looks up at me and he says, "I dropped my pen." I guess in his state of shock he thought it was important to pick up his pen. And as I'm running, I'm saying to myself, "Jump into the river, jump into the river, but be careful, there may be rocks there and you're going to land on them." It was weird because when we hit the river, the cloud basically dissipated. Maybe it was the water temperature, maybe it was the air coming down from the Hudson, I don't know. But I didn't have to jump in.

By Tuesday and Wednesday, I'm bouncing around the morgue, bouncing here and there, all detective bureau stuff. On Thursday, they tell me go up to the landfill. Chief William Allee, the chief of detectives, called me and said, "Jimmy, you're in charge of the Fresh Kills landfill." And I've been here ever since.

The night I got here I called Lieutenant Bruce Balldino from Staten Island, and Ray Ferrari, who's in charge of the fugitive enforcement division, and they came here. Then I met my counterpart from the FBI, Richard Marx, a great guy, and he's here. Me, Richie, and Bruce built this place. We got a lot of help from Sanitation, and then the Army Corps of Engineers came. To date, we have processed about 1.2 million tons of debris. We've recovered about thirty-seven hundred pieces of human remains and thousands upon thousands of pieces of property. The debris comes over by barge—at the beginning it was also coming over by truck, but now it's just coming over by barge. It's then taken out by crane and put into trucks, which then come up the hill. The debris is then dropped into machines, compost and recycling machines, quarry machines.

The three categories we're most concerned with are human remains, personal property, and evidence. The human remains range from fingers to torsos. We haven't had one intact body up here yet. For a while people were saying we were coming up with bodies, full bodies, but that was never true. We've had everything from teeth to torsos, but never an intact body. We'll get torsos without a head. We'll get torsos without legs and arms. We've identified seventy people already. As the DNA comes back, we'll identify more.

Then the evidence is categorized and vouchered, along with the personal property. The human remains are sent off to the morgue.

At a certain point we started coming up with faces, just faces. They looked like Halloween masks, but they were human faces with nothing in between. You'd have just the front part of a face that was ripped off. We got quite a few of them. We've seen a lot of bad things here. It just doesn't stop.

I wasn't killed on September 11. And maybe there's a reason I wasn't. I have a task to do up here. Family members who lost people come up here all the time and it's pretty emotional. I never really understood the expression, "Can't see the forest for the trees," but we're so involved up here that sometimes I don't even think we realize what we're doing. Maybe when all this is over, it will come to us. But for now you have to just keep on going. You really don't have an option.

WILLIAM ALLEE

60, Chief of Detectives, NYPD

"SHE WOUND UP TAKING ROSARY BEADS AND PUTTING THEM ON A FIRE TRUCK."

I was in my office at 1 Police Plaza, on the thirteenth floor, facing the window, which was open. I was being interviewed by a writer who had his tape recorder on. We had just started the interview, and I heard what initially sounded like a missile. And then seconds later I heard an extraordinary explosion. I looked out the window and saw what looked like a mushroom cloud without the top, without the cap, and the remainder of the World Trade Center above it.

I got my raid jacket on, a windbreaker that says NYPD on it, and I left the reporter. One of my aides was getting my car gassed, so I ran down the elevator with five or six people from my office. We ran over to Vesey Street, and naturally there were sirens and everybody was coming. There were hundreds of people on Vesey Street, between Church and Broadway, so I told a bunch of uniformed officers to clear the spot. And we continued west. When we got to what would have been right across from the northeast corner of the World Trade Center, I heard people scream. I heard a second explosion and looked up and saw the second tower with the same configuration of smoke and fire. I hadn't heard or seen a plane, but people were yelling that that's what it was. There were things spiraling down out of this dark cloud. I was like a deer caught in the headlights, staring up, and my sergeant said to me, "Boss, you better get out of here. We better get out of here."

Everybody's running and people are knocking into us, but they're going one way and we're going the other way. We're trying to hug the walls because one of the things that was spiraling down was one of the components of an airplane engine. It was coming down like a Frisbee and it smashed down right near where we were.

I was concerned about the possibility of toxins or chemical agents. The smoke was going south, out over the water, which I thought was a good thing. Whatever was up there, if it was something that had some toxicity to it, it would be getting into an area that was away from the buildings and toward the bay.

I tried to get a command post at 99 Church, which is a block north. We went into the building and I found a phone that worked, and called home. I told my wife I was okay. She asked, "Where are you?"

I told her, "Downtown." And I said, "I'm probably not going to be able to call you for a while."

She said, "Okay, be careful."

One of my drivers showed up and I told him, "Go get the helmets." I had helmets in the car, including my Kevlar helmet. We were trying to organize ourselves and everybody was getting separated. I needed to get the bomb squad together and start the process of preserving the crime scene. A lot of the smaller plane parts had come down on Vesey Street and bounced. Some of them went through the plate-glass window of building 7. So we're walking in the middle of the street, and we found a leg, found some other body parts, and I'm telling my guys to cover it because we have to preserve it. I went into building 7 and this maintenance guy was sweeping up the plane parts. And I'm again thinking, Crime scene. Don't sweep it. Leave it the way it is. We have to get pictures, we have to preserve the evidence, not knowing, of course, that the building was going to fall down.

I then went down to West Street thinking I was going to see where the police commissioner is, so I can let him know what we were doing. Ironically, when I go home at night, I go down Vesey Street to West and make a left to go into the tunnel to Brooklyn. So I know the block very well, and there's the Verizon building on the corner, a beautiful old building that I always admire as I go past. It later turned out to be more important than I ever would've thought.

But now we're walking down the middle of the street and I heard the most godawful sound I ever heard in my life. And it was tower 2 starting to come down. I looked up and the sky was full. The whole thing was coming down. So my driver and I ran. And the only place we could go was under the archway. Any other place would have been a mistake. We ran under the archway and hugged the arches. And as the building came down, another detective who had run behind us came under. The sound was deafening. In fact, my ear is still ringing from it. But I held onto that building, and I could feel the ground underneath me vibrating from stuff hitting it. And the column I was holding onto didn't move and didn't shake. Later on I found out that large beams had hit the Verizon building above us. And the building didn't move. I said to my wife, "I'll never complain about paying another Verizon bill again," because that old building was great.

So I opened my eyes and there was nothing, absolutely nothing. All I could see was my driver's hand reaching out. I didn't realize it, but the other detective had reached out and grabbed my driver's other hand. So the three of us were holding hands. And the saving grace was that I knew where I was. And I knew that if we kept the building to our right shoulder, and then get to the end and make a right, it was going to take us north, away from this.

Keeping our eyes open was useless. Breathing was like drowning dry. It's like somebody had come along and said, "Take spoonfuls of dry dirt and swallow them." I felt like an hourglass filling up. And it was the weirdest feeling in the world. I've been involved with a lot of things. I've been scared to death many, many, many, many, many times. I've been on the street my whole career. I've had many very, very close encounters. But in this case, I guess I frightened the fright out. It just went away. It was a feeling of "I'm going to die. I'm not afraid to die. But this is a shitty way to die." I mean, I'm swallowing this stuff and it's killing me.

Then we turned the corner, and I started thinking, Are there holes? Did the manhole covers blow? Are we going to fall into a crater? Are we going to walk into something that's on fire?

Then with our feet we found a fire hose that was going north. It was fully inflated with water, pressurized. I put my feet on it like a little kid on a rail. And we took little baby steps with the hose between our feet. And the fact that we were holding hands made a big difference. Having someone else with you was a lot better than being alone.

Then all of a sudden there was a tiny, little, itsy-bitsy red light. It turned out to be the back taillight of a big mobile trailer, and people pulled us in. They gave us water and oxygen, and we started feeling a little better. So we waited there a few minutes and when we could see, I said, "Let's go." We went back out and started finding people and bringing them in to 99 Church to patch them up: an officer who was hurt, an old-timer who we thought had had a heart attack.

Now we're back outside on Church and somebody yelled that the second building was coming down. So we ran back inside, down into the basement on an escalator that was stopped.

When we got back outside, I really started seeing the fires for the first time, starting by the post office at Vesey and Church. A little postal truck caught on fire and spilled its gas tank. It spread to the next truck, and then the next truck, and the next. The fires were spreading north by means of the cars that were parked on the street. Contrary to what most people believe, gas tanks don't explode. Tires explode. A gas tank would probably explode if it was almost empty, but in this case the trucks were spilling fuel, and it went *poof,* but it was not a big explosion.

We found a fire truck pumper, and we said, "We have to stop these fires because they're just going to keep going and going." The fires had already spread around the back. There was fire all over. That was really the first time I smelled fire. All the other times it was just the dust and the debris.

Then I called for my bomb squad. The cars that hadn't caught fire had to have the bomb squad check them out to make sure there were no explosives, as a secondary thing that a terrorist might have left to get the rescuers. Then I was going to get the cars towed and prevent them from catching fire and having the fire spread.

One of my bomb guys and I got in a truck and I was coated with this stuff and he was cleaning me off. And he asked, "Are you all right, guy? Are you all right?" Then all of a sudden he recognizes that it's me, and he said, "Oh, Chief, what happened to you?"

And I said, "What happened to me? The frigging building fell on me, that's what happened to me. You look nice and clean."

Later I sent some of my detectives to the morgue and I eventually went to New York Hospital on Thirty-third Street. That was strange because I walked in and there had to be one hundred to 150 medical people waiting, and my driver and I were the only two patients. We had scratched corneas, ringing ears, and all kinds of nasty stuff. I wound up being in the hospital twice, once in November and once in December. I had an uncontrollable cough during the night. My airway actually closed up and I couldn't breathe. It was spooky.

But mostly one day went into the next, and then the next. We organized the Fresh Kills landfill and the morgue and Missing Persons. The detectives who run Fresh Kills work for me. I set it up. It was dirt. There was nothing there. We created a city.

I live in Staten Island so even now, if I take a Sunday off, I'll take a ride to the landfill just to say hello. It's a funny thing. It'll be nine o'clock at night, and my wife says, "You've been at work since six o'clock in the morning."

And I'll say, "All right, I'm just going to make a stop at the landfill before I come home." She would expect me home in, say, an hour, and I wouldn't come home for three or four.

And my wife would say, "What's the matter with you? You say you're going to be home, and it's three hours later and you're not home. You're always up there. What are you doing up there?"

And one time I said, "You know what, I'm going to take you up there. Do you want to go up there?" And she said okay. So I took her up there and we had this little all-terrain vehicle and I drove her around. I drove in and out of the piles of the wrecked cars and the fire trucks, and she was being very quiet. And I didn't say anything. And then she said, "Now I know why you don't come home. This is sacred. This is almost like being in a cathedral. It's special, sacred ground."

She wound up taking rosary beads and putting them on a fire truck. And then she met people up there, and she loved them and she was kissing them and crying. And she said, "I'll never question again why you're up there."

Then I took her down to the Verizon building. And she got very uneasy. And I said to her, "What's wrong?"

And she said, "I can't. I don't want to go under there. I'm just afraid."

I said, "Listen, Diane, that was not my tomb. That was my bunker. That's what saved my life."

MICHAEL SCAGNELLI
55, Chief of Transportation, NYPD

"I WAS DRAWN TO THIS ONE: A HEART ABOUT THE SIZE OF A QUARTER. IT WAS DONE IN DARK PENCIL AND IT REALLY STANDS OUT. THERE'S THE RUBBLE, HERE'S THE RAILING, AND THERE'S AN ARROW. BUT IT'S NOT GOING THROUGH THE HEART. IT'S GOING JUST BEYOND THE HEART, POINTING TO THE RUBBLE. AND THE WORD IN THE HEART IS 'DADDY.' "

On September 11, I was a thousand miles north of Montreal in the Quebec tundra. I was on a caribou-hunting trip and I had been there for a couple of days. I'm at an outfit called James Bay Adventures, which runs caribou hunts up there, and I was bow hunting not very far from the camp.

There were sixteen of us there. Most of us were from New York. There were one or two fellows from Jersey, and I think two people from Pennsylvania. So we're out there hunting and the camp manager somehow finds me, brings me back to the camp, and says, "We have a radio telephone here. Arthur Taillon, the owner of James Bay Adventures, is on this satellite phone and he wants to talk to you."

I get on the phone, and he said, "Michael, it's Arthur. There's been a terrorist attack in the United States. Both towers of the World Trade Center have been hit by airplanes. It looks like they're commercial planes. And the Pentagon has been hit by an airplane. There's all kinds of craziness going on in all of North America, and I don't know if I can, but I suppose you want me to get you back to New York City, if it's possible."

I said, "Get me out of here. You have to get me back to New York City. Somehow you have to get me back." He said he would make some phone calls and then get back to me.

In the meantime, we gathered everybody. We fired a couple of shots so people would come back to camp. We sent some scouts out, and we assembled everyone in the mess tent. These were all hunters, friends of mine—two police officers, and the rest were all civilians. Just as I'm about to tell them what happened, the phone rings again. It's an oddball phone. I don't even know how to answer it, so the camp manager answers it. It's Arthur. He says, "Michael, it's gotten worse. Both towers have collapsed. There are untold numbers of people dead."

I'm hearing this, but the guys don't hear it, even though they're standing right there in the room, because I have the phone pressed to my ear, and I'll never forget the things that went through my mind at that point. It was a terrible, terrible feeling. All I thought of was, Oh, my God, I can't believe that people would do this, that these animals would do this. There could be forty thousand or fifty thousand people dead. I didn't even look at the time. I was out there hunting and time didn't mean anything to me. But I was picturing virtually everybody being in the World Trade Center. And I was picturing no time for rescue to have occurred. And this terrible sadness came over me that all these people were dead, and I wondered whether this was World War III.

All these things were going through my mind. I really didn't know what was happening at that point. And then Arthur said he had already been in contact with the Royal Canadian Mounted Police and the FBI, two agents of whom are permanently stationed in Ottawa. He said he'd get back to me again, and we hung up.

Then I spoke to the group about it. These are rough-and-tumble hunters, and you could hear a pin drop in the room. Some of us were openly crying. It was really terrible and touching. This is going to sound odd, but it was a terrible feeling and wonderful feeling at the same time, that everyone felt the same way. And you could just understand, right at that moment, a thousand miles north of Montreal in the wilderness, that this was going to pull the country together.

I wanted to jump out of my skin, because I knew that I should be there taking action and dealing with this disaster. I felt absolutely helpless. I was helpless. And then, a little while later, the phone ran again, and Arthur said, "I got the ball rolling with the RCMP and the FBI, and we'll take it one step at a time. We already have a float plane in the air."

The plane had to come 150 miles to get me and it landed on the lake next to the camp. I got on the plane. I took some of my equipment with me: a bag of clothing, because I knew that when I got to New York I'd need clean clothes, and I brought my shaving equipment, and my toiletries, but I left my bow and arrow and my rifle and my caribou with the other fellows who stayed behind. They were able to take a handful of us in the float plane, and we went 150 miles back to a hunter's base station, which was a little peninsula where they have a landing strip for larger planes that can hold around forty people. On the tarmac of this isolated landing strip, there were thirty-five or forty hunters in another plane, which was scheduled to take off to go home. Their hunts were completed. They were at different campsites. And now they were grounded because all commercial airlines in North America were grounded, and very rightfully so.

So I got there, and our plane was grounded too. Now I was stuck on this wilderness landing strip, still 850 miles from Montreal. And there's nothing but wilderness for the first five hundred of those miles.

I wound up on a telephone talking to the superintendent of the Royal Canadian Mounted Police. I also spoke to an FBI agent in Ottawa. We discussed the fact that it was really important for me to get back, and they were able—after about a half hour—to get air clearance for a hunter commercial flight. They had no extra seats on the plane, and I wound up sitting with the pilots on a little jump seat. Usually planes with hunters on them are rather noisy. Everyone's talking about the hunt and how wonderful it was, or how not-so-wonderful it was. This time, nobody talked the entire flight. For 850 miles, nobody talked. It was the eeriest feeling.

And then, when we came to Montreal International Airport, I looked down and saw an airport that had no movement. It was still daylight, late morning or midday, and you could look down and see that nothing on the ground was moving. You see these old movies where God forbid you had nuclear war and everybody's dead and you and only a handful of people are alive. That's how I felt, as if that had happened, because this airport had no movement.

I got off the plane, as did the other hunters. Now we were all stranded in Montreal. Once again, I spoke to the Royal Canadian Mounted Police and the FBI and I asked them if they could get me a police car to drive me to the border, and then the New York State Police could meet me and then drive me to New York City.

Well, the Royal Canadian Mounted Police did one better than that. They sent one of their Learjets from Ottawa to Montreal to pick me up. I got on the plane alone, and we got clearance from Canada and the United States for that plane to go to La Guardia.

It landed at La Guardia, and now it was dark. It's dark, there's no movement, there are practically no lights because they shut them off, and again, I'm in one of those 1950s movies, as if we're the only ones alive. It was an absolutely terrible feeling.

The plane lands and makes a U-turn on the tarmac and goes back toward the Port Authority police building. I didn't know about casualties at this point. I didn't know about police gone, about firemen gone. I knew nothing of that. I got out of the plane and was met by two Port Authority police cars. I thanked the pilot. I said hello to the people meeting me and I asked one of them, "How is my friend, Inspector Tony Infante?" He was the commanding officer of the Port Authority police at Kennedy Airport.

And one of the fellows looked at me and said, "Chief, he's dead." And reality really sunk in at that point. There I was asking about one individual, and the individual I picked is one of the deceased, one of our heroes that died. All the blood rushed out of my head, just right down to my feet. I was speechless.

I was physically standing in the rubble at 9:20 P.M. I looked around and I just couldn't believe that human beings could do that. And you had to cry. If you were at that scene and you didn't cry, you weren't human. It was absolutely devastating. There were rescue workers all over the place. The thing was still on fire. Smoke was coming out from everywhere. The stench was horrible. If you smell marijuana for the first time when you're young, and then don't smell it again for two hundred years, you'd still recognize it the next time you smelled it. Well, the World Trade Center had a smell that I will never forget. It was a unique smell, the World Trade Center smell. It was terrible.

I recall that we collectively rescued people that night and the next day, and then that was it. There were no live people after the second day. You just had this horrible feeling that there were people to be saved and it was almost an impossible task to save them because everything weighed a ton. And it was hot and looking like hell. Since those days, I've brought people over there to see it, and before they turn the corner I would use the words "Welcome to hell." It was absolutely devastating.

In the days that followed, I was proud to be a New Yorker and proud to be a citizen of the United States. As I said before, this country came together in a way that I never thought I'd see in my lifetime. We had people from all walks of life coming to New York. I met people from just about every state in the union. And they came right away. And the only way to come here was to drive, so they drove from California and from everywhere. For weeks, nobody gave up hope of finding live people, which may have been unrealistic, but I think we needed to think that.

You've seen that wooden viewing platform that was built on the water side of West Street. It has wooden rails all around it, and just about every inch of those wooden rails has been written on now. And every time I went there—and I went there a lot—I was drawn to this one: It was a heart. I get goose bumps and I cry when I think of this. But there's a heart about the size of a quarter. It was done in dark pencil and it really stands out. There's the rubble, here's the railing, and there's an arrow. But it's not going through the heart. It's going just beyond the heart, pointing to the rubble. And the word in the heart is "Daddy."

I like to say, maybe for effect, that hunting, which is my passion in life, saved my life. And maybe it did. At the very least, I might have been running for my life. We had firemen, policemen, and civilians running for their lives, and by the grace of two feet, some are dead and some are alive. You either made it or you didn't. And when you had to run, there was no analysis, no thinking. You were just lucky or not lucky.

I don't think 9/11 changed me. Most people are going to say it did. I'm still Mike Scagnelli, and I don't think I've changed since the third grade. I think deep down inside I always knew there were evil people in this world who could do things like that, even though I was shocked that it actually happened. I don't know, maybe there's something wrong with me, maybe it should have changed me. Probably it has changed me and I just don't want to admit it.

LAURA GLADING

45, Union Representative, Association of Professional Flight Attendants

"ONE OF THE GIRLS, AMY SWEENEY, HAD A FOUR-YEAR-OLD
AND A FIVE-YEAR-OLD AND A HUSBAND AT HOME. AND TO THINK
THAT SHE WOULD BE ON THE TELEPHONE HELPING THE COMPANY
AND GIVING THEM INFORMATION WHEN SHE WAS IN SUCH DANGER.
THAT WAS A REAL ACT OF HEROISM IN MY MIND."

I am the union's representative for the northeast division, which includes New York, Boston, and Washington. We had been negotiating a contract with American Airlines. The flight attendants' contract had expired. A previous team had gone in and negotiated an agreement, and it got overwhelmingly voted down. The board of directors and the team met, and the team wound up resigning, and the board wound up appointing a new team, and the president of the union appointed me to chair that new negotiating committee. And we went back in to negotiate a better contract.

Our negotiations lasted a record two years. There really were no breaks in the negotiations, and it was very stressful. Flight attendants for American Airlines had not had a raise in many, many years. The senior flight attendants hadn't had a substantial raise since the 1970s, and it was very important to get a good contract for them and others.

We did come to a tentative agreement in June of 2001. It was overwhelmingly ratified on September 12, 2001. But on September 10, I flew down to Dallas for a meeting with American Airlines to discuss the implementation schedule for the contract, and to be in Dallas for the ballot count. I was in my hotel room on September 11, preparing to meet with the company and the vice president of the union, when I saw on the television that a plane had hit the World Trade Center. I called the vice president of the union and asked whether this would delay our meeting when they started talking on TV about it being an American Airlines jet. We were on the phone when the second plane struck.

I immediately went to APFA headquarters and I couldn't even count how many flight attendants had come just to be with other flight attendants. We watched the news as it unfolded. It was surreal, I guess. I mean, I had grown up in New York. I still live in New York. I knew people who worked in the World Trade Center. I knew firemen. My father and my uncle were both retired firemen. And I was certain I knew people who were probably killed, but I don't think I let my mind go to that at the time. I just basically watched the news, and I don't even know what I was thinking, to tell you the truth. All I know is that for two whole years I was obsessed with the contract and suddenly it seemed so unimportant. It was twenty-four hours before the ballot count, and nothing seemed to matter anymore.

I did get an early heads-up on who was on the airplane, although I wasn't allowed to divulge that information, which was difficult because there were many people in APFA who were asking me if I knew who the victims were. But I didn't tell anyone who was on the plane because the company asked me not to.

The company was trying to get approval from the FBI and the FAA to get a plane in the sky on the night of September 11, so they could relocate some of their executives and care people. They asked me if I wanted to head to the northeast if they got a plane, and I said yes. The plane departed at approximately 6:30 P.M., Dallas time. It very eerie because the Dallas–Fort Worth airport was completely evacuated. There was nothing but dogs and military people and police.

There were maybe twenty or thirty people on the plane with me. I went to my seat and immediately started writing a letter to my son, who is seven years old. And in the letter I wrote to him about what had happened that day. I said I knew that I would have to talk to him about it one day, but I wasn't sure how. I just wanted to give him an account of what happened.

I kept thinking, What's going to happen next? I wasn't sure. I felt no fear going on that flight. It never even dawned on me to be fearful, yet there were people on the flight going, "Are we crazy? Should we really be in an airplane? This is nuts." We had an air force escort, which I found kind of eerie. People were talking to the captain. I told the captain to make sure that he kept his hands on the wheel. I think one of my concerns was that if we made a sharp turn of any kind, we'd probably be shot right out of the sky. I think I was more fearful of the air force escort than anything.

We flew into Boston. The airport was closed. There were troopers in the operations area. We were briefed by the base manager immediately on what transpired that day, about the telephone calls that had come in from the crew, and all the information they knew. They were very thorough and they briefed us on a lot of information. It was confidential and I wasn't to share it, but I had a very vivid idea of exactly what had happened on those planes that day.

I don't know that anything is really confidential anymore.

Passengers were disabled and anyone who stood up was cut. A flight attendant did speak with a supervisor from the air, and she walked him through it in a very calm way. She said a man in business class had stood up, and they had cut his throat. They had also cut two flight attendants, and they got in the cockpit and she was sure that they had disabled or killed the pilot. She was sure they were in control of the airplane. She said, basically, that a lot of the passengers in the back weren't sure what was happening. The flight attendants were incredibly professional. Two of their coworkers had been stabbed, and were lying bleeding on the floor. They paged for a doctor and a nurse, and the flight attendants administered oxygen while the doctor and nurse tried to stop the bleeding.

What impressed us most during the briefing we got that night in Boston was that the flight attendants had remained so calm. They tried very desperately to contact somebody even though they were risking their own lives. They remembered seat numbers. They gave descriptions. They really attempted to do their job under those circumstances.

One of the girls, Amy Sweeney, had a four-year-old and a five-year-old and a husband at home. And to think that she would be on the telephone helping the company and giving them information when she was in such danger. That was a real act of heroism in my mind. And I wish that her story had come out. I wish the flight attendants' experiences had come out a little bit more because there were so many mothers and fathers with real stories on those airplanes.

We had very big problems with getting the flight attendants back to work. Understandably, they were petrified. I thought that we would never get people back to work. I guess I was surprised at how many people just bounced right back and returned.

On the night of September 12, I got a telephone call from Dallas informing me that the contract had passed by 96.5 percent, which I believe is a record-breaking contract ratification from any union. I've never heard of a ratification that went that high. The contract included a very good retirement package and an early out. I thought a lot more people would take it, but the numbers were not overwhelming. We did not have a mass exodus. I think everyone was so brave to come back to work.

And it's been so tough for the flight attendants, because we had the crash in Belle Harbor shortly after September 11. I knew that the flight attendants were reeling from September 11, and I didn't know how this would affect them. I felt such overwhelming pride to be a flight attendant, and to be based in New York and see these courageous people who not only came right back after September 11, but were now marching back in after yet another incident only two months later. It was amazing to me. I'm very proud to be one of them.

The resiliency of America was never more evident than it was during the days and months following the September 11 attacks. People stopped what they were doing, put their lives on hold, and traveled to New York and Washington from nearly every corner of the United States.

And everyone's mission seemed to be the same: They suited up and showed up and came with food and water, cranes and front loaders, pick axes and jackhammers, flashlights and air masks, massages and AA meetings, money and talent, tears and messages of hope.

And what they found, above all else, was a purpose and a deeper commitment to what Thomas Jefferson described in the Declaration of Independence as our unalienable rights: life, liberty, and the pursuit of happiness.

It used to be that June 6, 1945, was America's longest day. But not anymore. September 11, 2001, is longer. And, unfortunately, for a lot of us, it's not over yet.

SETH CASTLEMAN
29, Volunteer

⟶

"SHE WAS JUST LETTING OUT THE MOST VISCERAL RAW EMOTION
THAT I HAD EVER SEEN, WITH SUCH BROKENHEARTEDNESS AND
SO COMPLETELY THAT IT JUST CRUMBLED ME."

I teach meditation and spiritual practice in the prisons, working with incarcerated youth and women in New York and California. My role in prisons is very similar to a chaplain's. When I arrived at Ground Zero the firemen and counselors said I should use "chaplain" to identify myself because it is easier to understand than "meditation teacher."

I was ironing a shirt in my apartment on the Upper West Side before heading to J&R Music and Computer World, which is right next to the World Trade Center, when I got the phone call that we were under attack. So I turned on the television and watched for about twenty or thirty minutes, then got on my cushion and did my morning davening, or Jewish prayer, for another thirty minutes. I felt that if there was ever a time for me to be meditating and praying, this was it. During my meditation, I realized that by some strange coincidence, my car was completely out of gas and I literally had no cash. We had no idea at that point what was happening and how long it would last and whether we were going to war and if things like banks and ATMs and gas stations would be open. So, realizing that first I needed to get myself into a position of some security and functionality, I went out, jumped in the car, drove to the nearest bank, withdrew a thousand dollars off my credit card, and then filled up at the gas station. At that point I felt like I was set. Now I could start thinking about how to help.

I started by heading from hospital to hospital to see if blood was needed. Of course, there were already long lines and there was no need. And as we know, there were very few victims walking out of the hospitals. So I spent most of the afternoon just schlepping around from one hospital to another, and by about four o'clock was ready to head home when I heard on the news something about a possible morgue being set up at Chelsea Piers. I figured, if there's a morgue, there will be people showing up. So I drove as close as I could and then walked the last two miles. Actually, Chelsea Piers was also being set up as a triage unit. Much of it had been taken over by doctors. But there was a small group of crisis counselors and chaplains hanging out in the corner with nothing to do. So I started putting up signs and schlepping chairs and helping with whatever needed to be done. Later that afternoon the triage unit closed down. Everybody else left, but we counselors stuck around and I ended up coordinating and directing a crisis center for families looking for missing persons. Families would come there as the last stop, having already visited the seven urban hospitals in New York. Sadly enough, we had very little information to give them.

The most memorable experience was meeting people. One Indian family came in with thirty people. I would ask for a photograph and a name and maybe some stories about this person, and they would tell me things and we would cry together and laugh together. Sometimes we would spend ten minutes together. Sometimes a family would stay for an hour or two or even longer. It was very much like a kidnapping situation where you didn't know whether to have hope or whether to mourn.

Eventually, the rescue workers started coming in as well. There was one National Guardsman who came in a state of complete crisis, screaming and yelling and vomiting from his experiences of scooping out guts and pulling out hands and sorting fingers into different bags.

A few days later I got to Ground Zero, where I spent the next forty days coordinating five different supply stations that offered food and equipment and medical help, and beds and massages and counseling and boots and respirators and such to firemen, rescue workers, and volunteers. I walked on the rubble doing one-on-one counseling, or one-on-four, or one-on-five. It was often a group of firemen or policemen. I'd also find people sprawled out on the rubble sleeping. I'd bring them blankets or hot food.

While my role was mostly about being of service to others, I went through my own process of grief and shock. I had been trying not to absorb a lot of other people's agony, to hold it but not take it on. On day five, I came out of the little St. Joseph's Chapel, where I was stationed to help coordinate the food and the clothing, and I was just exhausted. I stepped outside to get some fresh air, and a firewoman was wailing, and she was being supported by about four or five other firemen. She was barely walking and they were lifting her up as they went by. I started to approach to see if I could be of any help as a chaplain, and one of the firemen told me that they had just found her husband's body. He was a fireman too. And she was just letting out the most visceral raw emotion that I had ever seen, with such brokenheartedness and so completely that it just crumbled me. And I fell to the ground and started weeping. It was the first time I had cried since I had been down there, and I just had so much to let out, that I just cried and cried. That image of her being supported and her face and her terror and her tears is so stark.

The other image that comes to mind is a fireman from upstate New York. I never knew his name. It was about three o'clock in the morning at Ground Zero. He was covered in dust and he was sitting against his long wooden hook pole, asleep. I threw a blanket over him and just sat there until he woke up. He asked if we could pray together, so we did for a while and he really wanted to talk, so I stayed there. He told how his wife didn't want him to be down there and was so upset. But his son understood. He said his five-year-old son really knew on some level, and he knew his son would respect the fact that he was down there. And he had something else he needed to tell me. It didn't come out for a while and I just sat there. Finally he looked me in the eyes and I can just picture his face. He was completely covered in that gray soot. He said he had just crawled out of the rubble about a half hour before and had fallen asleep after doing rescue work all night. And he had found a body. He was crawling along with his light on his head and he came across a body that had been completely flattened to about four inches thick. And it was covered with another inch of cement dust. It was in a very tight space, but the fireman just wedged his way in there and found the body.

He was about to crawl out to get help to pull it out when he turned his head and caught a glimmer of light. It was the wedding ring on the man's finger. He was an Asian man, about thirty years old. The wedding ring caught the light because there was no dust on it. At first, the fireman thought another fireman must have come and wiped the dust off the ring, but then he realized that if someone else had found the body, they would have called for help and dragged it out. He could only imagine that an angel had done it. And he still had this image of the finger and everything else being gray except for this bright light. And I could picture it so clearly because here was this fireman who was also covered in dust, and yet his eyes were so bright. On some level there was this sparkle. The one part of him that still seemed alive were his eyes.

ROBERT GAYER
42, Volunteer

━━

"I WOUND UP JUST GETTING OVERWHELMED WITH EXHAUSTION, AND
I DROVE HOME. IT WAS ONE, TWO O'CLOCK IN THE MORNING, AND I
COLLAPSED IN MY WIFE'S ARMS ON MY FRONT STOOP."

I'm a coffee roaster. I roast and ship coffee. I was home in Wantagh, not far from
Jones Beach, and as I was getting out of the shower, I heard about the Trade
Center on the radio. When the second plane slammed into the second tower, I
just looked at my wife and said to her, "I gotta go."

I just felt compelled to go. I had this overwhelming need to help people. I just
told my wife that I loved her and the girls. I put on a really good pair of jeans, a
big belt, and some appropriate work boots. I have a four-by-four Durango and I
felt that they may be able to use my car for a makeshift ambulance. I stopped by
my local King Kullen and they donated six or seven cases of spring water. I then
made my way to the Long Island Expressway, which was at a total standstill.
Chaos. Cars in every direction.

I looked to my left and I noticed what appeared to be two doctors in their
scrubs. They had their stethoscopes around their neck, and I could see that they
had IDs clipped on their pocket area. I made a motion to the guy. He opened his

window and I asked him if they were going into the city, and he said they were trying to. And right away I knew that if I could get these doctors in my car, I would stand a better chance of getting in myself. So I persuaded them that it would be better if they came with me in my car because of the capabilities my truck had versus their car. And they agreed.

There were also two unmarked police cars in front of me with their lights on, also trying to get in. The traffic was so bad that I actually was able to get out of my car. I ran up to one of the police cars and told him that I have two doctors in my car and a lot of water supplies. They said great, follow them.

A Jeep Cherokee driven by a guy with an emergency personnel jacket on joined our little caravan, along with a couple of other unmarked cars. You couldn't move on the expressway, so we took the side streets and eventually got down to the Queens area. The guy in the Jeep hit a pothole and blew his tire out. He took his red emergency light, ran over to me, and said, "Here, keep this on your car. You're going to need it. Good luck. Go."

Now I had a light and I'm behind one of the police cars. I'm on the closed westbound portion of the Long Island Expressway doing approximately eighty, ninety miles an hour, with these two doctors, going toward Manhattan. And what a gruesome sight. As we got closer and closer toward the Midtown Tunnel, you could see the smoke just billowing into the sky.

As we came out of the tunnel, everything was in chaos. I made a left and was driving down Broadway, when all of a sudden the second building must have collapsed because it was just unbelievable. We went through that wave of ash. I pulled up down near City Hall. I don't know how I even made it there. It was just by luck. I was meant to be there.

The two doctors jumped out of my car and just went on their own. We actually hugged each other good-bye and wished each other luck. A policeman approached me and asked me what I was doing there. I told him I had cases and cases of water. And he said, "Fine. Just do what you gotta do." I took out the water, one case at a time, and I ran down Broadway throwing the bottles to the firemen so they could wash that ash off their faces.

After I depleted my supply of water, I raced back down Broadway and got to a Burger King, which was already being used as an evidence-slash-triage scenario. I got right down to the 10-10 firehouse, next to the Trade Center, and a guy said, "Let's go. We could use your hand here."

All you heard was the beeping of the alarms from the firemen's jackets, all over the place. And firemen were crying. I got upset. It was like a war zone.

I remember just taking a water tank with one of the firemen and throwing it up on my shoulder, and climbing right down into the pile. We went down into this big crater, and we came across a woman who was decapitated. We saw lots and lots of pieces of people. It was horrible.

I probably spent about twelve hours that day helping out in any way I could. I remember hearing one of the EMS guys saying that they needed more senior personnel. I said, "How can I help?" I said, "I got my four-by-four parked right by the street."

They said, "Can you drive us to the Staten Island Ferry," where the New York City Fire Department had set up headquarters. I said I would. One of the EMS guys then handed me an EMT helmet. We picked up three high-ranking police officials. I put them side by side in the back of my truck, full gear and everything. I was going back and forth, still helping out in any way I could.

I wound up just getting overwhelmed with exhaustion, and I drove home. It was one, two o'clock in the morning, and I collapsed in my wife's arms on my front stoop. I reeked. I smelled so bad that she made me get undressed right on the stoop. I had to take two showers to get the smell off of my body.

The next day I couldn't really do too much. My eyes were so swollen I had to pretty much lay quietly on day two. The morning of day three I got up very early and I told my wife that I was going back down there, and that I was going to bring in more supplies because I knew what was needed. I went to a few different supermarkets and they were pretty much carte blanche, whatever you wanted. I got cases of bananas and oranges and granola bars. Two of my customers from the coffee business each donated twenty-five cases of Poland Spring sixteen-ounce waters. My company donated 250 T-shirts. And I went right back down to Ground Zero where I proceeded to do the same exact stuff: helping out, handing out supplies, yelling and screaming for people, looking through the rubble, and climbing through any hole that I could find.

At around eight-thirty on the night of day three, I was standing around the Burger King next to a couple of guys and they were all talking to Deputy Police Commissioner Tibor Kerekes. I didn't know who he was at the time. I just knew he was a high-ranking cop. I was listening to the conversation and this one gentleman shows them a Port Authority police hat that had some sort of blue substance melted all over it. He says, "I was just down in the fifth-floor parking lot of building number 5. There are a lot of cars down there, and there could be people. We need to go back."

I ran into the Burger King and I got Deputy Kerekes some flashlights. We duct-taped them to his helmet. I had lights on my helmet. We were joined by an auxiliary police officer and a Red Cross worker who put some extra bottles of water in his backpack. We all grabbed some picks, shovels, and stuff and started to walk toward building 5. That was the same building that burned for approximately two days.

We walked down the main escalator into the mall complex under building 5 and we approached a Tourneau jewelry store. Keep in mind, the entire downstairs area was totally destroyed. Ceilings were hanging down. But some stores were okay.

Deputy Kerekes said to us, "Hold up a minute, guys." He noticed that there was some flashlight movement in the store.

We walked in the store and a gentleman was standing on the left side of the store. Deputy Kerekes asked him to identify himself. And right away the guy seemed very nervous, and he says, "I'm in here with my associate and we're looking for people."

With that, Tibor said to him, "Bullshit, you son of a bitch. You're looting the store. You're going to be put under arrest."

And he said, "Bob, hold onto him."

I grabbed the guy's arm, and I could actually feel him trembling. A few minutes later, from the back door of the store, another gentleman walked out and he was holding what appeared to be two boxes, which we found out later were disposable cameras. Deputy Kerekes asked him to identify himself. And he made some form of reference that he was a police officer.

Tibor said to him, "Well, you're not anymore. You're looting the store, you son of a bitch. You're being put under arrest. Put those two boxes down. We're going upstairs." And then he said, "Bob, you get this one, and I'm taking him," and we proceeded to walk up the escalator. Once we got out of the building, Deputy Kerekes identified himself to a police lieutenant and told him to place these two gentlemen under arrest for stealing.

One of these guys turned out to be an ex–corrections officer who was pretty much put out of a job in '99. He used false identification to get to the scene. I wound up testifying against him. I was a character witness for the State of New York, and he was found guilty on all three counts.

MARGIE EDWARDS

40, Volunteer

"ONE OF THE POLICE OFFICERS WALKED UP AND SAID, 'Y**OU LOOK
LIKE YOU ARE HOLDING ONTO SOMETHING FOR DEAR LIFE.'
"I** TOLD THEM, 'I**T'**S MY FRIEND T**ODD'**S DNA SAMPLES.'
"A**ND THEY SAID, 'G**IVE IT TO US.
W**E WILL TAKE IT WHERE IT NEEDS TO GO.' "

I watched the first building on fire, the second building being hit, and then from my office I watched both buildings fall.

One of my very good friends, Todd Rancke, who worked for Sandler O'Neill on the 104th floor of 2 World Trade, was killed in the attacks, but at the time I did not know that. I was afraid he was up there. When I got home later that afternoon, I started calling Todd's wife. We all live in New Jersey.

We searched all day long the next day, going from hospital to hospital, trying to find Todd. On Friday, two of my friends—one who lived down in Battery Park City and was now homeless—and I decided that we would volunteer. So we started walking to the city. We went to the American Red Cross, tried to sign up there, and went by the Salvation Army, but they said they didn't need anyone else. We went to St. Vincent's Hospital. They told us they would love for us to go out and find frozen food. So we started going around to grocery stores, but a lot of them had been tapped out. We ended up at Burger King and got them to donate four hundred beef patties and hamburgers. We did a little bit more begging and then decided that wasn't for us. So we ended up over at Pier 40, which is on Houston and the West Side Highway. They had what was called "Tent City" set up outside the pier. And we stood outside the pier, and no one would let us in. They said they didn't need any volunteers, but we wouldn't move.

Eventually, someone asked us to come in the back and make sandwiches. We stayed there for the next two and a half months calling restaurants three times a day to get them to donate food to feed the police officers. Soon we started taking the supplies we had at Pier 40 down to the site at Ground Zero. Then we worked at what we called "Site Two," which was right at Liberty and West Streets. We had shifts: we'd work until two o'clock in the morning and then on weekends. We had barbecues for the rescue workers at Pier 40. If they were running out of shoestrings, we would call a company to get them to donate shoestrings. We would try to get anything the guys needed down at Ground Zero for them.

Everyone is so emotional down there. These police officers, with tears in their eyes, would talk about their experiences, talk about being away from their families, talk about what they were going through. And when I needed to cry, they were there for me.

One of the captains called me into his office, and he goes, "I need to talk to somebody." This is a man, a captain to all these men, and he needs somebody to talk to, and he calls me in. We were just like a family. It's just so hard to put into words. A lot of my friends didn't understand what I was doing. Some of them never went down there and they could never understand why I kept going down there. I'd work all day at my job and I'd leave there and go directly over to Pier 40, or down to Ground Zero, and work until one o'clock in the morning. And if I didn't go one night, I'd feel guilty. I don't think I stopped for two months, and the one night I did I felt guilty. I felt like I needed to be down there, to be with those men. When you are down at Ground Zero, you weren't there to tell them what to do. You were there to listen to them. When they came off that pile, they wanted to see a smiling face. They wanted to talk about their families and where they were from. It was just amazing.

I did a lot of things I never thought I would have to do. I had to pick up my friend Todd's DNA samples from his family. Police officers saw me carrying the bag with his toothbrush and hair and everything. One of them walked up and said, "You look like you are holding onto something for dear life."

I told them, "It's my friend Todd's DNA samples."

And they said, "Give it to us. We will take it where it needs to go." They were just so incredible.

A lady walked in one day, I think she was Italian. She walked in with her next-door neighbor and her next-door neighbor's two daughters. And we all said, "Can we help you?"

She asked if this was family assistance. She said, "I'm looking for my brother." This was right at the beginning.

We said, "We think you're looking for Pier 94." And all these police officers sat down with this woman and they were all in tears listening to her tell about her brother, who was a window washer for twenty-seven years. And to see the compassion they gave to these women. I'm sitting here tearing up right now.

You always feel like you've got something inside yourself that you want to do, but it always seemed like I had an excuse: I'm working so much. I don't have time. But for this I just felt that I had to get my hands dirty. I had to do something for my friend Todd. And for all the other people. I saw what his wife was going through and going down to Ground Zero meant being closer to him. I'm so glad I did it, because it changed me as a person.

DREW NIEPORENT
46, Volunteer

"SOMETIMES WE JUST MADE SANDWICHES AND
PUT THEM IN SHOPPING BAGS TO TAKE AROUND.
SOMETIMES WE PUT CHAFING DISHES OF FOOD INTO
POLICE VEHICLES AND DISTRIBUTED THEM."

I live in Ridgewood, New Jersey, and my mode of travel for many years was always the PATH train to the World Trade Center—Ridgewood to Hoboken, and Hoboken to the World Trade Center.

On September 11, I left my house prior to knowing that a second plane hit the Trade Center. So I was on the train, going to Hoboken, and the guy next to me told me they just hit the Pentagon.

I said, "The Pentagon?"

He said, "Yeah, they just hit the Pentagon."

Then there was an announcement that they were going to stop the train. No transportation was allowed to go into New York, which at the end of the day if you think about it, saved a lot of people's lives. The PATH trains come right under the base of the Trade Center.

When I got off the train, you could see downtown Manhattan on fire. I jumped in the first cab I could get into. There were other people in the cab, and I talked my way into it. A woman in the cab was absolutely beside herself. Her husband worked in the Trade Center. Another guy in the cab, a young guy, was some sort of counterterrorism expert. There was no way we were getting into Manhattan at that point, so all we could do was go the other way. I made it back to Ridgewood, to a street called Crest Road. From that vantage point you can see the entire skyline of Manhattan, right from the George Washington Bridge to lower Manhattan.

Nobody was being allowed down near Ground Zero without identification that proved you lived down there. It didn't matter that I own restaurants down there. So I got in touch with a retired police captain friend of mine, and he brought me down there the next morning. That's when the restaurant community really started banding together to help out with food.

Just getting down there and assessing the situation made you realize how monumental it was. It was just an unbelievable sculpture, if you will, of mangled steel and debris and papers and dust. There were thousands of relief workers, rescue workers. The efforts to find anybody alive in the wreckage were extraordinary, and that was the initial absolute priority. You realized that you could be of assistance in a number of ways. One was morale. Another was providing any kind of food, hot food, to these people. They weren't looking to take any breaks. They were working around the clock trying to save whatever life they could find. And the effort was sustained twenty-four/seven.

I have six restaurants down there, so initially we cleaned out the refrigerators and cooked up whatever we could. We made Tribeca Grill the home base, but all the restaurants—Montrachet, Nobu—all brought food to Tribeca. There were three things that we had in mind: You needed access. You needed supply. And you needed distribution. Now keep in mind, there was very little access. They weren't letting anybody in. Number two, everyone wanted to donate food, so the supply wasn't a problem. Distribution was the biggest problem because once you had access, you had to be able to get around to give out the food.

After the first day, we realized it would've been a major hassle to try to get up to the restaurants above Canal or Houston Street. One of my ex-employees who's the chef at Tonic, Joseph Fortunato, said, "Why don't we just have the food come to you? We'll get trucks donated, and then with a police escort, we'll get it down to Tribeca where we'll distribute it." So those three things—access, supply, and distribution—made a really well-coordinated effort possible. After that day, people like Daniel Boulud, Le Cirque, and Bobby Flay delivered food. Then at Tribeca, we would distribute it all around the periphery. Sometimes we just made sandwiches and put them in shopping bags to take around. Sometimes we put chafing dishes of food into police vehicles and distributed them.

Obviously, as the days progressed, it became increasingly difficult to get in because they kept changing credentials and access. That's when we hooked up with people in the Office of Emergency Management. We got tremendous cooperation from John Odermatt, the deputy to OEM head Richard Sheirer. We got friendly with Manny Peppier, who was one of Rudy Giuliani's deputies. We saw things being done which prohibited access to the area, which we really needed.

While we were doing this sort of hands-on, ground-level work, Don Pintabona came up with a brilliant idea: Because of all the bureaucracy we were encountering on land, why not try to do something via the water? And that's when they came up with the idea with the Spirit of New York cruise line to dock a cruise ship in the harbor right behind the World Financial Center, and we'd ferry the food from the Twenty-third Street Chelsea Piers over to that boat. Once that operation was in effect, they served in excess of probably ten thousand people a day. Plus, it was an opportunity for the firemen and the rescue workers to come off the pile and literally rest, get massages and all kinds of refreshments on a four-hundred-seat luxury cruise ship. That was a brilliant idea.

This went on for about the next three months.

We gave away an extraordinary amount of food. But we felt good about it because at the end of the day, if there's a flood in Iowa, or a hurricane in Florida, everyone gets a bologna sandwich and an apple and is happy with that. But here we were in New York, where food is front and center, an important part of our culture, and we weren't going to be satisfied. We wanted the restaurant community to really show itself. And sometimes we were inhibited by bureaucracies along the way. We had meetings where they told us, "The health department is not going to let you do this. You should stop now. The Red Cross is in charge." We tried to interface with the Red Cross, with the Salvation Army, and they stiffed us. So we just said, "Fuck it. We're going to do what we've been doing," which is hand-carry food in. One day I walked in with a bunch of roast beef sandwiches, and Bill Clinton walked over to me. I was thinking, Oh, my God, there's Clinton with a construction hat on.

And he said, "I'll have one."

We had tremendous assistance from Governor Pataki's guys, Rob Antonek and Rob Ryan, in particular, who had scooters. We piled food onto them and because they had access, we could get right in. If we hadn't had the help from them and the people from OEM, we wouldn't have been able to do anything. The whole thing was a concerted effort.

ARTIE COLLINS
47, Detective, NYPD

<hr>

"AND THEN I FOUND A GOLF BALL THAT SEEMED TO
BE BRAND NEW. . . . I FIGURED IT WAS A BALL FROM SOMEBODY'S
DESK, AND IT MIGHT MEAN SOMETHING TO SOMEBODY WHO
HAD LOST EVERYTHING."

I was at the Brooklyn Army Terminal. We have a training facility there, and we were doing a basic narcotics entry course for some law enforcement agencies from different parts of the country. When I got there, the first plane hit the World Trade Center. When the second plane hit, I was down on the water where you can see Manhattan. We saw the second plane hit. We took some people from the class, from Massachusetts law enforcement, gave them guns, and headed toward Manhattan.

We were just about there when the building came down.

I was there personally for two months after September 11. Every day. We dug and climbed on the rubble with a group of people. Most of us were instructors and investigators. We usually formed a roster with our lieutenant and our captain, and whoever wanted to sign up would go into the pile every day and we'd start digging—by hand, with shovels and gloves, whatever we had.

Seven days after the towers came down we were digging on Liberty Street, toward the corner of West Street, just digging by hand, when somebody thought they smelled what could possibly have been a DOA. So we started digging by hand in that area. It was all basically cement, dust, and dirt. Everything was broken.

And then I found a golf ball that seemed to be brand new. It had some dirt on it. I brushed the dirt off, and it was a Titleist golf ball in perfect condition. And on the side of it, I noticed there was a company logo: Fiduciary Trust International. I took the ball home with me, which I probably wasn't supposed to do. But I figured it was a ball from somebody's desk, and it might mean something to somebody who had lost everything.

I went on the Internet and found out that Fiduciary had indeed lost seventy people, so I felt really badly. (The number has since been revised upward, to eighty-seven.) After seven days of not finding anybody, you get very frustrated. You get angry and upset.

So I decided to look up where Fiduciary Trust was in the towers. I looked on the Internet, and got to the directory of the World Trade Center, and I found that they were up pretty high in the South Tower.

I wrote Fiduciary a letter. It was a kind of therapy for me to contact somebody that was actually in the building. I e-mailed a note to Fiduciary saying if somebody wanted the golf ball, I'd be glad to mail it to them.

I wrote, "I know most of you must be destroyed by this disaster, but it touched me to find something I think came from your office, somebody's desk. There is really nothing in one piece that I have observed except this."

The CEO of the company, Anne Tatlock, contacted me by e-mail with a nice letter. She said if I wanted to send it to her, to please do so. So I sent it to them. She was very appreciative.

A couple of weeks later, I got a call from Mark Meyer, who is with Fiduciary. He told me that the ball I found had probably been his. He'd had a sleeve of Titleist balls, marked with the Fiduciary logo, in his desk. He asked, "Do you want to get together?"

I said, "Yeah."

He said, "Do you play golf?"

I said, "Yeah." We haven't played yet, but we're planning it. He's been busy with reestablishing the business. But I'm going to go to New Jersey one day and we're going to meet and have a golf game.

It was amazing. Everything was destroyed and this ball didn't have a mark on it. We were finding bits and pieces of things, and when we did, we'd hand them to the NYPD for the lost and found. But I knew that if I handed this in, it would just be thrown into a box and nothing would ever be done because there was really no importance in contacting anybody about a golf ball. Nobody would do that. It wasn't like somebody's driver's license, or an ID. But it felt good that I could do this.

The first couple days you would see the victims' families come down to Ground Zero. They were escorted by the police department, who would walk them right up to the edge of tower 2. I remember this one Asian woman. She was walking and somebody was holding her. She got right to the edge and she almost collapsed. We were standing there watching her. It really affected me not to be able to do anything for her. Other families came to the site and they just crumbled. And I would come home and talk to my wife about the frustration of not being able to find anyone. And then came this golf ball. It was a small thing, but it made me feel good.

GREGG NOLAN
47, Maintenance Foreman, Ground Zero

"BUT AFTER SIX OR SEVEN DAYS [AT GROUND ZERO], I REMEMBER
CROSSING SOME KIND OF A BOUNDARY IN MY OWN HEART."

I arrived down here on September 12 with my brother and a half-dozen other guys who work for me. I left a job as the foreman on a light rail over in Queens and I brought some of those guys with me. I came in from the north side, by West and Vesey, and I was totally blown away. I walked through the American Express building and looked through the Winter Garden at what was left of the Trade Center. It was smoldering and on fire. I was totally in shock at what was going on. Everywhere I walked there was total devastation.

Most people were on bucket brigades. Cranes were being brought in from different outfits. Trucks were trying to come in from everywhere. It was pretty much total chaos anywhere near the pile. There was equipment lined up and down the streets. Anybody who owned a backhoe, a dozer, or a loader was there. Rigs were stacked in the street all the way north of Canal waiting to come in. There was so much confusion. Everybody wanted to do something, but it was really out of hand. We were putting machines together, putting them on the pile, and people were getting run over by them. We'd put together a crane and try to get it close to the pile, and the operator would start swinging it around and suddenly fifteen people who were trying to look for loved ones would be knocked over by it. We didn't even realize what was happening because there were so many people, so much confusion everywhere we went. It was like that the first few days, people all over the pile, people coming in on their own, with their own front loaders, who had no idea what they were doing. People were going to the medical stations hurt from being in the wrong place at the wrong time. They'd hit a girder on one side that would kick loose a girder on another side and three people would get hit and fall down. The chaos was unbelievable. It was understandable because everybody was in such a panic to save somebody, and just trying to help, but for the first few days, it was just totally out of control.

We knew that some people were still alive, but there was no way to get to them because there was so much on top of them. There was one guy who we knew was alive. He had a lighter. He was down in a hole, but he kept flashing his lighter. We knew he was there, but there was so much stuff on top of him, there was no way we could get to him. And then after a while we didn't see his lighter anymore and we knew the guy had passed away. We didn't get to him for probably another two weeks.

Not a lot of people are trained to pick up body parts and put them in bags, but that's what we were dealing with, the horrific part of a disaster like this, death in this magnitude. The first few weeks we were surrounded by a smell we couldn't get away from. The smell was in the air, the decomposing flesh, the stench of what was burning and so many bodies. We had Vietnam vets who had to leave the job because they were having flashbacks from thirty years ago. There were some days that the wind would shift and all you could smell was death. Some of the younger guys didn't even know what the smell was. People who live out in the country know what death smells like—roadkill, deer, and stuff like that. But the guys from the city, a lot of them had never smelled anything like this and they just assumed that it was the sewer. In the beginning, if there was a foot laying around, guys would get sick. But it's a disgusting job that needs to be done. There's no nice way of doing it. You're digging through piles of dirt and you're spreading dirt on the ground just looking for pieces that can be sent to a laboratory. There's no nice way, no gentle way of doing this.

The National Guard came in and started taking control. Soon anybody leaving the outside perimeter wouldn't be let back in if they didn't have the right badges. Most of the guys working with me stayed because we knew that once we left we wouldn't get back in. So we found places to sleep for a couple of hours in hallways. The American Express building had a hallway that we slept in. Cots were set up at Stuyvesant High School, so we would sleep over there. The first night I came in I was sleeping on boxes of body bags in the American Express building. We were moved around, but most of us didn't sleep much anyhow. We would lie down at three o'clock in the morning and then we'd be back up at five o'clock in the morning working again. There was just so much work that had to be done. It was twenty-four hours a day, nonstop, assembling equipment. And as we're doing that, they're pulling dead bodies out and putting them in body bags. There were body bags stacked like cords of wood. Wherever you looked, there were body bags. The first few days I'd wonder, Who's in that body bag? I wonder if it's a woman. I wonder if it's a girl my daughter's age. But you didn't have time to keep on reflecting because somebody would be calling over, "Gregg, listen, we've got to get this rig in here." So I would tear myself away from the emotional part of it and get back to business, which was getting rigs together and moving debris.

But after six or seven days of doing that, I remember crossing some kind of a boundary in my own heart. I started feeling guilty that I was looking at these body bags as something that was in the way. I was having a tug of war with my conscience and it worried me because I thought I was losing it. At one point, I was putting a rig together and some firemen came up with three bodies on stretchers and lay them down behind me. At one point, I was backing a machine in and I tripped over a body and fell down. I'm looking at the body bag that I'd just tripped over and thinking, Who the hell put that body bag there?

And then I realized something wasn't right. I was losing it, getting pissed off because somebody put a body behind me, and I fell over it. It was in my way. Didn't they know that I was trying to get work done? I was becoming detached to the point where I needed to put some kind of reality back together. I knew I had to talk to somebody. So I called up a minister friend of mine. I live out in New Jersey, in farm country. I moved out there a few years ago and became pretty close to a minister in a Presbyterian church. His name is Tex Coleman. I spoke to him after those days at Ground Zero. I went down by the river and sat on a bench for a little while and just tried to collect my thoughts. I told him, "You know, I'm having a hard time separating people who are dying from people who are already dead from people we're still looking for."

And he told me that anything I had learned in my life up to that point had prepared me for the job that I needed to do now. He reminded me that in the Bible it says, "You pray for the sick and you bury the dead." He said, "You're doing God's work down there right now, and God is giving you a shock system that is going to help you separate what you need to do from the way you feel. And down the road somewhere, later on, you're going to deal with what you're feeling now. But right now he's helping you do what you need to do. And what you need to do right now is recover the dead."

After that, I was able to look at things differently. I was able to put some sense into what my job was, and it put a little more compassion back into me. From that point on, whenever I'd see a chaplain walking around, I'd say, "How ya doing, Father?" And if I had time, I'd say, "Hey, why don't we go over there?" And I'd say a quick prayer. I was also worried about my own guys, so I made it a point to show my men that we need to talk to these preachers, we need to talk to these rabbis, we need to talk to these people of God. Some of the younger guys might have been embarrassed to pray with a priest, but I know a lot of them looked up to the older guys, like myself, and they would watch how we handled it. I used to go out of my way to say to a couple of the younger guys, "Let's go and talk to Father Murphy for a little while." I would make them feel that it's not an embarrassing thing to cry. It's not an embarrassing thing to feel.

There came a point where I started feeling like this was a holy place, that this was hallowed ground and that God was here. Everywhere you went, you could feel the presence of God. I would walk around and people would come over to me and they would sit me down on a chair. They would take my muddy boots off and take my muddy socks off and throw them away and put clean socks on me, then put my boots back on. If I had a dirty T-shirt on, they'd take my shirt off and throw it away and put clean clothes on me. Everywhere you went there were miracles going on, people walking up to you that you didn't know. "How ya doing, brother? What's going on? You all right?" I felt like I crossed a lot of boundaries, just in my own prejudices. I came in contact with everybody there— black, Hispanic, Jews, Catholics, Chinese, American Indians, women. We were all here together as a brotherhood. We all knew what we had to do and we all did it. Every day, hour after hour, day after day, week after week, month after month, we stayed here. We were here for the long haul.

ANONYMOUS

"THE OUTSIDE WORLD WASN'T AT GROUND ZERO
AND HAD NO REAL IDEA WHAT WAS GOING ON THERE,
THE HORRORS AND THE URGE TO DRINK."

The Red Cross saw what was going on at Ground Zero. There was so much drinking and people were getting so fucked up that they knew something needed to be done. So the Red Cross called Alcoholics Anonymous and asked AA to come down there and start a meeting.

But it wasn't so simple. Ground Zero is a federal site, a war zone. Does AA go in under a mental health tag? Does it come in as spiritual? The Red Cross already has their rabbis, they have their counselors, their ministers, their priests. Do they bring AA in with the psychiatrists? Or under physical, with the doctors? You're talking politics here. You're talking insurance. Whose insurance? You're talking FEMA. Almost two weeks went by until somebody from Washington made a call, and boom, boom, boom, nine AA members from various New York groups came down.

They found a room, number 231, at St. John's, and they started to make up these big signs, FRIENDS OF BILL W [an AA slogan which refers to one of the founders], with arrows pointing to the empty school, which was evacuated on September 11. AA is famous for its placards and slogans, but we weren't allowed to deface any of the walls. Not only was this a school, it was also a crime scene, with rules and regulations. No cameras, no nothing. But we managed to slide a few slogans under the moldings, and little by little people started coming.

Working twenty-four hours a day at Ground Zero, with all the smoke, all the debris, just spun around everyone's biological clock. And the booze was just free. They were just handing out the booze. A volunteer comes in, he's all fucked up, they give him a tranquilizer, a big shot of booze. From an Alcoholics Anonymous perspective, this is not a good thing. But to a lot of people there's nothing wrong with a good shot, a good tranquilizer, to hold them together. These are people who were sleeping there, waking up and not knowing if it was day or night. They traveled here from Ohio and everywhere, and now suddenly there's an AA room for them to go to, open twenty-four hours a day, seven days a week.

I remember saying, "I never thought I'd be at Ground Zero talking at an AA meeting." That's when I realized, That's it. That's the name of the meeting, Ground Zero. There was this blackboard in the classroom, and the first few guys that came in signed their names up on a corner of the blackboard. As more and more people found out about the room, they showed up and they wrote in their names. Countless people filled that blackboard up—transit workers, Port Authority cops, firemen, construction workers. Some came for a hug and a cup of coffee, others came to share, or to fill out reports and sleep. More and more people showed up and we would all write our name and group on the blackboard there. We filled the place with different groups.

There was one guy I'll always remember. I was talking to someone in 231 when this worker comes in. I don't know what group he was from, but he had a helmet on and he was dirty. He looked around the room and saw this slogan hanging: THERE BUT FOR THE GRACE OF GOD. He dropped the helmet and put his head up against the slogan and started rocking, holding it, touching it. It reminded me of the Wailing Wall in Jerusalem. You could hear him crying as he rocked back and forth, stroking the slogan. Then he just got himself together, picked up his helmet, and walked out. Never said a word. I swear, it was one of the most spiritual things I've ever seen in my life.

Then they started a second meeting, Respite 2, over at the Marriott Hotel, for the people who had difficulty coming across the pile to St. John's. Between the two, the Ground Zero meetings became an important daily reprieve from the horrors of Ground Zero, and they kept me from going insane. I couldn't go home and relate a lot of what I saw to my family. I also had difficulty relating to the AA meetings that I've gone to for years because the outside world wasn't at Ground Zero and had no real idea what was going on there, the horrors and the urge to drink. And because of this group, because of the brotherhood and the dedication of other AA members at Ground Zero, I didn't drink. Whenever I needed a meeting it was there. To me, this was AA's shining moment. AA came to Ground Zero and saved my ass, and I believe that without the Ground Zero group a lot of people here wouldn't have been able to do what they needed to do. People needed that spiritual strength to carry on. The meetings eventually ended in December because St. John's needed to open up again, but I'll always remember the Ground Zero group of AA as a big part of the history of what happened down here. It's right up there with digging that cross out of the basement of World Trade 6 and hanging it up as a memorial. The Ground Zero group was a memorial too. I can't say enough about it.

GAIL PAIGE-BOWMAN
65, Psychotherapist

⌐➤

"THE ATTACKS HAVE CAUSED MANY PEOPLE TO QUESTION THEIR OWN PURPOSE IN LIFE."

The incident on 9/11 has in many cases exacerbated post-traumatic stress disorder, along with other disorders such as depression and anxiety. People who were very close to the World Trade Center and others who had been commuting into New York have been impacted profoundly. Family members and close friends of people close to the site have also been impacted. People have become hyper-vigilant and in varying degrees suffer from nightmares, sleeplessness, immobilizing depression, or extreme anxiety. In some ways, this hyper-vigilance is close to paranoia.

Fears include going into tunnels, subways, bridges, large crowds of people. The feelings of powerlessness and helplessness, which are part of post-traumatic stress disorder, become very acute. Some people have become more fearful for their safety, physical and emotional, and are having difficulty in maintaining what would be a normal balance of living.

From the clients I have, I note that people have been affected in varying degrees depending on their past history and their proximity to the actual Ground Zero area. Many people had to run for their lives, or were injured. Others lost dozens and dozens of friends in the World Trade Center. As a result of that kind of trauma, many people are going through what I call an extension crisis. They look at their lives, and they ask, "Who am I? What is the meaning of the life? What is the meaning of work? Is this really where I want to be living and working?" And this is not just because New York City was where these attacks occurred. But the attacks have also caused many people to question their own purpose in life. They reflect on who they are, where they've come from, where they're going, who they can trust, whether money is worth it, whether being locked into a particular career is worth it, whether the politics in many corporations are worth it.

I see a lot of people searching for solace in some of the creative therapies— music, art, writing, painting. A lot of people in the corporate world are turning toward those things as a way of expressing their feelings and trying to free their spirits in the aftermath of this kind of shock.

Some of the people who were directly involved, who ran for their lives, have been deeply traumatized and are struggling to regain an equilibrium. How long it takes is very difficult to estimate, and while there is some return to normalcy, many of them state that they feel they may never again be the way they were prior to 9/11.

Since 9/11, I've seen relapses in victims of past trauma and abuse, PTSD survivors and victims of child abuse, who had come a long way toward working through the trauma, dealing with their feelings, validating the situations that happened to them, and learning how to express anger, sadness, rage, and feelings of betrayal in a healthy way. People in those categories seem to be suffering most severely from the aftereffects of 9/11 because it has reactivated their previous PTSD and made it worse. Many of these people express their feelings that a lot of joy has gone out of life. They were unable to really enjoy holiday time in December. In many cases, these people aren't able to return to a state of normal functioning.

I also found that a number of clients who had completed therapy some time back called for appointments. Since most of my practice involves people who have experienced trauma in their past, many of these were so impacted by 9/11, even if they were not near the site, that they needed to come back for some trauma therapy after 9/11. Some are doing well and some are not doing well. But there is definitely a greater need for people to explore and look for ways to cope with a trauma in a constructive way. And in that sense there's a much greater urgency and much more emphasis on dealing with immediate trauma, grief, and mourning. Some people have been to funerals, several a week for almost every week since 9/11. And the enormity of that and the enormity of the amount of grief and mourning taking place is very unusual, and a lot of people really don't know how to grieve and how to mourn, and that it's okay to have those feelings. It's important to learn that instead of maintaining a stiff upper lip, and getting over it, and intellectualizing things away, coping is much more about feelings that come out, and accepting and learning how to process them.

I even talk to a lot of other therapists about it. Most of the therapists I know are very vigilant in getting their own help on a regular basis. We, as therapists who do deep trauma work, all need supervision and peer support. I think people who have burnt out may not have let themselves get the nourishment and the support that they need. These events have been pretty devastating, and it's hard to know whether other therapists have reached out, or if they have over-extended themselves. As a therapist, it's crucial for me not to overextend myself. You can do that in times of crisis for a short period of time, but ultimately you have to keep yourself balanced and supported and be able to process the feelings that come out, rather than keeping them bottled up.

The key for anyone having difficulty in the aftermath of 9/11 is to get help. Sometimes people who have the most serious implications are people who have never been in the habit of asking for help. These are people who are very high-functioning and have been able to get along very well in life. When they go through a trauma like this, they think just moving forward is enough, and they have a much harder time asking for help. There may be longer-term implications as a result. But if they do get proper trauma help, which may or may not include medication, and if they can learn to talk about feelings and know that they're not alone in what they're experiencing, in the long term they can resume not only life as they once knew it, but a fairly normal life as well.

TIM CAHILL
46, Construction Worker, Ground Zero

"IT FELT LIKE I WAS IN THE WOODS OF VERMONT, WHERE
I GREW UP IN THE SNOW, AND I FELT THIS QUIET COME OVER ME.
LIKE THIS GENTLE SNOW FALLING, ONLY IT WAS ASHES."

I've had some really positive experiences here, some unbelievable, spiritual experiences, and then I've had some of the most tragic, heartbreaking moments in my life too.

I remember standing on the crane and the fires were still really bad, so there was a lot of smoke. They were digging down below us and it started snowing ashes, like a fine snow, like a fine beautiful snow. And I held my hands out. It felt like I was in the woods of Vermont, where I grew up in the snow, and I felt this quiet come over me. Like this gentle snow falling, only it was ashes. But I felt that peace. I felt the presence of God in the midst of all that chaos and tragedy and pain and anger. It was unbelievable. I felt that some of the ash falling was the ashes of people who passed away. And for a moment I felt like everything was all right, that maybe everybody who died was okay.

I was here on a Sunday and our shift is seven days a week, twelve hours a day. You don't get any days off, you go until you just can't go anymore, and then you see if you can get somebody to cover your job for a day or two. I was here on a Sunday and I met this guy who had a cane. He was with another guy and he was getting out of a wheelchair. I came by in a "gator," which is like a golf cart. It's a four-wheel-drive kind of golf cart, big tires and a little pickup bin in the back so you can haul small stuff around.

So I came by and the one guy standing said, "Can you give him a ride?" I said yeah, so they hopped in and they were going to the east side of the job, and this guy with the cane started talking to me. He pulled out this silver flask and he said, "Do you want a drink?"

I said, "No thanks. I'm on duty. I don't drink."

He laughed and he said, "Yeah, I know, but have a drink with me." And he handed me this flask and I looked at it, and on it it said, "To Tim, with all my love. Your wife, Vanessa." I told him my name was Tim, too. He said his wife had given it to him, and she had died in the North Tower. She was twenty-nine years old and four months pregnant. And, you know, this chill went through me. I felt goose bumps. And I gave him back the flask and he started talking to me about everything. I was able to give him a ride over there, and I was actually able to bring him in front of the towers. And you can't do that normally because of the security. You have to have all the passes, but I guess they knew he was a victim, and they let me just drive him through to his car. He was overwhelmed. I'll never forget how stunned he was at the devastation, or the look of shock and horror on his face.

I brought him to his car and he asked for my name and address and said he would send me an invitation to his wife's funeral service. I told him, "I'd love to come if I'm not working. You know, we'll see what happens."

On the day of his wife's funeral, the wind downtown was gusting to more than fifty miles an hour. So they shut the cranes down and canceled work. I took a ride up to the cemetery, which is north of here, in Valhalla. I'm not familiar with that area, but there were about six or seven of the longest, blackest limos I've ever seen. There must have been five hundred or six hundred people there. I couldn't believe how many people were there. And they all came because they knew this girl, or knew her husband.

Before I went up there, I cut this little cross out of a steel beam from the North Tower, and I brought it with me. I brought it over to the church, where a priest put a blessing on it and wrapped it in a white cloth. I wanted to give her husband something. He had nothing but an empty casket. At first, I couldn't find him. Then I saw his friend, who remembered me. He said, "Hey, Tim, let's go find Tim."

We found him in the cemetery office, and he had his flask and he was having a drink. There were maybe five guys with him. I gave him the cross and told him it was from all of us down there. We wanted him to have something. He kissed my cheek with tears in his eyes. All these men who didn't know each other, men from different walks of life—businessmen; me, a construction guy; and this guy, a real smart young guy—we all had tears in our eyes.

Tim's brother-in-law was there. He lost his sister. And they were telling me stories about this woman, Vanessa, about her marriage to Tim and their wedding in Colorado. My brother lives in Colorado, so we were talking about that and they were telling me about how loving this woman was. It was just this great story about a good person. Then I came back to the job. Those are the kinds of things happening here that will break your heart. They just break your heart.

JOSEPH BRADLEY

57, Construction Worker, Ground Zero

"WE FOUND A LADY WITH A BLUE PIN-STRIPED SUIT ON.
A FIREMAN CLOSED HER EYES, FIXED HER LAPELS, AND
STRAIGHTENED HER SKIRT. . . . I KNOW ONE THING FOR SURE:
SHE NEVER THOUGHT SHE WAS GOING TO GO TO WORK THAT DAY
AND NEVER COME HOME AGAIN."

I'm an operating engineer. I run heavy equipment in New York City. I was at Kut-sher's playing golf when we got the call that a plane had hit the World Trade Center. We checked out of the hotel immediately and started making our way down to the city. When I got home, I called the union hall and they told me to come down and get on the volunteer list.

The next morning I went down to the hall at about 5 A.M., and four hours later I got the call to come down to West Street. I called my wife and told her not to expect me, and that I would stay in touch with her. I took the subway down. It stopped at West Fourth Street, so I had to walk the rest of the way. There was debris everywhere, paper everywhere, a cloud of dust, like six inches of snow on the ground.

And somewhere in there I became frightened. I was going into something I built. I first went to work down there in 1966 to move the utilities out of the way for the construction of the World Trade Center, right in the beginning. Now, on September 12, I was halfway down to Church Street and I was frightened. All I could think of was the Twenty-third Psalm, which says you walk through the valley of the shadow of death and you fear no evil. I prayed all the way down to Park

Place. Then I started to see all the devastation. My first look at the World Trade Center since the attacks, and it was a huge pile, maybe ten stories tall. And it was burning. I started to ask directions to where my crane might be when a whistle blew and suddenly fifty firefighters were running at me. I saw people scattering and I really didn't know what to do. So I ran and ran. It was as if they had let the bulls go in Spain and we were running through the street. People falling down, people picking them up as they came by, under the arms, dragging them, carrying them, just to get them out of the way, because something was collapsing. I didn't even look back. They thought 1 Liberty Plaza was coming down and that's why they blew the whistle. We stopped running when we got to the Battery Tunnel, and I caught my breath and said, "Oh, my God, I haven't even been here ten minutes and I'm going to die."

Then I settled down a little bit, made my way down to West Street and ran into a fellow who said, "Joe Bradley, how are you? How you doing?"

I said, "I don't even know who you are, or what your name is."

He said, "I'm Manny. I'm from Cranes Incorporated. Your rig is over there."

You have to remember, there were no companies down there, no supervision, no nothing, no money, no company hours. There were just volunteers. But I never felt the chaos. Everybody seemed to know what the heck they were doing. We ran into a fire chief and we said, "What can we do to help you?"

He said, "What do you have?"

I said, "A crane."

He said, "Okay, I want you to lift the beams off the debris field because that's the sidewalk and the plaza to the South Tower, and I have a feeling there are a lot of people under there." We hadn't even gone ten steps before we ran into a crew of ironworkers who said, "You guys got a rig? We'd like to work with you today, if you want a hand."

That's all it took to mobilize a crew. We got the crane in place and started cutting beams, and soon twenty-five firefighters showed up to help us dig through the rubble to get to the people. There were abandoned cars still sitting there with their signal lights blinking. It was like nothing I had ever seen.

We worked for about three days. I felt I had done my part. I started to make my way out of Ground Zero, the same way as when I walked in. At Canal Street, there were a lot of kids with piercings, tattoos, all different colored hair. They had made a bandstand and they started cheering when we came out. I just lost it. I started crying. Emotionally, I was completely spent. I cried for about four blocks and then made my way home. My wife took care of me—bath, food, then she put me to bed. And I slept about six or seven hours and then got up and dressed. She said, "Joe, where are you going?" and I said, "I've got to go back there." I went back and I've been here ever since.

It's interesting to see what the feelings and what just coming down here do to a man. Everything gets broken down. It's like putting meat on a spit. All the fat goes away and the only thing that's left is an honest man. No bullshit, no lying, no "I'm better than somebody else." The camaraderie was absolutely incredible. I've seen things here that I've never seen in my life. Any kind of squabble between trade unions disappeared. I've seen hate and resentment between men disappear. I saw such an amazing joint effort. Volunteers and people of all ages were carrying water or cold towels onto the pile; other people pulled your boots off and put dry socks on. Nothing drains down here. We were soaking wet the whole time. My feet looked like prunes. The conditions were terrible. You had to lay down anywhere you could, like in a doorway. All of a sudden you were homeless. The Salvation Army set up little bunks. They'd put a comforter and a pillow on the floor, and ask you what time you wanted to get up. They'd come to wake you with a cup of coffee and a smile. The humanity was just absolutely unbelievable.

Finding three crosses inside a collapsed building was even more unbelievable. They were in the Commodities Exchange, building 6. The center of the building collapsed, but the perimeter was still standing. Inside there were three crosses, one lying down on its side and two standing. It looked like Calvary, where Christ was hung. The crosses weren't doctored or dressed up. I went there in the evening and the light shone through the top. The moon was full, and it was very bright down there. And from the cars in the parking garage below, the reflections of license plates and headlights were like stars.

We took the center cross out and placed it on a bridge stanchion. It became the memorial for the World Trade Center. We didn't ask anyone's permission. We just did it. Because of the bureaucracy down here it's much better to ask forgiveness than permission. We had been there for weeks already, and got to a point emotionally where we knew we weren't going to take anybody out of there alive. We had gone down to rescue people. But the fires were so hot at the time.

I guess the first corpse was the hardest. The first one stays in my mind. We found a lady with a blue pin-striped suit on. A fireman closed her eyes, fixed her lapels, and straightened her skirt. They treated her with such dignity and I wondered what plans she might have had, where she was going on vacation. I know one thing for sure: she never thought she was going to go to work that day and never come home again.

We were probably there three, four weeks when the grapplers started coming up with money found in collapsed vaults. The money was perfect. It wasn't wet, it wasn't burned. Then we got a cache of drugs—cocaine, heroin, marijuana, all of it—in perfectly good condition. There were guns and ammunition and gold, guarded by the Secret Service, the FBI, and the police, with cameras and with personnel. There were at least fifty people there around the clock, watching and waiting, because they knew what was down there. It took them eight days and eight truck caravans to remove the gold, the drugs, the money, and the guns. I couldn't understand for the life of me how this survived and everything else was destroyed.

I was sitting in a respite center having a cup of coffee when I ran into a rabbi. He sat down and started to talk to me. After I related the story about the money, the drugs, and the ammunition found below Ground Zero, he said something in Hebrew. He basically said that evil does not destroy evil, but it does not destroy all the good either. He said the crosses we found were evidence that God is still here. And he used the example of the church, St. Paul's Chapel, which has been here since George Washington's time. It didn't sustain a single broken pane of glass on September 11. One block from the World Trade Center and it was completely untouched. Buildings were damaged six blocks away, but the church was fine. "Your cross is there," the rabbi said. "God is still listening."

Benjamin Garelick, right, with his younger brother, Noah.

BENJAMIN GARELICK
7, Second Grade, P.S. 41, the Greenwich Village School

"THEY LET US SIT IN THE FRONT OF THE TRUCK.
I FELT LIKE A HERO."

I saw smoke. My brother, Noah, saw it happen from our window. I put a big American flag up because my dad wanted an American flag in the window. Mom wanted it up because she didn't want to see the smoke. So I put it up and it blocked what you were looking at.

I raised seven hundred dollars for the firemen by selling lemonade. I did it because it's fun and I knew that the firehouse needed it. They needed some money to get a new truck. I like that they care about safety. I like that they put out fires.

The lemonade stand was my idea. I think most people would think that it was my mom and my dad's idea. But I just thought I could do something, and then I thought of making a lemonade stand.

We went to Staples and we got this big piece of cardboard paper, and we had this nice design on it. It was clouds in the sky. And then we wrote, LEMONADE— ONE DOLLAR. And it said EMT, FDNY, NYPD. We also put on stickers of firemen.

We worked for an hour each day. My friend, Sam, helped. We were standing out in front, and we would say, "Would you like lemonade?" We also said where the money goes. A man upstairs asked us how many cups we had left, and we said fifty. He gave us fifty dollars, but he didn't take any lemonade. People just made donations and they didn't buy lemonade.

I had fun. That's why I wanted to do it. And I knew Ladder 12 needed the money to get a new truck. Everybody came to the front of the firehouse and they shook our hands. They were cheering us, me, Noah, and Sam and his brother, Dylan. They gave us little bags of candy. They let us sit in the front of the truck. I felt like a hero.

I go there mostly every Wednesday now. I just like to visit them and say hi. They call me the lemonade kid.

ACKNOWLEDGMENTS

This book could not have been compiled without the help of many, many people, and the authors would like to gratefully acknowledge each and every one of them.

First and foremost is Judith Regan, who gave us office space, the use of her staff, and a thousand phone numbers to get us on our way.

Thanks, also, to our editors at Regan Books, Dana Albarella and Aliza Fogelson, and other key members of Judith's team, including Cal Morgan, Cassie Jones, Dan Taylor, Carl Raymond, Kurt Andrews, Evan Schoninger, Tom Wengelewski, Liz Lauricella, Conor Risch, and Ginger Ahn.

It would have been very difficult to find our interview subjects, much less prepare their first-person accounts, without our two tireless researchers, Tiffany Speaks and Gail Leicht.

Shelby Meizlik and Jen Suitor from HarperCollins gave us precisely the kind of PR help we needed.

And the list of helpers goes on: Brian Mynes, Peggy Reed, Francis X. Gribbon, Michael O'Looney, Sheldon Wright, Steve Stoute, Cindi Berger, Kevin Tedesco, Todd Gold, Jake Gibson, John Gibson, Richard Fink, Jeffrey Rubin, Sharon Hoge, Jill Martin, Randy Spector, Anna Strasberg, Diana Gould, Chris Weiller, Desiree Gruber, Sara Bauman,

Stacy Mizrahi, Ann Loew, Renee Spitz, Ann Paterson, Stephen Wilkes, Allen Grubman, Jess Drabkin, and Peter Grant.

Then there were others who stopped what they were doing to talk with us and give us a better understanding of what took place that day. They are: Laurent Dufourg, Wallace E. Miller, Donna DeFalco, Don Vadas, Jody Brown, William Ludwig, Tony Anthony, Pat Walsh, Kristan Exner, Rabbi Gary Guttman, Larry Silverstein, Frank Fournier, Julie Scelfo, Michael Orsa, Carmen Griffith, Arturo Griffith, Judith Grosz, Peter Davis, Frank Vollaro, Esther Harburg, Ed Fallon, William Beaury, Craig Taylor, Yolanda Acosta, Sal Carcaterra, Steve Haag, Dodie Gill, Judy Wein, Thayer Case, Michael Lomonaco, Dave Nolan, Paul Matulis, Tony Pecoro, Celia McCallum, and Jerry Iucci.

And we could not have taken the time to do this, expecially working together, without the love and support of our two children, Jesse and Brian Fink.

Finally, of course, there are the eighty-one men and women in this book whose September 11 stories became part of history and part of our lives forever. A sincere thank-you to all of them—for their courage, for their level of sharing, and for their belief that we could repeat their stories accurately, honestly, and compassionately.